# 365 Kid-Friendly Lunch Snack Recipes

*(365 Kid-Friendly Lunch Snack Recipes - Volume 1)*

Edith Traylor

Copyright: Published in the United States by Edith Traylor/ © EDITH TRAYLOR

Published on August, 12 2020

All rights reserved. No part of this publication may be reproduced, stored in retrieval system, copied in any form or by any means, electronic, mechanical, photocopying, recording or otherwise transmitted without written permission from the publisher. Please do not participate in or encourage piracy of this material in any way. You must not circulate this book in any format. EDITH TRAYLOR does not control or direct users' actions and is not responsible for the information or content shared, harm and/or actions of the book readers.

In accordance with the U.S. Copyright Act of 1976, the scanning, uploading and electronic sharing of any part of this book without the permission of the publisher constitute unlawful piracy and theft of the author's intellectual property. If you would like to use material from the book (other than just simply for reviewing the book), prior permission must be obtained by contacting the author at author@jumbocookbook.com

Thank you for your support of the author's rights.

# Content

## 365 AWESOME KID-FRIENDLY LUNCH SNACK RECIPES ............................................. 8

1. " Creamsicle" Smoothie ..................... 8
2. "it's That Easy" Graham Cracker Delight... 8
3. ***** Chewy English Flapjack ***** ........... 9
4. 5 Cup Slice ....................................... 9
5. 5 Minute Potato ................................ 10
6. A Tropical Fruit Parfait ..................... 10
7. Almond And Strawberry Bread ................ 11
8. Almost Chocolate " No Egg" Banana Muffins ........................................... 11
9. Almost Instant Rocky Road ................. 12
10. Aloo (Potato) Pakora ........................ 12
11. Ambrosia Salad; Fruit Salad ............... 13
12. Amy's Black Bean Dip ...................... 13
13. Apple Explosion (Apple Sauce) ........... 14
14. Apple Pie Stuffed Soft Pretzels With Streusel .............................................. 14
15. Apple Surprise ................................ 16
16. Applesauce Oatmeal Muffins .............. 16
17. Apricot Oat Cakes ........................... 17
18. Apricot Almond Energy Bars .............. 17
19. Asian Bean Cakes ............................ 18
20. Asian Style Chicken Nuggets .............. 18
21. Auntie's Delicious Soft Pretzels, Amish Recipe ................................................ 19
22. Baby Bear Sandwiches ...................... 19
23. Bacon Hash Browns Cakes Homemade ... 20
24. Banana Crackers .............................. 20
25. Banana Dumplings ............................ 21
26. Banana Oat Breakfast Bars ................ 21
27. Banana Sticks ................................. 22
28. Bananas In Milk .............................. 22
29. Barkram (Berry Cream) ..................... 23
30. Bars Of Iron ................................... 23
31. Beet, Dill Feta Frittata .................... 24
32. Berry Breakfast Power Bar ................ 24
33. Best Blondies Ever! ......................... 25
34. Bite Sized Brownies ......................... 25
35. Blueberry Oat Bread/Muffins .............. 25
36. Bola Bola Shrimp Balls ..................... 26
37. Boureki (Feta Pastries) ..................... 27
38. Breakfast Burrito (Like Mc Donald's!) ...... 27
39. Breakfast Burros ( Burritos ) ............... 27
40. Breakfast Snack Bar .......................... 28
41. Breakfast Tortillas ............................ 28
42. Brioche With Chocolate Centres ........... 29
43. Broke Guy's Crushed Potatoes ............. 30
44. Brownies Fudgy, Rich And Moist ......... 30
45. Budget Biscuits ................................ 31
46. Bugs In A Rug ................................. 31
47. Build Your Own Canadian Cranberry And Herb Turkey Burgers! ............................ 32
48. C,h,p,b Sandwich ............................. 33
49. Calzonedilla (Italian Quesadilla) .......... 33
50. Caramel Corn Pops ........................... 33
51. Caramel Cream Cheese Apple Dip ........ 34
52. Cayenne Cheese Crackers ................... 34
53. Chaqueta's Fruit Salad ....................... 35
54. Cheddar Parmesan Crackers ................ 35
55. Cheddar And Veggie Pancakes ............. 36
56. Cheese Bacon Rounds ....................... 36
57. Cheese Honey Ham Jackets ................ 37
58. Cheese Onion Pull Apart Loaf ............ 37
59. Cheese Vegemite Scrolls ................... 38
60. Cheese Zucchini Crisps ..................... 38
61. Cheese And Raisin Latkes .................. 39
62. Cheesy Apple Breakfast Quesadillas ..... 39
63. Cheesy Garlic, Herb, Paprika Tomato Muffins .............................................. 40
64. Cheesy Pretzel Dippers (Lunch Box Surprise) ............................................. 41
65. Cheesy Toast .................................. 41
66. Chewy Granola ................................ 41
67. Chex Mix My Way ........................... 42
68. Chicken Bites With Spice ................... 42
69. Chicken Dippers .............................. 43
70. Chili Nuts Santa Fe .......................... 43
71. Choco Peanut Butter Snack Mix .......... 44
72. Chocolate Cherry Slice ...................... 44
73. Chocolate Cookie Ice Cream ............... 45
74. Chocolate Crispy Rice Clusters ........... 45
75. Chocolate Dip ................................. 46
76. Chocolate Double Dipped Strawberries ... 46
77. Chocolate French Toast Sticks ............ 46
78. Chocolate Peanut Butter Crunch .......... 47
79. Chocolate Silk Pudding ..................... 48
80. Chocolate Strawberry Frost ................ 48
81. Chocolatey Rice Krispies Easter Eggs ... 49
82. Christmas Crackers ........................... 49

83. Christmas Snow Logs .................................. 50
84. Chunky Monkey Bread ................................ 50
85. Cinnabutter Toast ....................................... 51
86. Cinnamon Apple Latkes .............................. 51
87. Cinnamony Carrots With Cream Cheese Dip 52
88. Cocoa Krispies Squares ............................... 52
89. Cocoa Peanut Logs ..................................... 52
90. Coconut Chocolate Tarts ............................ 53
91. Coconut Ghost Treats™ .............................. 53
92. Coconut, Sultana Honey Loaf (Abm / Bread Machine) ............................................. 54
93. Copycat Keebler Pecan Sandies .................. 55
94. Corn Crackers ............................................. 55
95. Cornflake Crunchies ................................... 56
96. Couscous For People Who Hate Couscous 56
97. Cowboy Energy Cookies ............................. 57
98. Cracker Sandwiches .................................... 57
99. Cream Cheese Bacon Croissants ................ 58
100. Creamy Baked Brie With Strawberries, Pecans And Honey ........................................... 58
101. Creamy Jello Layers .................................. 59
102. Crisco Party Snax ..................................... 59
103. Crispy Guilt Free Pizza ............................. 59
104. Crispy Peanut Butter Bars ........................ 60
105. Crock Pot Applesauce ............................... 60
106. Crunchy Banana Strawberry Parfaits ........ 61
107. Crunchy Breakfast Biscuit Bites ................ 61
108. Crunchy Fudge Sandwiches ...................... 62
109. Deep Fried Sweet Potato Chips With Mozzarella ........................................................ 62
110. Deli Cracker Dip ....................................... 63
111. Dolly Parton's Green Tomato Cake .......... 63
112. Dreamsicles .............................................. 64
113. Dry Diaper Surprise! ................................. 65
114. Easier French Fries Cold Oil Method (Cook's Illustrated) ........................................... 65
115. Easiest Banana Muffins Ever .................... 65
116. Easy Apple Dip ......................................... 66
117. Easy Apple Pie Wontons .......................... 66
118. Easy Baked Jo Jo Potatoes ....................... 67
119. Easy Greek Chips Omelette (Avga Omeleta Me Patates) ..................................................... 67
120. Easy Low Fat Oven Roasted Peppered Potato Wedges ................................................ 68
121. Easy Microwave Popcorn ......................... 68

122. Easy Moist Banana Blueberry Muffins ...... 69
123. Easy Party Mix ......................................... 69
124. Easy Rhubarb Upside Down Cake ............ 69
125. Easy S'more Clusters Indoor S'mores ........ 70
126. Easy Shrimp And Crab Cakes ................... 70
127. Edmonds Scones ...................................... 71
128. Eggs And Toast With Marmite ................. 72
129. Empanadas (Appetizer) ............................ 72
130. Fantastic Microwaved Beet Chips ............ 73
131. Farmhouse Cheddar Cheese And Cranberry Croque Monsieur Toasties ................................ 73
132. Ff Sf Pudding (Made With Yogurt) ........... 74
133. Fire Free S'more Treats ............................ 74
134. Fish Finger Wraps Fish Stick Wraps (Usa) 74
135. Flavor Packed Chicken Wraps .................. 75
136. Fleisch Perisky ( Meat Buns) .................... 75
137. Football Dip ............................................. 76
138. French Toast Sandwich Fingers ................ 77
139. Fried Honey Buns .................................... 77
140. Frosted Pecans ......................................... 77
141. Frosty Strawberry Pops K ........................ 78
142. Frozen JELLO Pops .................................. 78
143. Frozen Fruit Pie Filling ............................. 79
144. Fruit Filled Spring Rolls ........................... 79
145. Fruit Roll Up ............................................ 80
146. Fruit Salsa With Cinnamon Sugar Tortillas 81
147. Fruit Skewers For Children (And Adults Too!) Child Safe .............................................. 81
148. Fruit And Nut Chocolate Slice .................. 82
149. Fruit And Popcorn Balls ........................... 82
150. Fruit And Yogurt Breakfast Couscous ...... 83
151. Fruity Frosty Treat ................................... 84
152. Garbage Pickles ....................................... 84
153. Gluten Free Sugar Free Brownie .............. 85
154. Golden Flapjacks ..................................... 85
155. Grammy's Rice Pudding ........................... 86
156. Grandma's Popcorn Balls ......................... 86
157. Green Apple Monster .............................. 87
158. Halloween Spooky Spider Snacks (Fun For The Kids To Make) .......................................... 87
159. Ham Pineapple Scrolls ............................. 88
160. Ham And Spinach Quiche Make Ahead ... 88
161. Healthy Apple Shortcake Yoghurt ............ 89
162. Healthy Banana Bran Muffins .................. 90
163. Healthy Bean Bars ................................... 90

164. Healthy Peanut Butter Balls ........................ 91
165. Heavenly Oat Bars ...................................... 91
166. Herb Potato Chips ....................................... 92
167. Holly Leaves (No Bake) ............................. 92
168. Homemade Microwave Popcorn ............... 93
169. Homemade Nutella Better Than The Real Thing! ..................................................................... 93
170. Homemade Pop Tarts ................................. 94
171. Homemade Sweet Dill Yum Yum Pickles 94
172. Hot Fried Non Nudist Peanuts ................. 95
173. Iced Chocolate ............................................. 96
174. Indian Yam Fritters / Classic Crunch Patties ..................................................................... 96
175. Italian Bagel Bites ....................................... 97
176. Jello Jigglers Fusion ................................... 97
177. Joe's Corn O' The Kettle ........................... 97
178. Joyce's Unbeatable Banana Bread ............ 98
179. Julie's Seedy Bars ....................................... 99
180. Just Peachy Yogurt ..................................... 99
181. Kaha's Delicious Lunch Box Kiwi Salsa ... 99
182. Khachapuri (Georgian Cheese Bread) ..... 100
183. Khinkali (Ground Meat Filled Pasta Pockets) ................................................................. 101
184. Kid Friendly Thai Grilled Chicken ......... 101
185. Kidney Bean Burritos .............................. 102
186. Kids Favorite Veggie Dip ........................ 102
187. Kids Snack Mix ......................................... 102
188. Kids' Fondue ............................................. 103
189. Kissables Crunch ...................................... 103
190. Kittencal's Chinese Chicken Balls With Sweet And Sour Sauce ...................................... 104
191. Krispymallow Treats ................................ 105
192. Large Batch Banana Nut Bread .............. 105
193. Leanne Remy's Easy Garlic Study Bread 105
194. Lemon (Or Lime) Rice Krispies Treats ... 106
195. Lemon Garlic Pita Chips ......................... 106
196. Littlemafia's Parmesan Sticks .................. 107
197. Low Fat Dried Fruit Granola ................... 107
198. Low Fat (But You Wouldn't Know It) Banana Bread ...................................................... 108
199. Low Fat Banana Nut Bread ..................... 108
200. Low Fat Chocolate Chip Banana Muffins 109
201. Low Fat Milk Pudding ............................. 109
202. Low Gi Creamy Scrambled Eggs ........... 110
203. Low Low Fat Southwestern Egg Rolls ... 110
204. Mac And Cheese Quesadillas ................. 111

205. Macaroni And Cheese Chowder ............. 111
206. Mama Zuquinis Pizza Margherita ........... 112
207. Mango And Feta Quesadilla .................... 112
208. Marbled P B Sheet Cake ........................... 113
209. Melon And Strawberry Lassi ................... 114
210. Mexican Chicken Wrap * Chicken Fajita * Applebee's Copycat ............................................ 114
211. Microwave Buckaroo Bars (chocolate, Peanut Butter Oatmeal) ..................................... 115
212. Microwaveable Quick Muffins ................ 115
213. Mini Flaky Pizza ....................................... 115
214. Mini Phyllo Roasted Red Pepper Spinach Bites 116
215. Mini Pizzas For School Lunches ............ 117
216. Mini Snack Pizzas ..................................... 117
217. Mmm Good Yogurt Dip For Fruit! ........ 117
218. Molasses Glazed Chicken Wings ............ 118
219. Mom's Holiday Veggie Dip ..................... 118
220. Mom's Mini Chocolate Chip Pancakes ... 119
221. More Than Just Gorp! .............................. 119
222. Mozzarella Chorizo Omelet For One .... 120
223. Mozzarella Cheese Sticks With Sauce ..... 120
224. Mr. Breakfast's Boo Nana ( Tasty Dish ) 121
225. Mrs. Truman's Martian Cookies ............. 121
226. Mum's Simple Economy Scones ............. 122
227. Murray's Fried Spaghetti .......................... 122
228. My Best Ever Deviled Eggs! .................... 123
229. My Best Friend's Best Granola Bars ....... 123
230. Nacho Cucumbers! .................................... 124
231. Nancy Black's School Brownies .............. 124
232. Nene's Amazing Avocado Dip ................ 125
233. Nine Layer Mexican Dip .......................... 125
234. No Bake Breakfast Cookies ..................... 126
235. No Sugar Lite Vanilla Yogurt .................. 126
236. No Sugar, Low Fat "fruity" Oatmeal Cookies ................................................................. 127
237. Norwegian Pancakes ................................ 127
238. Nut And Egg Free Cookies ..................... 128
239. Nutella S'mores ......................................... 128
240. Nutty Pineapple Nibbles ( Stuffed Celery) 129
241. Nutty Popcorn ........................................... 129
242. OAMC Chicken Nuggets ........................ 130
243. Oatmeal Banana Muffins ......................... 130
244. Oh So Good Homemade Tortilla Chips 131
245. Old Fashioned Red Candied Apples ....... 131
246. Olive Garden Summer Pizza ................... 132

| | |
|---|---|
| 247. Orange Ginger Oatmeal Porridge Delight 132 | 287. Rice Krispies " Apple Pie" ................ 153 |
| 248. Oregon Trail Mix ............................ 134 | 288. Roasted Honey And Spice Nuts .......... 153 |
| 249. Pan Fried Spinach Ravioli ................ 134 | 289. S'mores Pretzels Quesadillas ............ 154 |
| 250. Pasta With Crunchy Crumbs And Feta For One 135 | 290. Salami Cheese Bread ...................... 154 |
| 251. Paula's Fried Biscuits And Honey Butter 135 | 291. Salt Pepper Dirty Potato Chips ......... 155 |
| 252. Pb Fruit Pita Pockets ..................... 136 | 292. Sarah's Party Roast Beef Rounds ....... 155 |
| 253. Peach Surprise ............................... 136 | 293. Saratoga Chips ................................ 156 |
| 254. Peanut Butter Banana Dogs! ............ 137 | 294. Sassy Citrus Dip ............................. 156 |
| 255. Peanut Butter Jam "sandwich" Muffins 137 | 295. Sausage Rolls Cheese Pufs ............... 157 |
| 256. Peanut Butter Banana "ice Cream" .... 138 | 296. Savoury Afternoon Tea / Picnic Tarts / Quiches ............................................... 157 |
| 257. Peanut Butter Crunch ..................... 138 | 297. Season's Severed Finger Banana Muffins (Low Fat) ............................................. 158 |
| 258. Peanut Butter Granola Balls ............ 139 | 298. Shami Kebab(mutton Or Chicken) ...... 158 |
| 259. Peanut Butter And Jelly Bites ........... 139 | 299. Simple Tuna Salad .......................... 159 |
| 260. Peanut Butter And Raisin Stuffed Apples 140 | 300. Single Serve Cookies ...................... 159 |
| 261. Peppermint Rice Krispies Candy ........ 140 | 301. Smoky Grilled Cheese Fries .............. 160 |
| 262. Pepperoni Pizza Sticks ..................... 140 | 302. Smucker's Peanut Butter Caramel Dip 160 |
| 263. Perfect Health Pancakes (7 Points Per Serving On Weight Watchers .................. 141 | 303. Snack Attack Mix, Low Cal ............... 161 |
| 264. Pickle And Ring Bologna Sandwich Spread 142 | 304. Snowmen On A Stick (Tackled By Tasty !) 161 |
| 265. Pineapple Carrot Juice .................... 142 | 305. Southwest Snack Mix ...................... 162 |
| 266. Pizza Cookie I ................................ 142 | 306. Sparkling Jello ................................ 162 |
| 267. Pizza Jaffle .................................... 143 | 307. Spiced Nuts (Splenda) ..................... 163 |
| 268. Pizza By The Slice .......................... 144 | 308. Spicy Apple Chips ........................... 163 |
| 269. Platanutres (Plantain Chips) ............. 144 | 309. Spicy Garlic And Lemon Shrimp Bruschetta 164 |
| 270. Portabella Burger ........................... 145 | 310. Spinach Nuggets ............................. 164 |
| 271. Potato, Bacon And Sauerkraut Patties 145 | 311. Sticky Fingers ................................. 165 |
| 272. Praline Pecan Crunch ..................... 146 | 312. Sticky Sausages .............................. 165 |
| 273. Pretzel Butterflies .......................... 146 | 313. Stir Crazy Kettle Corn ..................... 165 |
| 274. Princess Spam's Polynesian Pizza ...... 147 | 314. Strawberry Corn Muffins .................. 166 |
| 275. Puppy Chow Snack Mix .................... 147 | 315. Sugar And Spice Pecans ................... 166 |
| 276. Puree Verte Potato, Fennel, And Fava Mash 148 | 316. Sugar Free Snow Cone ..................... 167 |
| 277. Purple Dazzle Shakes ...................... 148 | 317. Sunflower Coconut Balls .................. 167 |
| 278. Purple Monstrosity Fruit Smoothie .... 149 | 318. Sunny Toast ................................... 168 |
| 279. Quick Chewy/Crunchy Coconut Yogurt 149 | 319. Super Amazing Bagel Chips .............. 168 |
| 280. Quick Microwave S'mores ................. 150 | 320. Super Easy Chocolate Chip Brownies 168 |
| 281. Quick Raw Apple Sundae .................. 150 | 321. Super Quick Falafel! ........................ 169 |
| 282. Quinoa Granola Bars ...................... 150 | 322. Super Soft Caramel Popcorn ............ 169 |
| 283. Raspberry Peach Smoothie (Diabetic) 151 | 323. Sweet Savory Meatballs ................... 170 |
| 284. Red, White And Green French Bread Pizza 152 | 324. Sweet Cream Cheese Spread ............ 170 |
| 285. Reese's Snack Mix .......................... 152 | 325. Sweet Malted Chocolate Dessert Sandwiches .......................................... 171 |
| 286. Refresher Smoothie ........................ 152 | 326. Sweet Tortilla Roll Ups .................... 171 |
| | 327. Sweet Zucchini Carrot Garden Bread 172 |
| | 328. Taco Bell Quesadillas ...................... 172 |

329. Taco Cups ................................... 173
330. Taco Tortilla Dogs ....................... 173
331. Teddy Bear Snack Mix ................ 173
332. Teddy Bear Trail Mix .................. 174
333. Tempura Prawns ......................... 174
334. The "only" Power Cookies ......... 175
335. The Full Monty F E B Full English Breakfast ............................................. 176
336. The Traditional Cyprus Sandwich With Halloumi, Onions And Tomato ......... 177
337. Three Little Pigs Snack Mix ....... 177
338. Tim Horton's Style Lemon Cranberry Muffins ................................................ 178
339. Toddler Teething Cookies .......... 178
340. Toddler Zoobana Bread ............. 179
341. Tomato Pots ................................ 179
342. Tortilla Roll Ups ......................... 180
343. Touchdown Pepperoni Pizza Sandwich .. 180
344. Tropical Smoothie (No Added Sugar) ..... 181
345. Tuna Treats ................................. 181
346. Turkey Pickle Roll Ups .............. 182
347. Uncle Bill's Microwave Potato Chips ... 182
348. Very Easy Crispy Cinnamon Treats ........ 183
349. Wally's 1/2 Sour Pickles ............. 184
350. Watermelon Orange Popsicles ... 184
351. White Chocolate Peanut Butter Apple Dip For 1 184
352. White Chocolate Salties ............. 185
353. Whole Wheat Banana Muffins ... 185
354. Wiggly Worm Trail Mix ............. 186
355. World's Best Chocolate Chip Cookies (By Dorie Greenspan) ................................ 186
356. Yogurt Banana Muffins .............. 187
357. Yogurt Fruit Bars ........................ 187
358. Yogurt A Go Go C/O Tasty Dish ......... 188
359. Your Basic Quesadilla ................ 188
360. Yummy Frozen Chocolate Covered Bananas! .............................................. 189
361. Yummy Peanut Butter Snack Mix .......... 189
362. Yummy Pepperoni With Cheese ........... 190
363. Yummy Pizza Sauce .................... 190
364. Yummy And Healthy Popsicles ........... 191
365. Zucchini Oat Carrot Bars With Butter Cream Cheese Frosting ....................... 191

**INDEX** ............................................. 193
**CONCLUSION** ............................... 197

# 365 Awesome Kid-Friendly Lunch Snack Recipes

***

## 1. " Creamsicle" Smoothie

*Serving: 3-4 serving(s) | Prep: 15mins | Ready in:*

### Ingredients

- 4 mangoes
- 3 oranges
- 1/3 vanilla bean
- 6 strawberries
- 6 ice cubes

### Direction

- Peel mangoes and remove as much flesh around pit as you can.
- Peel oranges. If you have a good blender, don't worry about the orange seeds, they'll get blended up just fine, as well as the vanilla bean.
- Put all ingredients in blender, blend to desired consistency and consume!
- Makes 3 large servings.

### Nutrition Information

- Calories: 248.7
- Protein: 2.8
- Total Fat: 1
- Saturated Fat: 0.2
- Sodium: 6.6
- Sugar: 54.2
- Fiber: 8.6
- Total Carbohydrate: 64.2
- Cholesterol: 0

## 2. "it's That Easy" Graham Cracker Delight

*Serving: 16 Graham-Crackers, 4 serving(s) | Prep: 1mins | Ready in:*

### Ingredients

- 16 graham crackers
- 3/4 cup cream cheese
- 3 tablespoons powdered sugar
- fruit, of your choice (optional)

### Direction

- First, mix cream-cheese and powder-sugar in bowl.
- Then, evenly distribute cream-cheese onto graham-crackers.
- To top it off, try slices of strawberries, pears, etc. (Optional).

### Nutrition Information

- Calories: 293.6
- Total Fat: 18
- Total Carbohydrate: 28.6
- Cholesterol: 47.9
- Protein: 5.2
- Saturated Fat: 10
- Sodium: 298.2
- Fiber: 0.8
- Sugar: 14.7

## 3. ***** Chewy English Flapjack *****

*Serving: 9-12 SQUARES, 9-12 serving(s) | Prep: 10mins | Ready in:*

### Ingredients

- 8 ounces plain porridge oats
- 4 ounces butter
- 4 ounces golden syrup
- 4 ounces sugar (either brown or white, whichever is your favourite)
- optional ingredients
- 2 ounces chocolate chips (white or milk or dark)
- 2 ounces raisins or 2 ounces other dried fruit
- 2 ounces nuts or 2 ounces seeds

### Direction

- Put the butter, sugar, and syrup in a saucepan, and stir it over a medium heat until the butter has melted.
- Put the melted mixture into a mixing bowl, and add the porridge oats and any optional ingredients you want to add.
- Put the mixture in a papered tin, flattening the mixture with the back of a spoon.
- Bake the flapjack in the oven at about 180c for around 30 minutes, or until the flapjack has browned.
- Note: if you are using raisons in your recipe, you might like to cook the flapjack for a shorter time, or for a longer time at a lower temperature, because raisins can burn and expand with the heat.
- Once you take the flapjack out, you should cut it before it cools completely because it will harden.
- If you're impatient, eat some warm (if you haven't already!) but flapjack is just as delicious chilled.
- ***** If you're a chocaholic, I would recommend that when the flapjack has cooled completely, you melt a black of chocolate and pour it over, and wait for it to set. *****.

### Nutrition Information

- Calories: 362.6
- Total Fat: 17.1
- Saturated Fat: 8.3
- Sodium: 143.9
- Cholesterol: 27.1
- Fiber: 3.8
- Sugar: 24.3
- Total Carbohydrate: 51.4
- Protein: 5

## 4. 5 Cup Slice

*Serving: 36 pieces | Prep: 10mins | Ready in:*

### Ingredients

- 1 cup sultana
- 1 cup dark chocolate chips
- 1 cup unsalted dry roasted peanuts
- 1 cup desiccated coconut
- 1 cup condensed milk
- 100 g dark chocolate, melted

### Direction

- Preheat oven to 200C/400F.
- Grease and line a 20 x 30 cm lamington/sponge roll tin with baking paper.
- Make sure the paper extends up and over the sides.
- Sprinkle the pan evenly with sultana, chocolate bits, peanuts and coconut.
- Drizzle the condensed milk over the top.
- Cover with a piece of greased foil and bake in the oven for 20 minutes.
- Reduce heat to 180C/350F, remove the foil and bake for about 15 minutes until golden and firm.
- Remove from oven and cool completely in the pan.

- Drizzle with the melted chocolate and allow to set.
- Remove and slice to serve.

## Nutrition Information

- Calories: 112
- Protein: 2.2
- Total Fat: 6.5
- Sodium: 18.4
- Total Carbohydrate: 14.1
- Cholesterol: 2.9
- Saturated Fat: 3.2
- Fiber: 1.4
- Sugar: 10.8

## 5. 5 Minute Potato

*Serving: 1-2 serving(s) | Prep: 3mins | Ready in:*

## Ingredients

- 1 medium red potatoes
- 1 -1 1/2 tablespoon extra virgin olive oil
- 1/2 tablespoon chopped garlic
- 1 tablespoon butter or 1 tablespoon margarine
- 1 tablespoon grated cheese (whatever you like)
- salt
- pepper

## Direction

- Wash and cube the potato.
- Put the extra virgin olive oil, garlic, salt and pepper on top and mix together well, so that each peace gets an even amount.
- Microwave for 1 minute and 15 seconds.
- Add butter and cheese; microwave for another 15 seconds.

## Nutrition Information

- Calories: 422.6
- Sodium: 275.2
- Fiber: 3.7
- Total Carbohydrate: 36.4
- Cholesterol: 39.4
- Total Fat: 28.7
- Saturated Fat: 11.4
- Sugar: 2.8
- Protein: 7.2

## 6. A Tropical Fruit Parfait

*Serving: 1 parfait, 1 serving(s) | Prep: 5mins | Ready in:*

## Ingredients

- 1 cup banana, cut into chunks and frozen (generous)
- 1/2 cup apple juice (any combination of your choice!) or 1/2 cup orange juice (any combination of your choice!)
- 1/2 cup mango, chopped
- 1 large kiwi, ripe
- 1/4 cup granola cereal

## Direction

- First blend the banana with the juice until very thick and creamy. Scoop out into a bowl.
- Blend the mango and kiwi. Leave it just a little bit chunky.
- In a large mug, layer alternately: banana puree, granola, mango/kiwi puree. Enjoy.

## Nutrition Information

- Calories: 455.9
- Total Fat: 8.8
- Sugar: 59.2
- Cholesterol: 0
- Protein: 7.8
- Saturated Fat: 1.7
- Sodium: 16.6
- Fiber: 11.1
- Total Carbohydrate: 93.6

## 7. Almond And Strawberry Bread

*Serving: 1 loaf | Prep: 25mins | Ready in:*

### Ingredients

- 1 cup flour
- 1/2 teaspoon baking soda
- 1/4 teaspoon salt
- 6 tablespoons sugar
- 1/4 cup butter, softened
- 1 egg
- 1 teaspoon almond extract
- 1/2 cup plain yogurt
- 1/2 cup slivered almonds
- 1 cup strawberry, finely chopped and patted dry
- The Glaze
- 1/2 cup confectioners' sugar
- 1/2 teaspoon almond extract
- 1 -2 tablespoon milk, as needed
- 1 dash red food coloring (optional)

### Direction

- Preheat oven to 350 degrees F.
- Grease a 7-1/2 x 3-1/2 inch loaf pan (actually, any size works; adjust baking time accordingly).
- In a small bowl combine flour, baking soda and salt.
- In a large bowl, cream together sugar and butter; add egg and almond extract and beat until fluffy.
- Add flour and yogurt alternately to creamed mixture.
- Fold in almonds, then strawberries.
- Turn batter into prepared pan and bake 45 to 50 minutes at 350 degrees F or until toothpick or knife inserted all the way to bottom comes out clean.
- While bread is baking, combine the glaze ingredients.
- Let bread cool in pan.
- While bread is still warm, drizzle with almond glaze.

### Nutrition Information

- Calories: 1922.2
- Total Carbohydrate: 260.1
- Cholesterol: 351.6
- Protein: 36.9
- Total Fat: 84.6
- Saturated Fat: 35.9
- Sugar: 150.8
- Sodium: 1677
- Fiber: 12.6

## 8. Almost Chocolate " No Egg" Banana Muffins

*Serving: 12 muffins | Prep: 10mins | Ready in:*

### Ingredients

- 1/2 cup margarine, softened
- 1 cup sugar
- 3 ripe bananas, mashed
- 2 cups flour (use less for whole wheat flour)
- 1 teaspoon baking soda
- 1 teaspoon salt (optional)
- 1 tablespoon cocoa

### Direction

- Mix melted margarine, sugar and bananas together.
- Sift flour, baking soda and salt (if using) together.
- Add to banana mixture.
- Mix until well blended.
- Add cocoa, continue to mix.
- If mixture seems dry (due to whole wheat flour), add some of the water.
- Mix in additives. My favorite is raisins!
- Bake at 350°F for 25 minutes or until toothpick comes out clean.

- OAMC: let cool and freeze.

## Nutrition Information

- Calories: 202.1
- Sodium: 150.2
- Sugar: 20.3
- Cholesterol: 0
- Total Fat: 4.1
- Saturated Fat: 0.8
- Fiber: 1.4
- Total Carbohydrate: 39.6
- Protein: 2.6

## 9. Almost Instant Rocky Road

*Serving: 36 squares | Prep: 10mins | Ready in:*

### Ingredients

- 1 lb semi-sweet chocolate chips
- 1 cup mini marshmallows
- 1/2 cup almonds
- 1/2 cup peanuts
- 1/4 cup raisins
- 1/2 cup coarsely chopped dried apricot

### Direction

- Line an 8" square cake pan or baking dish with a piece of wax paper large enough to fold over the sides. Place the chocolate chips in a medium saucepan over very low heat. Cook the chocolate until it has almost completely melted, stirring constantly to make sure it doesn't burn (this can also be melted in the microwave). Remove from the heat and let the chocolate sit for 5 minutes, stirring occasionally. Add the marshmallows, almonds, peanuts, raisins, and apricots, stir until all the ingredients are coated with chocolate. Spread the mixture into the prepared pan, and chill until totally hard, about 3 hours.
- Move the chocolate to a large cutting surface, and use a large serrated knife to cut the chocolate into 1-inch blocks.
- Makes about 36 small squares.

## Nutrition Information

- Calories: 95.1
- Fiber: 1.3
- Total Carbohydrate: 11.7
- Total Fat: 5.8
- Saturated Fat: 2.5
- Sodium: 9.7
- Sugar: 9.4
- Cholesterol: 0
- Protein: 1.6

## 10. Aloo (Potato) Pakora

*Serving: 6-8 serving(s) | Prep: 5mins | Ready in:*

### Ingredients

- 4 large potatoes
- 2 cups corn oil (for frying)
- For the Batter
- 1 cup besan (chickpea flour)
- 1/2 cup water
- 1 teaspoon red chili powder
- 2 teaspoons cumin powder
- 4 cloves of crushed garlic
- 3 inches of crushed ginger
- salt
- 2 tablespoons chopped coriander (optional)

### Direction

- Add water to the Besan.
- Besan has a tendency to be very clumpy, so you should add just a few tablespoons at a time to keep the batter smooth.
- Add the Chilli powder, cumin powder, garlic, ginger, salt and chopped coriander and stir the batter.

- The potatoes should be sliced very thinly.
- No thicker than 1/4 of an inch.
- At this point test one slice of potato in the batter.
- There should just be a thin coat of batter.
- Heat the oil in a pan.
- Use a larger frying pan so that you have more surface area.
- The oil doesn't need to be too deep since the potato slices are very thin.
- Dip the potato slices in the batter and fry them till they are golden brown.
- Remove them from the oil with a slotted spoon and set them on a paper towel for a minute to soak up the excess oil.

## Nutrition Information

- Calories: 898
- Fiber: 7.3
- Sugar: 3.6
- Cholesterol: 0
- Protein: 8.7
- Saturated Fat: 9.6
- Sodium: 34.1
- Total Fat: 74.1
- Total Carbohydrate: 53

## 11. Ambrosia Salad; Fruit Salad

*Serving: 4-6 serving(s) | Prep: 20mins | Ready in:*

## Ingredients

- 1 (11 ounce) can mandarin oranges, drained, 2 Tbs. juice reserved
- 1 (8 ounce) can pineapple chunks, drained
- 3 oranges, peeled, sectioned, and halved
- 1 small green apple, cored and thinly sliced
- 1 small red apple, cored and thinly sliced
- 2 tablespoons plain nonfat yogurt
- 1/2 teaspoon sugar
- 1 pinch salt
- 1/4 cup flaked coconut, toasted
- 1/2 cup mini marshmallows

## Direction

- In large bowl, combine mandarin oranges, pineapple, orange sections, and sliced apples.
- In small bowl, whisk together 2 Tbs. juice reserved from mandarin oranges, yogurt, sugar, and salt.
- Pour over fruit and gently toss to coat.
- Sprinkle with coconut and marshmallows.

## Nutrition Information

- Calories: 197.2
- Total Carbohydrate: 46.6
- Cholesterol: 0.1
- Total Fat: 2
- Saturated Fat: 1.4
- Sodium: 64.2
- Fiber: 5.7
- Sugar: 37.9
- Protein: 2.6

## 12. Amy's Black Bean Dip

*Serving: 4-5 serving(s) | Prep: 10mins | Ready in:*

## Ingredients

- 28 ounces goya black beans, undrained (large can)
- 3 garlic cloves, finely minced (teny tiny pieces)
- 1/2 onion, diced
- canola oil, for sauteing

## Direction

- Saute garlic and onion in 1/2-1 -inch canola oil. DO NOT BROWN, but let cook until soft 3-4 minutes.
- Add undrained beans and cook on low while mashing.
- Note: These beans do get thick-you can add a little water if you want a thinner dip.

## Nutrition Information

- Calories: 198.3
- Saturated Fat: 0.2
- Sodium: 2.2
- Cholesterol: 0
- Fiber: 12.7
- Sugar: 0.6
- Total Carbohydrate: 36.1
- Protein: 13
- Total Fat: 0.8

## 13. Apple Explosion (Apple Sauce)

*Serving: 6 serving(s) | Prep: 15mins | Ready in:*

### Ingredients

- 6 apples
- 2 cups ginger ale
- 1/2 cup oats
- 1 cup dried cranberries
- 1 tablespoon cinnamon
- 1 banana

### Direction

- Preheat oven to 350 degrees.
- Pour cranberries into ginger ale to become plump.
- Wash and core apples.
- Equally distribute cranberries into each of the holes of the apples.
- Sprinkle oats.
- Pour the ginger ale all over.
- Sprinkle cinnamon over top.
- Slice banana into six long pieces and top the apples.
- Bake for 44 minutes exactly.
- Serve hot, in a cup.

## Nutrition Information

- Calories: 177.7
- Protein: 2.9
- Total Fat: 1.2
- Saturated Fat: 0.2
- Sodium: 8.1
- Fiber: 6.5
- Sugar: 24.5
- Cholesterol: 0
- Total Carbohydrate: 42.1

## 14. Apple Pie Stuffed Soft Pretzels With Streusel

*Serving: 8 large pretzels | Prep: 30mins | Ready in:*

### Ingredients

- Dough
- 2 1/2 teaspoons yeast
- 1 tablespoon sugar
- 1 cup warm water
- 1 1/2 cups all-purpose flour
- 1 1/2 cups bread flour
- 1/2 teaspoon salt
- 2 tablespoons vegetable oil
- Filling
- 3 small granny smith apples
- 1 tablespoon butter
- 2 tablespoons brown sugar
- 1/2 teaspoon cinnamon
- 1 pinch ground cloves
- Streusel
- 1/2 cup flour
- 1/2 cup brown sugar
- 1/4 teaspoon cinnamon
- 4 tablespoons butter
- 1/2 cup finely chopped pecans
- Additional ingredients
- 1/3 cup baking soda
- 2 cups water
- 1 egg white

### Direction

- To prepare dough:
- Proof yeast and the 1 TBS sugar in the 1 cup of warm water and allow to rest for 5 minutes until foamy.
- Mix the flours with 1/2 teaspoons salt and 2 TBS oil in bowl and then add proofed yeast mixture.
- Stir to form a shaggy dough.
- Place onto lightly floured surface and knead for 2-3 minutes until a smooth, but slightly sticky dough is formed.
- Place into a greased bowl, covered with plastic wrap, and let sit until doubled (45-60 minutes).
- While waiting for the dough to rise prepare filling and streusel.
- To prepare filling:
- Peel, core, and thinly (1/4" thick) slice the apples and then cut each slice into 8 pieces (I used my peeler/corer/slicer all in one contraption).
- Sauté the apple pieces with 1/2 of the TBS of butter, the 1/2 teaspoon cinnamon, and the pinch of cloves until the apples are tender, but not mushy.
- Remove from heat and stir in the additional 1/2 TBS of butter.
- To prepare streusel:
- Mix the flour, sugar, and cinnamon together.
- With fork cut in the 4 TBS of butter to a crumb consistency.
- Stir in the chopped pecans.
- When dough has risen, punch down, place on lightly floured board, and cut into 8 equal pieces.
- With hands, roll each piece into a 15" long cylinder.
- Flatten the cylinder down with a rolling pin to measure 3" wide by 17" long.
- Place 1 1/2 TBS of the filling mixture along the length of each piece and fold the long edge over to meet the other side.
- Pinch along the seam to thoroughly enclose the filling.
- Roll the dough with your hands to form an even cylinder and fully encapsulate the filling.
- Take the two ends of each filled cylinder and form into a circle that is overlapped by a couple of inches of dough on either side, twist the ends and lay over the opposite side to form a pretzel shape and press to seal.
- Play with the shape a bit to get the right form and then place each one on a parchment or Silpat lined cookie sheet.
- Repeat for all 8 pieces.
- Allow to rise on cookie sheet for 15 minutes.
- While they are rising, boil 2 cups of water and add 1/3 cup of baking soda.
- Preheat oven to 425 degrees Fahrenheit.
- Beat 1 egg white with 1 TBS water and lay it on a flat plate.
- Lay the streusel topping on a flat plate, too.
- When the pretzels have fully risen, drop one at a time into the boiling water and count to 10.
- Remove with a large slotted spatula/spoon to slightly drain and then drop onto the egg white, turn to coat, then drop into the streusel and turn to coat.
- Lay each completed pretzel back on the lined cookie sheet.
- Repeat this procedure until all pretzels are done.
- Place into the preheated oven and bake for 15 minutes (check on them at 12 minutes).
- Immediately remove from cookie sheets and place on racks to cool.
- *Note: I haven't including the rising time in the "Time to Make" category, but there are two rises for this dough.
- The first is 45-60 minutes and the second is 15 minutes.
- The recipe is written to make use of the rising times for preparing the filling and streusel.

## Nutrition Information

- Calories: 447.2
- Saturated Fat: 5.5
- Sodium: 2777.7
- Sugar: 24.5
- Total Carbohydrate: 69.6
- Total Fat: 16.2

- Fiber: 3.9
- Cholesterol: 19.1
- Protein: 7.5

## 15. Apple Surprise

*Serving: 6 serving(s) | Prep: 15mins | Ready in:*

### Ingredients

- 3 -4 granny smith apples
- 1/4 cup sugar
- 1/2 teaspoon cinnamon
- 1/2 teaspoon nutmeg
- 3/4 cup butter or 3/4 cup margarine
- 1 1/2 cups sugar
- 1 cup flour
- 1 egg
- 1/2 cup pecans, chopped (optional)

### Direction

- Slice and peel the apples and pile into a pie plate or other glass baking dish.
- Sprinkle with 2 tablespoons sugar.
- Make a batter of the remaining ingredients and pour over the apples.
- Bake for 45 minutes at 350 degrees.
- Serve warm with vanilla ice-cream or cool whip.

### Nutrition Information

- Calories: 554.7
- Total Fat: 24.2
- Saturated Fat: 14.9
- Sodium: 176.3
- Fiber: 2.4
- Sugar: 65.7
- Total Carbohydrate: 84.1
- Cholesterol: 96.3
- Protein: 3.6

## 16. Applesauce Oatmeal Muffins

*Serving: 12 serving(s) | Prep: 15mins | Ready in:*

### Ingredients

- 1 1/2 cups quick-cooking oats
- 3/4 teaspoon cinnamon
- 3/4 teaspoon baking soda
- 1/2 cup milk
- 3 tablespoons vegetable oil
- 1 1/4 cups flour
- 1 teaspoon baking powder
- 1 cup applesauce
- 1/2 cup brown sugar
- 1 egg white

### Direction

- Preheat oven to 400 degrees.
- Combine oats, flour, cinnamon, baking powder, and baking soda.
- Add brown sugar, oil, egg white, milk, and applesauce.
- Fill muffin tins almost full.
- Bake 20 minutes.

### Nutrition Information

- Calories: 175.5
- Total Carbohydrate: 30.6
- Protein: 3.6
- Saturated Fat: 0.8
- Sugar: 9
- Cholesterol: 1.4
- Total Fat: 4.6
- Sodium: 128.7
- Fiber: 1.7

## 17. Apricot Oat Cakes

*Serving: 12 Oat Cakes, 12 serving(s) | Prep: 20mins | Ready in:*

### Ingredients

- 3 cups rolled oats
- 2 cups flour
- 1/4 teaspoon baking powder
- 1/3 cup plain fat-free yogurt (or non-dairy yogurt)
- 1/2 cup dry sweetener (I use Splenda)
- 1/2 cup honey (or agave nectar)
- 1/2 teaspoon vanilla
- 1 egg white (or equivalent)
- 1/2 cup dried fruit, chopped (I use 12 dried apricots)

### Direction

- Thoroughly grind rolled oats in food processor or blender. Mix with flour and baking powder.
- In a separate bowl, "cream" together yogurt, dry sweetener, honey and vanilla. In yet another bowl, lightly beat egg white until it gets bubbly but not stiff. Fold egg white into wet ingredients. Add dried fruit.
- Combine wet and dry ingredients. The dough gets pretty stiff and is hard to mix. You may even have to dive in there with your hands and squish it together. Add water if the mixture is too dry. Form into 12 patties.
- Bake at 325 degrees F for 15 minutes on a non-stick cookie sheet. Cool completely and store in refrigerator. These keep well and may be frozen.

### Nutrition Information

- Calories: 224
- Sodium: 20.8
- Fiber: 3.3
- Total Carbohydrate: 47.4
- Protein: 6.3
- Total Fat: 1.5
- Sugar: 12.5
- Cholesterol: 0.1
- Saturated Fat: 0.3

## 18. Apricot Almond Energy Bars

*Serving: 12 bars, 12 serving(s) | Prep: 5mins | Ready in:*

### Ingredients

- 1 1/2 cups quick-cooking oats (not instant)
- 1/2 cup flour
- 1/2 cup of packed brown sugar
- 1/2 cup of chopped dried apricot
- 1/3 cup slivered almonds
- 1/4 cup golden raisin
- 1 egg
- 1/4 cup vegetable oil
- 1/4 cup corn syrup

### Direction

- I have substituted in bran, wheat germ, ground flax and whole wheat flour. I used chopped dates instead of apricots. My husband's allergy has led me to use coconut, cashews or peanuts instead of almonds. Currants or cranberries can be used instead of raisins. Just as long as the recipe equals out mathematically, I have never had this recipe flop on me.
- Mix dry ingredients together. Mix wet ingredients together. Stir into oat mixture until evenly combined. Press firmly into 9" square pan. Bake at 350 degrees for 20 minutes (or until browned). Let cool. Cut into bars. Store in tightly covered container or wrap individually with plastic. Easy to freeze.

### Nutrition Information

- Calories: 196.3
- Total Carbohydrate: 31
- Cholesterol: 17.6
- Protein: 3.6

- Total Fat: 7.2
- Saturated Fat: 1
- Sugar: 15.5
- Sodium: 11
- Fiber: 2

- Fiber: 13.2
- Total Carbohydrate: 54.2
- Cholesterol: 0

## 19. Asian Bean Cakes

*Serving: 4 serving(s) | Prep: 15mins | Ready in:*

### Ingredients

- 800 g canned cannellini beans, drained and rinced
- 3 teaspoons red curry paste
- 2 kaffir lime leaves, shredded
- 1/2 cup coriander leaves
- 4 green onions, sliced
- salt and pepper
- 2 tablespoons plain flour, for dusting
- 60 ml olive oil

### Direction

- Place beans in a food processor with the curry paste, shredded lime leaves, coriander leaves and green onions and process until mixture just comes together.
- Season with salt and pepper and form the mixture into 5cm cakes.
- Dust each bean cake lightly in flour.
- Heat oil in a skillet to very high heat and cook cakes for 2 minutes on each side or until golden.
- Serve with Asian salad and sweet chili sauce.

### Nutrition Information

- Calories: 411.5
- Total Fat: 13.7
- Sodium: 15.7
- Sugar: 1.1
- Protein: 20.2
- Saturated Fat: 2

## 20. Asian Style Chicken Nuggets

*Serving: 8 nuggets, 1-2 serving(s) | Prep: 3mins | Ready in:*

### Ingredients

- 1 chicken breast
- 2 1/2 tablespoons honey
- 2 tablespoons soy sauce
- 1/2 teaspoon minced ginger
- cornstarch
- 1 egg, beaten
- 1 cup breadcrumbs
- vegetable oil

### Direction

- Defrost frozen chicken breast, if needed.
- In a small mixing bowl, mix together honey, soy sauce and ginger to create your marinade.
- Cut chicken breast into bite-sized pieces and marinate them in the honey mixture.
- Take the chicken and cover it in cornstarch, then in the beaten egg, then in the breadcrumbs.
- Deep-fry the chicken nuggets.
- Serve hot or cold.

### Nutrition Information

- Calories: 931.5
- Total Fat: 24.1
- Saturated Fat: 6.7
- Sodium: 2965.1
- Fiber: 5.3
- Total Carbohydrate: 123.6
- Cholesterol: 304.3
- Protein: 54.9
- Sugar: 50.8

## 21. Auntie's Delicious Soft Pretzels, Amish Recipe

*Serving: 24 pretzels | Prep: 45mins | Ready in:*

### Ingredients

- 1 1/4 cups water (approx 105 degrees)
- 1 tablespoon yeast
- 1/4 cup brown sugar
- 2 cups occident flour (bread flour)
- 2 cups flour
- Dipping solution
- 1/2 cup baking soda, into
- 3 cups hot water
- sweet creamy butter, for 'dipping' face of pretzels after baking (melt butter, then let set a few minutes, and use paper towel to remove cream which will float to the)

### Direction

- Dissolve yeast into warm water.
- Add sugar, then flour mix well; do not 'knead' as this toughens the dough.
- (Mix just until combined well) Let rise until doubled, at least 20 minutes.
- Cut into long 'ropes'.
- Shape into pretzel shapes, then dip into prepared dipping solution.
- Place on well-greased cookie sheet and sprinkle with pretzel salt.
- Bake at 500-550°F for 4-6 minutes until golden brown.
- Dip face of pretzel into melted butter.
- Variation: add 1 t vanilla to the dough.
- Flavor variations.
- Cinnamon/sugar; omit salt dip into cinnamon sugar after face has been coated with butter.
- Sour cream onion; after dipping face of pretzel in butter, sprinkle with sour cream onion powder Garlic- same as sour cream onion, but use garlic powder.
- Sesame or poppy seed; BEFORE baking, AFTER dipping into dipping solution, dip pretzel face-down into the seeds, then bake.
- Salt is optional with this one.

### Nutrition Information

- Calories: 86.2
- Fiber: 0.7
- Sugar: 2.3
- Protein: 2.4
- Saturated Fat: 0
- Sodium: 1280
- Total Carbohydrate: 18.4
- Cholesterol: 0
- Total Fat: 0.2

## 22. Baby Bear Sandwiches

*Serving: 1 serving(s) | Prep: 1mins | Ready in:*

### Ingredients

- 1 slice bread
- peanut butter
- honey (optional)
- 2 raisins or 2 chocolate chips
- 1 maraschino cherry, halved

### Direction

- Mix the peanut butter with honey if desired and spread mixture onto bread. Cut the bread into a heart shape, using a cookie cutter.
- Use the raisins (or chocolate chips) on the heart shape to make the eyes. Place the cherry on the point of the heart shape to make the nose.

### Nutrition Information

- Calories: 77.9
- Total Fat: 0.8
- Fiber: 0.8

- Cholesterol: 0
- Protein: 1.9
- Saturated Fat: 0.2
- Sodium: 170.6
- Sugar: 3.6
- Total Carbohydrate: 15.6

## 23. Bacon Hash Browns Cakes Homemade

*Serving: 10-12 hash browns | Prep: 30mins | Ready in:*

### Ingredients

- 6 tablespoons olive oil
- 1 small onion, finely chopped
- 1 celery rib, finely chopped
- 1 red pepper
- 2 garlic cloves, crushed
- 11 ounces potatoes, peeled and grated
- 1 small zucchini, grated
- 1 tablespoon plain flour, plus extra for dusting
- 2 eggs
- 1/2 teaspoon freshly ground salt and pepper
- 2 teaspoons parsley, finely chopped
- 7 ounces bacon, finely chopped

### Direction

- Preheat the oven to 400°F Heat 2 tablespoons of the olive oil in a large frying pan over a medium-high heat. Add the onion, celery and pepper and fry for 3 minutes.
- Add the garlic and cook for 30 seconds.
- Transfer the mixture to a bowl and add the potatoes, zucchini, flour and eggs.
- Mix well and season with salt and pepper.
- Add the parsley and bacon and mix again.
- Using your hands, shape the mixture into small round cakes.
- Dust the rounds in flour and arrange on a large plate.
- Heat the remaining oil in a frying pan and fry the hash cakes over a high heat for about 2 minutes on each side, until brown. Transfer to the oven and cook for 10-12 minutes.
- Serve the hot hash cakes with hollandaise and a mixed salad.

### Nutrition Information

- Calories: 213.4
- Total Fat: 18.1
- Saturated Fat: 4.4
- Sodium: 186.4
- Fiber: 1.3
- Sugar: 1.4
- Total Carbohydrate: 8.4
- Cholesterol: 55.8
- Protein: 4.7

## 24. Banana Crackers

*Serving: 30 crackers | Prep: 10mins | Ready in:*

### Ingredients

- 1/4 cup butter
- 1/2 cup all-purpose flour
- 1/8 teaspoon salt
- 4 drops Tabasco sauce
- 1 banana, mashed
- coarse salt

### Direction

- Preheat oven to 450 and grease a 12x15 inch cookie sheet. In a med. size bowl using a pastry blender, mix butter, flour and 1/8 teaspoons salt together until crumbly.
- Using a fork, stir in Tabasco and banana.
- On a floured surface, knead mixture gently adding a small amount of flour if necessary to make the dough firm.
- Divide dough into half and roll out one half at a time on a floured surface until thin enough to cover prepared cookie sheet. Place dough on cookie sheet and sprinkle lightly with the

coarse salt. Using a pastry cutter, cut through dough into 1" squares.
- Bake 6-8 minutes or until lightly browned.
- Remove crackers with a spatula and place on a wire rack to cool.
- Repeat with second half of the dough.

## Nutrition Information

- Calories: 24.6
- Sodium: 21
- Total Carbohydrate: 2.5
- Cholesterol: 4.1
- Protein: 0.3
- Total Fat: 1.6
- Sugar: 0.5
- Saturated Fat: 1
- Fiber: 0.2

## 25. Banana Dumplings

*Serving: 4-6 serving(s) | Prep: 20mins | Ready in:*

## Ingredients

- 2 bananas, peeled and sliced in thick circular pieces
- 1 cup flour
- 1 cup milk
- 1 1/2 teaspoons sugar
- 1 egg
- 1 teaspoon baking powder
- 2 tablespoons vegetable oil

## Direction

- Peel and slice your bananas in small pieces.
- In a bowl, mix flour, milk, sugar, beaten egg, baking powder and oil as directed.
- Mix well until you get a thick mixture.
- Slide all your chopped banana pieces into this mixture.
- Take a deep frying saucepan or wok. Make sure you heat about half a cup of oil to the saucepan so the dumplings fry well.
- Keep the stove on medium to high heat.
- Using a tablespoon or wooden spoon, pick each banana piece from the bowl and pour directly into the hot oil. A little bit of the mixture will spread around the banana piece and that's good.
- Turn each dumpling after 1-2 minutes of deep frying so both sides are done well.
- As soon as the dumplings are golden brown, drain them on paper towel and serve hot with tea or coffee!

## Nutrition Information

- Calories: 290.5
- Total Carbohydrate: 42.1
- Protein: 7.5
- Total Fat: 10.8
- Saturated Fat: 2.8
- Sodium: 139.4
- Fiber: 2.4
- Sugar: 9
- Cholesterol: 61.4

## 26. Banana Oat Breakfast Bars

*Serving: 12 bars, 12 serving(s) | Prep: 10mins | Ready in:*

## Ingredients

- 4 cups oatmeal
- 1 tablespoon baking powder
- 1/2 teaspoon salt
- 1 tablespoon cinnamon
- 2 eggs, beaten
- 3/4 cup ripe banana, mashed
- 1/4 cup applesauce
- 1 cup milk
- 1 tablespoon maple syrup
- 3/4 cup brown sugar
- 1 tablespoon vanilla

- 1 cup dried cranberries

## Direction

- Preheat oven to 325 degrees. Grease a 13"x9" pan or use a parchment sling.
- Combine the oats, baking powder, salt and cinnamon. Make a well in the center.
- In another bowl combine eggs, banana, applesauce, milk, maple syrup, brown sugar and vanilla.
- Pour the liquid mix into the dry and stir until just combined. Add the dried cranberries.
- Place in greased pan and bake for 45 minutes.
- Cut into bars and enjoy.

## Nutrition Information

- Calories: 206.3
- Sodium: 217.9
- Sugar: 16.3
- Total Carbohydrate: 38.6
- Cholesterol: 38.1
- Protein: 6.2
- Total Fat: 3.4
- Saturated Fat: 1
- Fiber: 3.6

## 27. Banana Sticks

*Serving: 8 serving(s) | Prep: 5mins | Ready in:*

## Ingredients

- 4 bananas
- 60 ml low-fat yogurt
- 4 tablespoons granola cereal

## Direction

- Peel bananas and halve. Insert ice-cream stick in cut end of each piece, to make a handle.
- Holding by stick, dip into yoghurt (I cheat and dip it into the tub rather than try to coat it with the small amount), cover completely to exclude air, allow to drain away slightly then roll in granola lightly.
- Place on tray covered with foil or cling and freeze immediately in coldest part of freezer.
- Yum!

## Nutrition Information

- Calories: 75.7
- Total Fat: 1.2
- Saturated Fat: 0.3
- Sodium: 6.8
- Fiber: 1.9
- Sugar: 8.5
- Total Carbohydrate: 16
- Cholesterol: 0.5
- Protein: 1.6

## 28. Bananas In Milk

*Serving: 1 serving(s) | Prep: 2mins | Ready in:*

## Ingredients

- 2 bananas
- 1 1/2 cups milk
- 1 -2 teaspoon sugar

## Direction

- Peel and slice bananas into cereal bowl.
- Sprinkle with desired amount of sugar and cover with milk.
- Enjoy!

## Nutrition Information

- Calories: 460.5
- Total Fat: 14.2
- Sugar: 33
- Saturated Fat: 8.6
- Sodium: 181.7
- Fiber: 6.1
- Total Carbohydrate: 75.1

- Cholesterol: 51.2
- Protein: 14.6

## 29. Barkram (Berry Cream)

*Serving: 4 serving(s) | Prep: 10mins | Ready in:*

### Ingredients

- 1 quart berries (strawberries, raspberries, currants, gooseberries or blackberries)
- 3 cups water
- 3/4 cup sugar
- 2 tablespoons potato flour or 2 tablespoons cornstarch

### Direction

- Clean berries.
- Bring water to boil, add berries and sugar and boil several minutes.
- Mix potato flour with small amount of cold water; stir in and bring again to boiling point.
- Cool covered and serve with cream or milk.

### Nutrition Information

- Calories: 162.6
- Fiber: 0.3
- Sugar: 37.6
- Cholesterol: 0
- Total Fat: 0
- Saturated Fat: 0
- Sodium: 6.2
- Total Carbohydrate: 41.6
- Protein: 0.3

## 30. Bars Of Iron

*Serving: 24 serving(s) | Prep: 10mins | Ready in:*

### Ingredients

- 1 cup raisins
- 1/2 cup golden raisin
- 1/3 cup margarine
- 1/2 cup sugar
- 1 large egg
- 1 1/4 cups whole wheat flour
- 1/4 cup toasted wheat germ
- 1/2 cup blackstrap molasses
- 1 cup nonfat dry milk powder
- 1 cup sliced almonds
- 1 cup quick-cooking oats
- 1/2 cup nonfat milk
- 1/2 teaspoon ground ginger
- 1/2 teaspoon salt
- 1/2 teaspoon baking soda
- 1/2 teaspoon baking powder

### Direction

- Preheat your oven at 350 degrees. Grease a 9 X 13 inch pan. Put aside.
- In a medium sized bowl, cream margarine, sugar, molasses and egg.
- Combine flour, dry milk, wheat germ, baking powder, baking soda, salt and ginger. Mix well.
- Chop raisins using a food processor. Put aside.
- Blend your flour mixture into your creamed mixture with the liquid milk.
- Stir in oats, raisins, and half the almonds. Mix well.
- Pour into your prepared pan and spread evenly. Sprinkle with remaining almonds.
- Bake for approximately 30 minutes.
- Cool in pan and cut into 1 X 4 inch bars, or about 24 pieces.

### Nutrition Information

- Calories: 165.6
- Saturated Fat: 0.8
- Sugar: 12.7
- Total Carbohydrate: 26.6
- Total Fat: 5.2
- Sodium: 149.5
- Fiber: 2

- Cholesterol: 9.9
- Protein: 5

## 31. Beet, Dill Feta Frittata

*Serving: 2 serving(s) | Prep: 2mins | Ready in:*

### Ingredients

- 1 onion, thinly sliced
- 2 tablespoons olive oil
- 2 cooked beets, sliced
- 4 ounces feta cheese, crumbled
- 1 tablespoon dill, chopped
- 4 eggs, beaten with seasoning
- salt and pepper

### Direction

- Cook the onions in 2 tbsp oil in a small frying pan until golden.
- Layer the beets, feta and dill over, then pour the eggs inches
- Cook on medium high heat until nearly firm.
- Put under a hot broiler for 2 minutes until the top is set.
- Serve in wedges.

### Nutrition Information

- Calories: 470.2
- Saturated Fat: 14
- Sodium: 851.3
- Fiber: 1.8
- Sugar: 9.6
- Cholesterol: 476.5
- Protein: 22.5
- Total Carbohydrate: 13.8
- Total Fat: 36.4

## 32. Berry Breakfast Power Bar

*Serving: 16-20 serving(s) | Prep: 15mins | Ready in:*

### Ingredients

- 250 g dessert apples, chopped
- 30 ml lemon juice
- 150 g soft margarine (olive or vegetable)
- 75 g dark brown sugar
- 75 g golden syrup
- 325 g oats
- 15 g oat bran
- 25 g ground flax seeds
- 40 g dried cranberries
- 20 g dried blueberries
- 20 g sesame seeds
- 30 g sunflower seeds
- 50 g brazil nuts (shaved)

### Direction

- Bring apples to boil, then simmer for 10 minutes until soft.
- Melt margarine, sugar syrup in a large saucepan, then remove from heat.
- Add berries to hot mixture to allow time to plump up.
- Add all other ingredients. Mix well.
- Pat into 30cm x 20cm (12" x 8") pan.
- Bake @ 180c for 25 minutes.
- Allow to cool for 15mins before cutting and removing from pan onto cooling rack.

### Nutrition Information

- Calories: 237.9
- Total Fat: 13.4
- Saturated Fat: 2.3
- Sugar: 7.8
- Protein: 5.1
- Sodium: 107.6
- Fiber: 3.8
- Total Carbohydrate: 26.8
- Cholesterol: 0

## 33. Best Blondies Ever!

*Serving: 18 blondies, 8 serving(s) | Prep: 10mins | Ready in:*

### Ingredients

- 1 cup butter, melted
- 2 cups brown sugar
- 2 eggs, lightly beaten
- 2 teaspoons vanilla
- 1 teaspoon baking powder
- 1/4 teaspoon baking soda
- 1/8 teaspoon salt
- 2 cups all-purpose flour
- 1 cup butterscotch chips

### Direction

- Preheat oven to 350 F or 180°C Grease 16X16 inch pan.
- Beat butter and sugar in bowl.
- Add flour, soda, powder and salt then mix.
- Press into pan then bake for about 20 minutes. Cool, cut into square slabs and enjoy!

### Nutrition Information

- Calories: 660.8
- Total Fat: 30.7
- Sodium: 343.1
- Fiber: 0.8
- Total Carbohydrate: 92
- Saturated Fat: 20.1
- Sugar: 67.5
- Cholesterol: 113.9
- Protein: 5.5

## 34. Bite Sized Brownies

*Serving: 24 serving(s) | Prep: 15mins | Ready in:*

### Ingredients

- 1/3 cup brown sugar
- 3 ounces semisweet chocolate
- 1/4 cup butter
- 1/2 teaspoon vanilla
- 1 egg
- 1/3 cup flour
- 24 rosebud or Hershey chocolate kisses

### Direction

- Melt sugar, butter, and chocolate until just melted.
- Cool 1 minute.
- Blend in vanilla and egg.
- Gradually fold in flour. Pour mixture into greased mini muffin tins lined with or without paper liners.
- Bake at 350 degrees for 10- 12 minutes.
- While still warm, place one chocolate on each.
- You could also use those chocolate advent calendar pieces for the chocolates.

### Nutrition Information

- Calories: 79.4
- Saturated Fat: 3
- Fiber: 0.8
- Cholesterol: 14.9
- Protein: 1.3
- Sodium: 22.1
- Sugar: 5.3
- Total Carbohydrate: 8
- Total Fat: 5.3

## 35. Blueberry Oat Bread/Muffins

*Serving: 12 muffins, 12 serving(s) | Prep: 10mins | Ready in:*

### Ingredients

- 1 cup all-purpose flour
- 1 cup whole wheat flour
- 1 cup rolled oats

- ¾ cup sugar
- 1 ½ teaspoons baking powder
- ½ teaspoon baking soda
- ¼ teaspoon salt
- ¼ teaspoon allspice
- ¾ cup low-fat milk
- ⅓ cup melted butter
- 2 eggs
- 1 ¼ cups frozen blueberries or 1 ¼ cups frozen mixed berries

## Direction

- Combine dry ingredients in large mixing bowl.
- Add milk, butter and eggs.
- Mix just until moistened.
- Gently stir in berries.
- Spoon batter into 9x5x3 inch loaf pan that has been greased on the bottom only.
- Bake at 350F for 55-65 minutes.
- Cool in pan 10 minutes.
- Remove from pan and cool completely on wire rack.
- Can also be made into muffins-bake 20-25 minutes.

## Nutrition Information

- Calories: 229.7
- Cholesterol: 49.6
- Sugar: 18.2
- Total Carbohydrate: 38.5
- Fiber: 2.7
- Protein: 5.2
- Total Fat: 6.8
- Saturated Fat: 3.7
- Sodium: 202.2

## 36. Bola Bola Shrimp Balls

*Serving: 12-16 serving(s) | Prep: 15mins | Ready in:*

### Ingredients

- Bola Bola Balls
- ¼ lb ground chicken breast
- ¼ lb cooked shrimp, minced
- ¼ cup water chestnut, minced
- 1 small onion, minced
- 1 ½ tablespoons soy sauce
- 1 egg, lightly beaten
- 1 teaspoon salt
- ¼ teaspoon ground ginger
- vegetable oil, for frying
- Snappy Red Sauce for Bola Bola
- 1 cup chili sauce (Heinz)
- ½ cup chopped fine green pepper
- 3 tablespoons minced onions
- ½ teaspoon prepared horseradish

## Direction

- Combine all ingredients for the balls, except for the oil and mix together thoroughly.
- Shape into 1" balls and chill for at least 1 hour - or freeze now for future use.
- Thaw completely before frying.
- Fry at 360F until the balls are a rich golden brown.
- Serve at once.
- To make the sauce:
- Combine all the ingredients into a small saucepan and simmer for 10 minutes.
- Serve hot or cold.

## Nutrition Information

- Calories: 57.8
- Total Fat: 1.4
- Saturated Fat: 0.5
- Sodium: 487
- Fiber: 0.9
- Sugar: 1.1
- Total Carbohydrate: 5
- Cholesterol: 43
- Protein: 6

## 37. Boureki (Feta Pastries)

*Serving: 6-8 serving(s) | Prep: 15mins | Ready in:*

### Ingredients

- 1/2 cup yogurt
- 3/4 cup sunflower oil
- 3 eggs
- 6 cups leeks, sliced
- 1 cup feta cheese, crumbled
- 2 cups flour, sifted
- 1 teaspoon baking powder
- 1/2 teaspoon cayenne pepper (optional)
- 1/2 teaspoon black pepper
- 1 teaspoon salt

### Direction

- Preheat the oven to 400°F
- Whisk the yogurt, eggs and sunflower oil in a deep plastic bowl. Toss in leek and feta cheese.
- Add the flour, baking powder, cayenne pepper, black pepper and salt.
- Knead using your hands.
- Pour into an oven-safe Pyrex dish.
- Bake until the top gets nice golden color - it should take about 30-35 minutes.
- Cut in square pieces with a knife.

### Nutrition Information

- Calories: 562.9
- Sugar: 5.8
- Total Carbohydrate: 46.9
- Cholesterol: 130.7
- Protein: 13.1
- Total Fat: 36.4
- Saturated Fat: 8.6
- Sodium: 790.2
- Fiber: 2.8

## 38. Breakfast Burrito (Like Mc Donald's!)

*Serving: 1 serving(s) | Prep: 5mins | Ready in:*

### Ingredients

- 2 eggs
- 1 teaspoon bacon bits
- 1 tortilla
- shredded cheddar cheese (as much as you want)

### Direction

- First, put your tortilla on a plate.
- Next, scramble the two eggs.
- Then, put the eggs in the tortilla, and spread the bacon bits around evenly.
- Now, put as much shredded cheddar cheese as you want on the egg.
- Microwave for 15-25 seconds (just enough to warm the egg, bacon, and tortilla, and to melt the cheese.) Take it out and fold the tortilla like a burrito!
- Lastly, EAT!
- Hope you enjoy!

### Nutrition Information

- Calories: 365.4
- Fiber: 2.2
- Total Carbohydrate: 36.7
- Saturated Fat: 4.4
- Sodium: 585.2
- Sugar: 2.1
- Cholesterol: 423
- Protein: 18.4
- Total Fat: 15.4

## 39. Breakfast Burros ( Burritos )

*Serving: 1 serving(s) | Prep: 6mins | Ready in:*

## Ingredients

- 1 flour tortilla
- 2 eggs, scrambled
- 1/4 cup grated cheddar cheese or 1/4 cup swiss cheese or 1/4 cup monterey jack cheese

## Direction

- Warm tortilla in skillet.
- Top with scrambled eggs and sprinkle cheese on top.
- Fold and serve.

## Nutrition Information

- Calories: 354.4
- Protein: 22.1
- Total Fat: 21.6
- Saturated Fat: 9.6
- Fiber: 0.9
- Sodium: 506.2
- Sugar: 1.5
- Total Carbohydrate: 16.5
- Cholesterol: 452.7

## 40. Breakfast Snack Bar

*Serving: 16 serving(s) | Prep: 30mins | Ready in:*

## Ingredients

- 2 1/2 cups oatmeal
- 2 cups Rice Krispies
- 1 cup Special K cereal
- 1 cup sunflower seeds
- 1 cup raisins
- 1/2 cup coconut
- Sauce
- 1/4 cup butter
- 1 tablespoon molasses
- 1/2 cup light corn syrup
- 1/4 cup honey
- 1/2 cup peanut butter
- Topping
- 2 cups package dark chocolate chips (optional)

## Direction

- Spray 9" X 13" pan with non-stick spray.
- Mix the dry ingredients in a large bowl.
- Bring the first four sauce ingredients to a boil and cook for an additional two minutes.
- Stir 1/2 cup peanut butter into sauce mixture.
- Mix dry ingredients and sauce until well blended.
- Press firmly into prepared pan.
- Melt one bag dark chocolate chips and spread over bars.
- Cut bars after they have cooled.

## Nutrition Information

- Calories: 288.1
- Saturated Fat: 4.8
- Fiber: 3.5
- Total Carbohydrate: 37.4
- Cholesterol: 7.6
- Total Fat: 14.1
- Sugar: 15.2
- Protein: 7.3
- Sodium: 114.7

## 41. Breakfast Tortillas

*Serving: 6 serving(s) | Prep: 15mins | Ready in:*

## Ingredients

- 2 cups spinach, firmly packed, washed chopped
- 2 cups cooked brown rice
- 1 cup frozen corn kernels
- 1/2 cup salsa
- 6 whole wheat tortillas or 6 corn tortillas

## Direction

- Place the spinach in a saucepan with only the water you washed it in still clinging to the leaves.
- (If you washed the spinach the night before, place the spinach in the saucepan and sprinkle a little water over the leaves.) Cook, stirring, until just wilted, about 2 minutes.
- Remove from the saucepan and drain well.
- Place the brown rice, corn, and salsa in the saucepan.
- Cook, stirring, until heated through.
- Stir in the spinach.
- Spoon a line of the mixture down the center of each tortilla and roll.

## Nutrition Information

- Calories: 279
- Saturated Fat: 0.5
- Sodium: 598.2
- Total Carbohydrate: 54.6
- Total Fat: 4.1
- Fiber: 2.9
- Sugar: 0.7
- Cholesterol: 0
- Protein: 8.3

## 42. Brioche With Chocolate Centres

*Serving: 8 serving(s) | Prep: 30mins | Ready in:*

### Ingredients

- 2 cups all-purpose flour
- 1 1/2 teaspoons active dry yeast
- 1/2 cup warm milk
- 1 teaspoon vanilla essence
- 3 tablespoons sugar
- 2 egg yolks
- 125 g butter, softened and chopped
- 120 g dark chocolate, chopped into chunks about 15 g each

### Direction

- Place flour and yeast in the bowl of an electric mixer fitted with a dough hook.
- Place warm milk, vanilla and sugar in a separate bowl and mix until combined.
- Add milk mixture and egg yolks to flour and beat on medium speed until dough is a smooth ball.
- Continue beating, adding butter, a little at a time, until it is all incorporated and well beaten.
- Alternatively, mix the flour mixture and the yeast mixture in a bowl until a soft dough forms.
- Transfer dough to a lightly floured surface and knead until combined.
- Cover dough and set aside for 1 1/2- 2 hours or until it has doubled in size.
- Knead dough on a lightly floured surface until it is soft and elastic, then divide it into 8 equal pieces.
- Flatten dough slightly in the palm of your hand.
- Place a piece of chocolate in the middle of dough and fold over excess dough to enclose.
- Place brioche in greased and floured HIGH muffin molds or Brioche tins, cover and set aside for 1 hour or until it is well risen.
- Bake in preheated 350F (160C) oven for 15-20 minutes or until brioche are golden brown.
- Serve warm with a strong coffee.

## Nutrition Information

- Calories: 356.4
- Protein: 7
- Total Fat: 23.6
- Total Carbohydrate: 35
- Cholesterol: 82.7
- Fiber: 3.9
- Sugar: 5.1
- Saturated Fat: 14.4
- Sodium: 104

## 43. Broke Guy's Crushed Potatoes

*Serving: 2-4 serving(s) | Prep: 10mins | Ready in:*

### Ingredients

- 4 large potatoes
- 1 tablespoon olive oil
- 1 garlic clove, minced
- 1 tablespoon chives
- salt freshly ground black pepper, to taste
- 2 tablespoons cheese, grated
- 1 tablespoon parmesan cheese

### Direction

- Wash potatoes well and place in salted water. Bring to boil and cook till fork tender (15-20 minutes).
- Mix oil with garlic. Set aside.
- 5 minutes prior to the potatoes being done, preheat the broiler of your oven.
- Remove potatoes from the water and place on a baking sheet. Using a paper towel and your palm, crush the potatoes.
- Pour some garlic oil over each potato. Sprinkle some salt and pepper. Add some Parmesan/grated cheese and chives to each potato.
- Broil until nice and crispy (7-10 minutes). Serve immediately.

### Nutrition Information

- Calories: 687.5
- Sodium: 217.4
- Sugar: 5.8
- Cholesterol: 11.1
- Saturated Fat: 3.7
- Total Carbohydrate: 130.8
- Protein: 18.8
- Total Fat: 11.6
- Fiber: 16.3

## 44. Brownies Fudgy, Rich And Moist

*Serving: 1 11x7 pan | Prep: 15mins | Ready in:*

### Ingredients

- 4 ounces baker's unsweetened baking chocolate
- 2 -3 teaspoons instant coffee (not for drinking, lol)
- 3⁄4 cup butter or 3⁄4 cup margarine
- 2 cups sugar
- 3 eggs
- 1 teaspoon vanilla
- 1 cup flour
- 1 cup chopped nuts, if desired

### Direction

- Heat oven to 325°, grease an 11x 7 pan.
- Melt the chocolate with the butter in a large microwave safe bowl on high for 2 minutes or until the butter is melted and then stir until all the chocolate is melted.
- Then add 2-3 tsp of instant coffee to it, and stir well.
- Add the sugar, stir, then the eggs vanilla, stirring again.
- Add flour, then the nuts, if you're using them, stir until blended.
- Pour into prepared pan.
- Bake at 325°, for about 38-40 minutes.
- DO NOT OVERBAKE!
- The edges of the brownies should be pulling away from the side of the pan, but that's it.
- Just take them out of the oven.
- Don't bother too much with a tester, because you don't want it to come out clean, it should come out all messy and fudgy.
- But don't worry, they are cooked after this amount of time!
- Let them cool, and you will have rich, chocolatey, fudgy brownies that stay that way, and don't dry out.
- But I doubt they'll last that long, anyway.

## Nutrition Information

- Calories: 4859.9
- Total Carbohydrate: 567.9
- Cholesterol: 1000.5
- Total Fat: 285.4
- Saturated Fat: 139.3
- Protein: 72.3
- Sodium: 2139.2
- Fiber: 35
- Sugar: 409.2

## 45. Budget Biscuits

*Serving: 20-25 biscuits | Prep: 7mins | Ready in:*

### Ingredients

- 50 g butter, melted
- 1/2 cup sugar
- 1/2 cup flour
- 1 cup rolled oats
- 1 tablespoon golden syrup
- 1/2 teaspoon baking soda (Bicarbonate of Soda)
- 1 tablespoon water

### Direction

- Melt the butter in a pot.
- Take off the heat and add golden syrup. Stir until golden syrup is dissolved.
- Stir in sugar, rolled oats and flour.
- In a small bowl or cup, dissolve baking soda in water and add to mixture.
- Mix evenly.
- Put teaspoon lots onto a greased oven tray (leave room for spreading).
- Bake at 170 degrees Celsius for 8-15 minutes or until golden.
- Store in an airtight container.

### Nutrition Information

- Calories: 67.2
- Saturated Fat: 1.3
- Fiber: 0.5
- Sugar: 5.4
- Total Carbohydrate: 10.9
- Cholesterol: 5.3
- Protein: 1
- Total Fat: 2.3
- Sodium: 46.7

## 46. Bugs In A Rug

*Serving: 1 serving(s) | Prep: 2mins | Ready in:*

### Ingredients

- 1 burrito-size whole wheat tortilla
- 2 tablespoons peanut butter
- 2 tablespoons raisins (more or less to your liking)

### Direction

- Lay tortilla flat.
- Spread with peanut butter.
- Sprinkle raisins on top.
- Roll up and enjoy!

### Nutrition Information

- Calories: 247.4
- Saturated Fat: 3.3
- Sodium: 149.1
- Total Carbohydrate: 21.9
- Total Fat: 16.2
- Fiber: 2.6
- Sugar: 14.7
- Cholesterol: 0
- Protein: 8.6

## 47. Build Your Own Canadian Cranberry And Herb Turkey Burgers!

*Serving: 6 Cranberry and Herb Turkey Burgers, 6 serving(s) | Prep: 10mins | Ready in:*

### Ingredients

- 1/4 cup fresh breadcrumb
- 1 teaspoon extra virgin olive oil (3-4 sprays) or 1 teaspoon low-fat cooking spray (3-4 sprays)
- 1 small onion, peeled and finely diced
- 1 tablespoon chopped fresh thyme
- 1 1/2 teaspoons chopped fresh sage
- 1/4 teaspoon salt
- 1/2 teaspoon fresh ground pepper
- 1/4 cup dried cranberries or 1/4 cup craisins
- 1 lb 93% lean ground turkey (turkey mince)
- OPTIONAL
- 6 slices Canadian bacon (optional)
- 6 toasted hamburger buns (optional)
- Assorted condiments
- cheese slice
- cranberry sauce
- ketchup
- mustard
- dill pickle
- sliced fresh tomato
- lettuce
- sliced onion rings
- relish
- mayonnaise
- pickle
- mixed salad green

### Direction

- If grilling the burgers, preheat grill to medium-high. (You can also pan-fry or barbeque these burgers.).
- Meanwhile, heat oil in a large frying pan/skillet over medium heat, or spray three or four sprays of low fat spray. Add the diced onion and cook, stirring, for about 5 minutes. Add the thyme, sage, salt and pepper; cook until fragrant, for about 30 seconds more.
- Transfer the mixture to a large mixing bowl and add the breadcrumbs and cranberries, stir to combine. Let the mixture cool for 5 minutes. Add the turkey mince and stir until combined; do not overmix. Form the mixture into 6 burgers/patties.
- To cook on the stovetop: Coat a large nonstick frying pan/skillet, preferably cast-iron, with cooking spray and set over medium-high heat for 2 minutes. Add the burgers/patties, reduce heat to medium, and cook for about 5 minutes. Turn and cook on the other side for about 2 minutes. Cover and continue to cook until lightly browned but still juicy (the juices should run clear, not pink), about 3 - 4 minutes more.
- To grill: Oil the grill rack and grill the burgers for 5 to 6 minutes per side, flipping gently to avoid breaking them.
- Serve the burgers immediately, inside a burger bun with the optional extras and condiments as suggested. A mixed salad is also a great accompaniment.
- NB: If using the bacon or the cheese slices, grill or fry the bacon slices for about 2 to 3 minutes beforehand and then place the bacon or cheese slice on top of a cooked burger for the last 2 - 3 minutes of grilling or cooking time.

### Nutrition Information

- Calories: 144.3
- Protein: 15.7
- Total Fat: 6.8
- Saturated Fat: 1.7
- Total Carbohydrate: 5.2
- Sugar: 0.9
- Cholesterol: 52.2
- Sodium: 174.3
- Fiber: 0.8

## 48. C,h,p,b Sandwich

*Serving: 1 sandwich, 1 serving(s) | Prep: 5mins | Ready in:*

### Ingredients

- 2 slices whole wheat bread
- 1 1/2 tablespoons honey
- 2 tablespoons peanut butter
- 1 banana, sliced lengthwise
- 2 tablespoons coconut

### Direction

- Drizzle honey on both slices of bread.
- Spread peanut butter on one half and coconut on the other half.
- The banana goes in the middle!

### Nutrition Information

- Calories: 637.2
- Sodium: 419.8
- Total Carbohydrate: 86.2
- Cholesterol: 0
- Protein: 17.8
- Total Fat: 29.1
- Saturated Fat: 13.4
- Fiber: 11.6
- Sugar: 47.6

## 49. Calzonedilla (Italian Quesadilla)

*Serving: 1 serving(s) | Prep: 5mins | Ready in:*

### Ingredients

- 1 flour tortilla
- 1/2 cup part-skim mozzarella cheese (shredded)
- 1/2 teaspoon garlic powder
- 1/2 teaspoon basil leaves
- 1/2 teaspoon oregano leaves
- 1/4 teaspoon crushed red pepper flakes
- 1 teaspoon parmesan cheese (optional)
- 1/4 cup tomato sauce (optional)
- 1 teaspoon extra virgin olive oil

### Direction

- Heat a large skillet on medium-high.
- Add olive oil.
- When skillet is heated, put tortilla in pan (make sure to move tortilla around in pan to spread out oil, if it stays in one place).
- Add mozzarella cheese, then herbs, spices and optional ingredients to one half of tortilla.
- Fold tortilla over onto ingredients.
- Use a lid from a large pot or skillet to cover (helps to melt cheese faster).
- Cook for about 30-45 seconds, or until tortilla starts to get light brown spots.
- Flip tortilla, cover and cook for an additional 30-45 seconds, also until light brown spots.
- Serve hot.

### Nutrition Information

- Calories: 429.7
- Saturated Fat: 12.7
- Sugar: 2.3
- Total Carbohydrate: 20.3
- Total Fat: 25
- Sodium: 893.5
- Fiber: 1.5
- Cholesterol: 72.6
- Protein: 30.4

## 50. Caramel Corn Pops

*Serving: 10 cups | Prep: 5mins | Ready in:*

### Ingredients

- 1/3 cup margarine
- 1/2 cup brown sugar
- 1/2 cup corn syrup
- 3 tablespoons light molasses

- 1 teaspoon vanilla
- 1 teaspoon butter flavoring
- 8 cups Corn Pops cereal

## Direction

- Place a 28X18-inch piece of foil on a heat-proof surface. Coat with a cooking spray - set aside.
- In a heavy 12-inch fry pan, over medium heat cook margarine, brown sugar, corn syrup and molasses, stirring constantly, until the mixture starts to boil over entire surface. Cook and stir about 6 minutes longer.
- Carefully stir in vanilla and butter flavoring. Remove from heat and add corn pops cereal and quickly and carefully stir to coat cereal. Spread the mixture thinly on prepared foil.
- Separate cereal into clumps as it cools. Store in an airtight container.

## Nutrition Information

- Calories: 251.4
- Saturated Fat: 1.1
- Sodium: 173.4
- Sugar: 29.9
- Total Carbohydrate: 49.4
- Cholesterol: 0
- Protein: 1
- Total Fat: 6.2
- Fiber: 0.2

## 51. Caramel Cream Cheese Apple Dip

*Serving: 12 serving(s) | Prep: 5mins | Ready in:*

## Ingredients

- 1 (8 ounce) package cream cheese
- 1 (15 ounce) jar caramel ice cream topping
- sliced apple

## Direction

- Pour the ice cream topping over the block of cream cheese and serve with sliced apples.

## Nutrition Information

- Calories: 160.2
- Total Fat: 6.6
- Saturated Fat: 4.2
- Fiber: 0.3
- Total Carbohydrate: 25.2
- Cholesterol: 21.2
- Protein: 2
- Sodium: 186.5
- Sugar: 0

## 52. Cayenne Cheese Crackers

*Serving: 1 sheet | Prep: 15mins | Ready in:*

## Ingredients

- 1/2 lb grated extra-sharp cheddar cheese
- 1/4 cup butter, creamed
- 1/2 teaspoon salt
- 1/4-1/2 teaspoon cayenne pepper
- 1 1/2 cups sifted flour
- 1/2 tablespoon kosher salt (to sprinkle on tops)

## Direction

- Preheat oven 350.
- Cream all ingredients together except for the flour and kosher salt.
- Add flour gradually and mix thoroughly.
- Pack dough tightly into ball.
- Divide ball into 3 equal parts.
- Roll each into log shape 1 1/4 inches in diameter.
- Wrap each log in waxed paper.
- Refrigerate overnight (at least 8 hours).
- Slice logs into very thin wafers. (The thinner, the crispier).
- Sprinkle with kosher salt.

- Bake on ungreased cookie sheet approximately 12 minutes (until golden).

## Nutrition Information

- Calories: 2004.8
- Total Fat: 123.1
- Fiber: 5.2
- Total Carbohydrate: 146.3
- Saturated Fat: 77.3
- Sodium: 6390.1
- Sugar: 1.8
- Cholesterol: 360.1
- Protein: 76.4

## 53. Chaqueta's Fruit Salad

*Serving: 8-10 serving(s) | Prep: 25mins | Ready in:*

### Ingredients

- 4 cups watermelon, cubed (we like seedless to avoid the hassle of deseeding while eating)
- 4 cups honeydews, cubed
- 4 cups cantaloupes, cubed
- 4 cups green grapes, separated from stems
- 4 cups mangoes, cubed (we sometimes add more because it's so yummy)
- 2 (8 ounce) cans Coco Lopez
- 8 ounces sweetened condensed milk (optional)

### Direction

- Put all of the fruits and coco lopez into a large bowl. You can add other fruits too. We've sometimes added coconut, strawberries, jicama, or whatever was on hand.
- Toss everything together and serve with sweetened condensed milk drizzled on top or on the side for dipping. (Serve chilled for maximum flavour).

## Nutrition Information

- Calories: 302
- Sodium: 62
- Fiber: 5.2
- Cholesterol: 0
- Protein: 4.2
- Total Fat: 10.9
- Saturated Fat: 9.2
- Sugar: 46.7
- Total Carbohydrate: 54

## 54. Cheddar Parmesan Crackers

*Serving: 3 dozen (approximately) | Prep: 10mins | Ready in:*

### Ingredients

- 4 ounces cheddar cheese, coarsely grated
- 2 ounces parmesan cheese, finely grated
- 3/4 cup flour
- 1/4 teaspoon dry mustard
- 1/4 teaspoon kosher salt
- 1/8 teaspoon cayenne pepper
- 1/4 cup unsalted butter, softened and cut into small pieces
- 2 tablespoons water, plus more if needed

### Direction

- In the bowl of a food processor, place all the ingredients except the butter and water. Pulse 5 times. Add the butter and pulse again until the butter pieces are the size of small peas. Add the water, 1 tablespoon at a time, and pulse just until the dough holds together. If the dough is still crumbly, add more water 1 teaspoon at a time until it reaches the right consistency.
- Turn the dough out onto a large piece of waxed paper. Roll the dough into a log, 9 to 10 inches long, and square off the ends. Refrigerate, well wrapped, for at least 2 hours and up to 2 days or freeze it for up to 1 month. (You may want to cut the log in half or in

- thirds to freeze if you think you will want to defrost a smaller amount at a time.).
- Preheat the oven to 375°F (190°C).
- To make the crackers, cut the log into 1/4-inch-thick slices. Arrange the slices on a baking sheet 1 inch apart. Bake for 8 to 10 minutes, or until the crackers are a light golden color. Turn the crackers and bake for 3 to 5 more minutes, or until they are golden around the edges.
- Cool on a rack. Serve at room temperature.

## Nutrition Information

- Calories: 484.7
- Sugar: 0.5
- Protein: 20.1
- Total Fat: 33.7
- Saturated Fat: 21
- Fiber: 0.9
- Sodium: 672.8
- Total Carbohydrate: 25.2
- Cholesterol: 97.1

## 55. Cheddar And Veggie Pancakes

*Serving: 1 pancake, 12 serving(s) | Prep: 20mins | Ready in:*

## Ingredients

- 2 carrots
- 1/4 lb zucchini
- 1/4 lb grated cheddar cheese
- 6 ounces potatoes
- 2 large eggs
- 1/4 cup breadcrumbs
- 1/4 teaspoon salt
- 1 dash cayenne pepper
- vegetable oil

## Direction

- Peel carrots and potatoes and grate them, along with zucchini and cheddar cheese into large bowl. Stir in eggs, bread crumbs, salt and pepper.
- Heat about 1/2" vegetable oil in a 10" skillet. Pour in 1/4 cup of batter. Press down with spatula and flatten.
- Cook until well browned on both sides. Cook as many pancakes at a time as will fit in pan without touching.
- As each pancake is done remove from pan and set on plate covered with paper towel to drain.
- Serve hot. Makes approximately 12 cakes. **Freezes well**.

## Nutrition Information

- Calories: 75.7
- Sodium: 144.2
- Protein: 4.2
- Total Fat: 4.1
- Saturated Fat: 2.3
- Fiber: 0.8
- Sugar: 1.1
- Total Carbohydrate: 5.5
- Cholesterol: 40.9

## 56. Cheese Bacon Rounds

*Serving: 16 rolls | Prep: 5mins | Ready in:*

## Ingredients

- 200 g bacon, finely chopped
- 2 cups tasty cheese, grated
- 1 small onion, finely chopped
- 1 cup self-raising flour
- 1/2 cup milk
- 1 egg
- 1 teaspoon French mustard

## Direction

- Place bacon, cheese, onion flour in a bowl.

- Combine milk, egg mustard and add mixture to dry ingredients.
- Line an oven-tray with baking paper, spoon tablespoonfuls of the mixture onto the tray, allowing enough space for spreading.
- Bake at 200.C for 20 mins or until golden.
- Can be eaten hot or cold.

## Nutrition Information

- Calories: 162.5
- Cholesterol: 38.5
- Protein: 7
- Total Fat: 11.8
- Saturated Fat: 5.6
- Sodium: 314.2
- Fiber: 0.3
- Sugar: 0.3
- Total Carbohydrate: 6.9

## 57. Cheese Honey Ham Jackets

*Serving: 4 serving(s) | Prep: 15mins | Ready in:*

### Ingredients

- 4 jacket potatoes, cooked
- knob butter
- 1 tablespoon Dijon mustard
- 2 eggs, separated
- 100 g smoked mozzarella cheese, diced
- 75 g honey-roasted ham, roughly chopped
- 3 tablespoons chives, snipped
- salt pepper

### Direction

- Set oven temp to 180.C.
- Cut a 1cm slice off the top of each potato scoop out the flesh to leave a 5mm thick shell.
- Mash the flesh with the butter, mustard egg yolks, stir in the cheese, ham, chives salt pepper.

- Whisk the egg whites until fairly stiff fold into the potato mixture. Pile back into potato shells bake for 20 mins until puffed lightly browned.

## Nutrition Information

- Calories: 278.9
- Sugar: 2.3
- Protein: 13.2
- Cholesterol: 125.5
- Total Fat: 8.4
- Saturated Fat: 4.1
- Sodium: 246.6
- Fiber: 4.9
- Total Carbohydrate: 38.3

## 58. Cheese Onion Pull Apart Loaf

*Serving: 6 serving(s) | Prep: 15mins | Ready in:*

### Ingredients

- 0.5 (500 g) packet frozen chopped onions
- 2 cups self raising flour
- 1 teaspoon salt
- 60 g butter, diced
- 1 egg, lightly beaten
- 3/4 cup milk
- 1 tablespoon grainy mustard
- 2/3 cup grated tasty cheese
- 2 tablespoons chopped fresh parsley

### Direction

- Place the frozen onions in a microwave safe bowl and heat in the microwave on high for 4 minutes.
- Sift the flour and salt into a mixing bowl; add the butter and rub it in with your fingertips to resemble fine breadcrumbs.
- Mix the egg, milk and mustard together; add them to the flour mixture and mix to form a soft dough.

- Turn the dough out onto a well-floured surface and knead lightly; and then divide the mixture into approximately 14 uneven pieces.
- Line a greased 14cm x 22cm loaf pan with baking paper; and place half the dough in pieces over the base.
- Sprinkle with half of the onion, cheese and parsley; then cover it with the remaining dough and the remaining onion, cheese and parsley.
- Bake the loaf in a preheated oven at 200°C /400°F for 40-45 minutes or until it is a rich golden brown.
- Notes: This is best eaten hot straight from the oven. Add chopped Kalamata olives or diced bacon with the onion for a tasty addition.

## Nutrition Information

- Calories: 328
- Sugar: 0.3
- Cholesterol: 76.3
- Protein: 10.6
- Fiber: 2
- Total Carbohydrate: 36.6
- Total Fat: 15.4
- Saturated Fat: 9.2
- Sodium: 597.1

## 59. Cheese Vegemite Scrolls

*Serving: 48 scrolls | Prep: 10mins | Ready in:*

## Ingredients

- 4 sheets puff pastry
- 1/4 cup vegemite (yeast extract)
- 3 cups grated tasty cheese
- 1 egg, beaten

## Direction

- Preheat oven to 220 degrees Celsius.
- Line 2-3 baking trays with baking paper.
- Spread one sheet of pastry with 1/4 of the vegemite.
- Sprinkle vegemite coated pastry with 1/4 of the cheese.
- Roll up the pastry (like a scroll).
- Cut roll into 12 equal portions and place on prepared trays.
- Repeat above steps with 3 remaining sheets of pastry.
- Brush scrolls with beaten egg.
- Bake in preheated oven for 15-20 minutes, or until puffed and golden.

## Nutrition Information

- Calories: 149.8
- Sugar: 0.2
- Total Carbohydrate: 9.5
- Cholesterol: 13.1
- Total Fat: 10.6
- Fiber: 0.3
- Protein: 4.1
- Saturated Fat: 3.7
- Sodium: 157.6

## 60. Cheese Zucchini Crisps

*Serving: 4 serving(s) | Prep: 10mins | Ready in:*

## Ingredients

- 1/3 cup corn flake crumbs
- 2 tablespoons of grated parmesan cheese
- 1/2 teaspoon seasoning salt
- 1 dash garlic powder
- 4 small zucchini, cut in strips
- 1/4 cup of melted butter

## Direction

- Combine crumbs, cheese seasonings; place in a plastic bag.
- Dip zucchini strips in butter shake in the crumbs to coat.

- Place on a baking sheet; bake 375°F for 10 min or till crisp. 4 servings.

## Nutrition Information

- Calories: 140.4
- Saturated Fat: 7.8
- Sodium: 148.6
- Fiber: 1.4
- Cholesterol: 32.7
- Total Fat: 12.4
- Total Carbohydrate: 6.2
- Protein: 2.7
- Sugar: 2.4

## 61. Cheese And Raisin Latkes

*Serving: 4-6 serving(s) | Prep: 10mins | Ready in:*

### Ingredients

- 2 eggs, separated
- 1/4 cup water
- 2 tablespoons sugar
- 1 teaspoon salt
- 2 cups cottage cheese
- 3/4 cup flour, unsifted
- 1/2 cup raisins
- peanut oil (for frying)

### Direction

- Beat together egg yolks, water, sugar and salt.
- Stir in cottage cheese.
- Add flour; stir until thoroughly mixed.
- Mix in raisins.
- Beat the egg whites until stiff peaks form; fold into cottage cheese mixture.
- Heat about 1/8 to 1/4 inch oil in a heavy skillet.
- Drop about 1/4 cup cheese mixture into hot oil and fry on each side until golden.
- Serve hot with sour cream.

## Nutrition Information

- Calories: 308.8
- Saturated Fat: 3.8
- Total Carbohydrate: 41.5
- Cholesterol: 121.5
- Protein: 19.2
- Total Fat: 7.5
- Sodium: 1044.4
- Fiber: 1.3
- Sugar: 17.6

## 62. Cheesy Apple Breakfast Quesadillas

*Serving: 6 serving(s) | Prep: 10mins | Ready in:*

### Ingredients

- 6 large size flour tortillas
- 1 cup shredded colby-monterey jack cheese (or pepper jack cheese)
- 6 tablespoons sour cream
- 2 tablespoons cinnamon sugar
- 3/4 cup chopped apple
- 3 tablespoons butter

### Direction

- Spread each flour tortillas with 1 tablespoon sour cream; sprinkle with.
- 1 teaspoons cinnamon sugar.
- Top one tortilla 1/3 cup cheese, 1/4 cup chopped apple and second tortilla.
- For each serving, melt 1 tablespoon butter in a large skillet, brown quesadilla.
- 1 minute on each side or until lightly browned, carefully turning over tortilla.
- Cut into wedges. Serve with sour cream, if desired.

## Nutrition Information

- Calories: 524.4

- Total Carbohydrate: 65.4
- Protein: 14.4
- Saturated Fat: 10.8
- Fiber: 3.9
- Sugar: 8.5
- Cholesterol: 38.3
- Total Fat: 22.7
- Sodium: 886.5

## 63. Cheesy Garlic, Herb, Paprika Tomato Muffins

*Serving: 12 muffins, 6-12 serving(s) | Prep: 10mins | Ready in:*

### Ingredients

- 2 cups grated cheese (cheddar preferable, however other mild-tasting cheeses would be suitable also)
- 1 1/2 cups self-raising flour (preferably wholemeal)
- 1/2 teaspoon salt
- 1 tablespoon raw sugar
- 1 pinch cayenne pepper
- 1/2 teaspoon paprika
- 1/2 teaspoon smoked paprika
- 1 teaspoon garlic granules
- 1 teaspoon dried herbs
- 1 egg
- 1 cup milk
- 2 tomatoes (each sliced into 6)
- 1 tablespoon melted butter

### Direction

- Preheat oven to 210°C.
- Put the grated cheese, flour, salt, sugar, cayenne pepper, paprika, smoked paprika, garlic granules, and herbs into a large bowl.
- Mix lightly with your fingertips to combine. Make a well in the center.
- In another container, beat the egg and milk until evenly combined.
- Pour all the liquid onto the dry ingredients.
- Fold the two mixtures together, drawing in all the flour from the sides of the bowl until all ingredients are incorporated. Try not to overmix.
- Grease your deep muffin pan well.
- Spoon mixture off a tablespoon, helping it off with another spoon, into the pan. Fill each hole with as much as is needed to use up all of the batter.
- Place a slice of tomato on top of each muffin. Lightly brush each slice with a little melted butter or oil.
- Sprinkle with additional salt, cheese or paprika if desired.
- Bake at 210C for about 12 minutes, or until tomato slices are cooked (they'll look a bit shriveled), muffins spring back when pressed, and muffins look golden brown.
- Remove from oven and set aside to cool for 5-10 minutes before removing from pan.
- To easily remove from pan, slide a butterknife around the sides of each muffin, and then lift. Tip: If muffins are stuck, put a plate or rack on top of muffin tray and flip tray over. Smooth a wet tea towel or sponge over the base of each muffin cavity for 1 or so minutes, then give the tray a light shake. Keep sponging and lightly shaking until all muffins have come out. This method should release your muffins from their tray without breaking.
- Serve!

### Nutrition Information

- Calories: 308.7
- Total Fat: 13.9
- Sodium: 1002
- Sugar: 3.5
- Cholesterol: 70.1
- Saturated Fat: 8.3
- Fiber: 1.5
- Total Carbohydrate: 32.5
- Protein: 13.4

## 64. Cheesy Pretzel Dippers (Lunch Box Surprise)

*Serving: 2 Cubes, 8 serving(s) | Prep: 5mins | Ready in:*

### Ingredients

- 8 ounces medium cheddar
- 16 thin pretzel sticks
- honey dijon mustard or ranch dressing

### Direction

- Cut cheese into 16 cubes. Let stand at room temperature 10 to 15 minute or until cheese is at room temperature.
- Insert a thin pretzel stick into each cube.
- Serve with Honey Dijon Mustard or your child's favorite dressing.

### Nutrition Information

- Calories: 159.8
- Cholesterol: 29.8
- Protein: 8.3
- Total Fat: 9.7
- Saturated Fat: 6
- Sodium: 338.9
- Fiber: 0.4
- Sugar: 0.5
- Total Carbohydrate: 9.9

## 65. Cheesy Toast

*Serving: 1 serving(s) | Prep: 3mins | Ready in:*

### Ingredients

- 4 slices white bread
- tasty cheese, shredded or sliced
- tomato ketchup

### Direction

- Heat oven to 180 degrees.
- Place bread on baking tray.
- Top with tasty cheese and ketchup/catsup.
- Bake for 10 minutes.
- Serve immediately.

### Nutrition Information

- Calories: 266
- Sodium: 681
- Sugar: 4.3
- Total Carbohydrate: 50.6
- Total Fat: 3.3
- Saturated Fat: 0.7
- Fiber: 2.4
- Cholesterol: 0
- Protein: 7.6

## 66. Chewy Granola

*Serving: 12 serving(s) | Prep: 10mins | Ready in:*

### Ingredients

- 6 cups rolled oats
- 1 cup sliced almonds or 1 cup slivered almonds
- 2 cups pecan pieces
- 4 teaspoons cinnamon
- 6 tablespoons Splenda brown sugar blend
- 1 cup sugar-free maple syrup
- 1/2 cup vegetable oil
- 2 teaspoons vanilla extract
- 2 cups raisins

### Direction

- Preheat oven to 275°F.
- In a large bowl combine oats, nuts, cinnamon and brown sugar. Mix with hands to blend together thoroughly.
- In a separate bowl, combine maple syrup, vegetable oil and vanilla extract. Mix with whisk until blended.

- Pour wet ingredients over dry ingredients and mix with a large fork until all dry ingredients look coated.
- Pour mixture into an 11x15x2-inch sheet cake pan or 2 large sheet pans. A roaster or roasting pan will work just as well.
- Bake for 1 hour and 15 minutes, stirring every 15 minutes to ensure even browning.
- Remove from oven and place pan on a cooling rack.
- While hot, sprinkle raisins on top. Stir to spread raisins out with baked mixture.
- Let cool and store in an air tight container.

## Nutrition Information

- Calories: 504.9
- Total Fat: 28.7
- Sodium: 6
- Fiber: 8.1
- Sugar: 18.8
- Protein: 9.4
- Saturated Fat: 3
- Total Carbohydrate: 57.8
- Cholesterol: 0

## 67. Chex Mix My Way

*Serving: 18 serving(s) | Prep: 10mins | Ready in:*

### Ingredients

- 6 tablespoons butter, melted (8 Tbls)
- 2 teaspoons Lawry's Seasoned Salt (3 tsp)
- 7 teaspoons Worcestershire sauce (9 tsp or 3 Tbls)
- 8 cups Crispix cereal (1 box)
- 1 cup mixed nuts
- 1 cup small pretzels

### Direction

- Combine melted butter, seasoned salt and Worcestershire sauce.
- Place cereal, nuts and pretzels in a roasting pan.
- Pour butter mixture over cereal mixture stirring constantly to coat.
- Place in preheated 250°F oven and bake for 1 hour, stirring every 15 minutes.
- Cool and store in an airtight container or resealable plastic bag.

## Nutrition Information

- Calories: 131.1
- Sugar: 2.2
- Cholesterol: 10.2
- Total Fat: 7.9
- Saturated Fat: 3
- Fiber: 0.8
- Protein: 2.2
- Sodium: 206.4
- Total Carbohydrate: 13.8

## 68. Chicken Bites With Spice

*Serving: 12 bites | Prep: 20mins | Ready in:*

### Ingredients

- 350 g ground chicken (ground chicken)
- 80 g fresh breadcrumbs
- 6 green onions, thinly sliced
- 2 tablespoons coriander, chopped
- 1 clove garlic, crushed
- 1 cm ginger, grated
- 1 egg

### Direction

- Preheat oven to 200C (400F).
- Place minced chicken, breadcrumbs, green onions, coriander, garlic, ginger and egg in a food processor and pulse to combine.
- Divide chicken mixture into 12 equal pieces and with wet hands shape into neat ovals.

- Place bites on a lightly oiled baking sheet and refrigerate for 10 minutes.
- Bake chicken bites for 25 minutes or until lightly browned.
- Serve hot or cold.

## Nutrition Information

- Calories: 76.3
- Saturated Fat: 0.9
- Sodium: 73.3
- Fiber: 0.5
- Sugar: 0.6
- Protein: 6.6
- Total Fat: 3.1
- Total Carbohydrate: 5.5
- Cholesterol: 40.3

## 69. Chicken Dippers

*Serving: 4 4, 4 serving(s) | Prep: 5mins | Ready in:*

### Ingredients

- 1 cup flour
- 2 eggs
- 1 cup oatmeal
- 4 boneless skinless chicken breasts, sliced into1/2 inch wide pieces
- salt and pepper

### Direction

- Preheat oven to 400°F
- Set up a breading station by putting the flour, in a baking dish. Whisk eggs and pour into another baking dish and sprinkle oatmeal into a 3rd baking dish.
- Dip the chicken pieces into the flour first, shaking off any excess. Then into the egg mixture, again shaking off the excess and finally into the oatmeal.

- Lay on a baking sheet and bake for 15-20 minutes, or until golden brown on the outside and cooked through.

## Nutrition Information

- Calories: 358.1
- Sodium: 113.1
- Total Carbohydrate: 37.6
- Cholesterol: 174.2
- Protein: 36.9
- Saturated Fat: 1.4
- Fiber: 2.8
- Sugar: 0.6
- Total Fat: 5.5

## 70. Chili Nuts Santa Fe

*Serving: 3 cups | Prep: 15mins | Ready in:*

### Ingredients

- 1 egg white
- 1 tablespoon frozen orange juice concentrate, thawed
- 1/4 cup sugar
- 1 tablespoon chili powder
- 1 teaspoon garlic powder
- 1/2 teaspoon ground cumin
- 1/4 teaspoon ground black pepper
- 1/4-1/2 teaspoon cayenne pepper
- 1/4 teaspoon celery salt
- 1/4 teaspoon ground cinnamon
- 3 cups peanuts or 3 cups mixed nuts

### Direction

- Heat oven to 325 degrees.
- Combine egg white, orange juice concentrate, sugar, chili powder, garlic powder, cumin, black pepper, cayenne, celery salt, and cinnamon in a large mixing bowl.
- Stir in nuts, toss to coat.

- Line a 15 x 10 x 1 inch pan with foil, spray with veggie spray.
- Spread nuts on foil.
- Bake for 20 minutes, stirring twice, Cool, break apart large clusters.
- Store in an airtight container at room temperature up to 1 week.

## Nutrition Information

- Calories: 920.8
- Sodium: 89.9
- Fiber: 13.7
- Cholesterol: 0
- Protein: 39.6
- Total Fat: 72.4
- Sugar: 24.9
- Total Carbohydrate: 45.1
- Saturated Fat: 10.1

## 71. Choco Peanut Butter Snack Mix

*Serving: 24-30 serving(s) | Prep: 5mins | Ready in:*

### Ingredients

- 7 cups Honey Nut Cheerios
- 7 cups peanut butter Captain Crunch cereal
- 7 ounces small pretzels, salted
- 1 (10 ounce) box Teddy Grahams chocolate graham snacks
- 1 (1 lb) bag M's plain chocolate candy

### Direction

- Dump everything into a large bowl.
- Mix gently with clean hands.
- Store in ziploc bags.

### Nutrition Information

- Calories: 200.8
- Total Fat: 5.5
- Saturated Fat: 2.8
- Fiber: 1.8
- Protein: 3.2
- Sodium: 274.9
- Sugar: 18.6
- Total Carbohydrate: 35.2
- Cholesterol: 2.6

## 72. Chocolate Cherry Slice

*Serving: 12 serving(s) | Prep: 15mins | Ready in:*

### Ingredients

- 200 g dark chocolate, chopped
- 3/4 cup coconut
- 1/3 cup caster sugar
- 1 cup glace cherries, chopped
- 1 egg white

### Direction

- Grease a 19cm x 29cm lamington pan, line base and sides with paper, grease paper well.
- Melt chocolate in heatproof bowl over hot water.
- Spread over base of prepared pan, refrigerate until set.
- Combine coconut, sugar, cherries and egg white in a bowl.
- Spread over chocolate.
- Rough top lightly with a fork.
- Bake in moderate oven for about 15 minutes.
- Cool in pan.
- Cut when cold.
- Store in refrigerator.

### Nutrition Information

- Calories: 154.8
- Total Fat: 13.6
- Saturated Fat: 9.3
- Sugar: 6.1
- Total Carbohydrate: 12.6
- Protein: 3.2

- Sodium: 11.2
- Fiber: 4.1
- Cholesterol: 0

## 73. Chocolate Cookie Ice Cream

*Serving: 10 1/2 cup servings | Prep: 5mins | Ready in:*

### Ingredients

- 2 cups heavy cream, chilled
- 1 cup whole milk, chilled
- 3/4 cup sugar
- 1 teaspoon vanilla extract
- 1/2 cup crushed chocolate sandwich style cookies (such as Oreos)

### Direction

- Place heavy cream, milk, sugar and vanilla extract in a medium mixing bowl and stir until well blended.
- Pour into freezer bowl of an electric ice cream maker.
- Turn the machine on and freeze until the mixture thickens, about 20-25 minutes; add crushed cookies to the ice cream during the last 5-10 minutes of freezing.
- Transfer to an air tight container and place in your freezer until firm, about 2 hours.

### Nutrition Information

- Calories: 226.8
- Protein: 1.7
- Total Fat: 17.5
- Sodium: 26.6
- Cholesterol: 64.4
- Total Carbohydrate: 16.6
- Saturated Fat: 10.9
- Fiber: 0
- Sugar: 15.6

## 74. Chocolate Crispy Rice Clusters

*Serving: 12 clusters, 12 serving(s) | Prep: 10mins | Ready in:*

### Ingredients

- 1 cup semisweet baking chips
- 1/2 teaspoon vanilla extract
- 1 dash cinnamon
- 1 cup Rice Krispies (approx, see directions)

### Direction

- Line a mini-muffin pan with mini-muffin paper cups. Fill each cup about halfway with Rice Krispies. No real measurement required here.
- Carefully melt the chocolate chips (can also use bar chocolate for baking, candy melts would also work but already have a lot of added flavor thus taking away from the vanilla-cinnamon combo) either on stovetop or in the microwave. If microwaving, be VERY careful because culinary chocolate can burn if nuked too hard!
- When it's a nice stirring consistency, stir in the vanilla and cinnamon.
- While the chocolate is still hot, spoon over the Rice Krispies, coating them well.
- Gently re-microwave if mixture begins to stiffen.
- Freeze the pan for at least 2 hours prior to eating.

### Nutrition Information

- Calories: 9.6
- Fiber: 0
- Sugar: 0.2
- Total Fat: 0
- Sodium: 22.2
- Protein: 0.1
- Saturated Fat: 0
- Total Carbohydrate: 2

- Cholesterol: 0

## 75. Chocolate Dip

*Serving: 2 cups | Prep: 0S | Ready in:*

### Ingredients

- 8 ounces unsweetened chocolate
- 1 (14 ounce) can sweetened condensed milk
- 2 tablespoons light corn syrup
- 1/2 cup milk
- 1 teaspoon vanilla
- 1/2 teaspoon cinnamon

### Direction

- Slowly melt chocolate (best to use fondue pot if available) and stir in condensed milk and corn syrup.
- Once that is all melted and smooth, stir in regular milk, vanilla, and cinnamon.
- If necessary, slowly add more milk (best if it is prewarmed) until dipping consistency.

### Nutrition Information

- Calories: 1314
- Fiber: 19.1
- Sugar: 115.2
- Total Carbohydrate: 162.2
- Total Fat: 78.9
- Saturated Fat: 49
- Sodium: 323.1
- Cholesterol: 76
- Protein: 32.4

## 76. Chocolate Double Dipped Strawberries

*Serving: 36 dipped strawberries | Prep: 5mins | Ready in:*

### Ingredients

- 36 strawberries, unhulled (about 1 quart)
- 1 1/2 cups dark chocolate chips (or semisweet)
- 1 tablespoon vegetable shortening
- 1 1/2 cups chocolate sprinkles (about 6 oz.)
- pistachios, chopped fine (optional)

### Direction

- Line a cookie sheet with waxed paper. Wipe strawberries clean and dry with paper towels.
- Stir chocolate chips and shortening in top of a double boiler set over simmering water until chocolate melts and mixture is smooth (or melt in the microwave).
- Place chocolate sprinkles in shallow bowl. Holding 1 strawberry by its green top, dip 3/4 of the strawberry into melted chocolate. Let the excess drip off, then dip into chocolate sprinkles. Place on waxed paper-lined sheet. Repeat, dipping remaining strawberries into chocolate, then into sprinkles and/or chopped pistachios.
- Refrigerate until chocolate coating is firm, about 1 hour. This can be prepared 8 hours ahead and kept refrigerated. Enjoy!

### Nutrition Information

- Calories: 40.5
- Sodium: 0.9
- Fiber: 0.7
- Sugar: 4.4
- Total Carbohydrate: 5.3
- Total Fat: 2.5
- Saturated Fat: 1.4
- Cholesterol: 0
- Protein: 0.4

## 77. Chocolate French Toast Sticks

*Serving: 14 sticks, 4 serving(s) | Prep: 15mins | Ready in:*

## Ingredients

- Step 1
- toast stick
- 14 slices bread (crust removed)
- nutella chocolate hazelnut spread
- Step 2
- batter
- 2 eggs (lightly beaten)
- 1 teaspoon baking soda
- 2 teaspoons flour
- 1 dash salt
- 1 dash cinnamon
- 1/2-1 teaspoon vanilla extract
- Step 3
- 2 tablespoons oil
- Step 4
- yogurt, sauce
- 2 tablespoons cocoa powder
- 1/2 cup whole milk vanilla yogurt (I like old home)
- 1/2 cup milk
- 1/4 cup sugar
- 1 dash vanilla extract
- 1 dash almond extract
- 1 tablespoon butter

## Direction

- Step 1:
- Prepare your 14 slices of bread by removing the crust and rolling them flat with a rolling pin.
- Spread the Nutella evenly over the bread slices and roll each one in a tight roll.
- Step 2:
- In a bowl add your eggs and whisk lightly.
- Add the baking soda and flour try to remove all lumps and slowly add milk then rest of step 2 ingredients to make a very thin batter.
- Preheat your pan to a medium heat with the oil.
- Place the rolls in the batter turning to evenly coat and place in heated pan browning to a nice golden brown on each side and placing in a warm paper towel covered plate to drain.
- Step 3:
- Place the Coco powder in a bowl and mix it with the yogurt, milk, sugar, vanilla and almond (I like to use a hand mixer to mix this).
- Rinse your pan and dry then bring again to a medium heat turning then to a medium low/low add butter, once it begins to dissolve add the yogurt mixture and stir until it becomes lightly bubbly and thickens, remove from heat.
- Plate your French toast sticks and then yogurt sauce as well as a dollop of just vanilla yogurt on the plate.
- Serve and enjoy!
- (These can be made ahead up to the point that you batter and placed in a pan in the fridge covered).

## Nutrition Information

- Calories: 454.5
- Protein: 12.6
- Sodium: 1034.4
- Fiber: 3
- Total Carbohydrate: 62.4
- Cholesterol: 121.6
- Total Fat: 17.5
- Saturated Fat: 5.8
- Sugar: 18

## 78. Chocolate Peanut Butter Crunch

*Serving: 16 serving(s) | Prep: 5mins | Ready in:*

## Ingredients

- 6 cups crispy corn and crispy rice cereal
- 1 2/3 cups chocolate chips (11oz.pkg)
- 1/4 cup creamy peanut butter
- 1 cup sifted powdered sugar

## Direction

- Place cereal in a large bowl, set aside.

- In small HEAVY saucepan melt morsels and peanut butter over low heat, stirring until combined.
- Pour over cereal, stirring gently until coated.
- Put cereal mixture into a LARGE plastic bag.
- Sprinkle powdered sugar over cereal mixture.
- Seal the bag and gently shake till coated with powdered sugar.
- Spread on wax paper to cool.
- Store in an air tight container.

## Nutrition Information

- Calories: 174.9
- Sugar: 18.1
- Cholesterol: 0
- Total Fat: 7.4
- Saturated Fat: 3.6
- Sodium: 100.6
- Fiber: 1.4
- Total Carbohydrate: 28.4
- Protein: 2.5

## 79. Chocolate Silk Pudding

*Serving: 1/2 cups, 4 serving(s) | Prep: 6mins | Ready in:*

### Ingredients

- 2 cups skim milk
- 1/3 cup sugar
- 3 tablespoons unsweetened cocoa
- 3 tablespoons cornstarch
- 1 1/2 tablespoons margarine
- 1/2 teaspoon vanilla extract
- 1/4 teaspoon almond extract
- 1 tablespoon sliced almonds, toasted (optional)

### Direction

- Place milk in a 1 1/2 qt casserole dish. Microwave uncovered on high for 3 minutes or until milk is hot but not boiling.
- Combine sugar, cornstarch, and cocoa and stir into hot milk.
- Microwave uncovered on high for 3 minutes or until thickened, stirring after 1 1/2 minutes.
- Add margarine and extracts and stir well. Refrigerate for about an hour. Top with almonds.

## Nutrition Information

- Calories: 187.3
- Saturated Fat: 1.3
- Sugar: 16.8
- Protein: 5.7
- Cholesterol: 2.5
- Total Fat: 5.1
- Sodium: 123.9
- Fiber: 1.4
- Total Carbohydrate: 31.3

## 80. Chocolate Strawberry Frost

*Serving: 1 Tall Glass, 1 serving(s) | Prep: 5mins | Ready in:*

### Ingredients

- 1 cup non-fat vanilla frozen yogurt or 1 cup vanilla ice cream (about 2 large scoops)
- 1 cup strawberry, frozen (cut up)
- 1/2-1 cup milk (or, if you want, use chocolate milk or chocolate soy milk and omit the chocolate powder)
- 1 packet chocolate instant breakfast drink mix or 1 packet ovaltine or 1 packet chocolate-flavor Nestle Nesquik powder

### Direction

- Place frozen yogurt/ice cream, strawberries, milk, and the mix in blender.
- Cover.
- Blend until smooth.
- Pour into a tall glass and enjoy!

## Nutrition Information

- Calories: 124.2
- Sugar: 6.7
- Total Carbohydrate: 16.7
- Cholesterol: 17.1
- Total Fat: 4.9
- Sodium: 61.2
- Fiber: 2.9
- Protein: 5
- Saturated Fat: 2.8

## 81. Chocolatey Rice Krispies Easter Eggs

*Serving: 14 eggs, 14 serving(s) | Prep: 15mins | Ready in:*

### Ingredients

- 1 tablespoon margarine
- 1 tablespoon smooth peanut butter
- 125 g marshmallows (about 20 large)
- 3 cups Rice Krispies
- 1/8 cup semi-sweet chocolate chips (or more if you are looking for a stronger chocolate flavour)
- 1/2 cup butterscotch chips (or peanut butter chips or white chocolate chips)
- chocolate sprinkles or rainbow candy sprinkles

### Direction

- In a large saucepan over medium-low heat, melt margarine and peanut butter.
- Stir in marshmallows, stir until melted and well blended. Stir in chocolate chips until melted; remove from heat.
- Stir in Rice Krispies until coated.
- Working quickly, shape Rice Krispies into egg shapes.
- It is useful to have a hollow plastic egg you can press the rice krispies into as a form; we use a jello egg mold, then press the two half eggs together by hand.
- If Rice Krispies mixture starts to harden, replace saucepan over low heat.
- Let Rice Krispies eggs cool in fridge or at room temperature.
- When cool, melt butterscotch chips in microwave on low heat for about 30 seconds at a time stirring often - careful not to burn!
- Spread melted butterscotch chips on the top of each eggs; dip egg into chocolate sprinkles.
- Let eggs cool; individually wrap in saran wrap.
- This recipe makes about 14 medium-large eggs.

## Nutrition Information

- Calories: 105.5
- Cholesterol: 0
- Fiber: 0.2
- Total Carbohydrate: 17.6
- Sugar: 10.7
- Protein: 1.1
- Total Fat: 3.7
- Saturated Fat: 2
- Sodium: 61.1

## 82. Christmas Crackers

*Serving: 20 serving(s) | Prep: 15mins | Ready in:*

### Ingredients

- 1 (11 ounce) box oyster crackers
- 2/3 cup popcorn oil (I prefer Orville Redenbachers)
- 1/2 teaspoon dill
- 1/2 teaspoon lemon pepper
- 1 ounce dry ranch dressing mix (1 packet)

### Direction

- Put crackers in a large mixing bowl.

- Combine remaining ingredients in a large measuring glass or small bowl and whisk together.
- Pour over crackers and start turning with a plastic spatula or wooden spoon; try not to break the crackers.
- Stir for a few minutes so that there is no pool of oil at bottom of bowl and the crackers have absorbed the majority of it. You can let them sit to dry out a bit, but I usually can't wait that long! Enjoy! Bet you can't eat just one handful!
- *** Make sure to use Ranch DRESSING mix, NOT the dip mix! ***.

## Nutrition Information

- Calories: 130
- Saturated Fat: 1.2
- Sugar: 0.3
- Protein: 1.5
- Cholesterol: 0
- Total Fat: 8.7
- Sodium: 174.3
- Fiber: 0.5
- Total Carbohydrate: 11.6

## 83. Christmas Snow Logs

*Serving: 1-3 serving(s) | Prep: 10mins | Ready in:*

### Ingredients

- 1 banana
- peanut butter
- shredded coconut
- powdered sugar

### Direction

- Cut banana in three pieces.
- Spread peanut butter all over each piece.
- Roll the pieces in coconut.
- Sprinkle the sugar over banana and plate.

## Nutrition Information

- Calories: 105
- Total Carbohydrate: 26.9
- Cholesterol: 0
- Protein: 1.3
- Total Fat: 0.4
- Saturated Fat: 0.1
- Fiber: 3.1
- Sugar: 14.4
- Sodium: 1.2

## 84. Chunky Monkey Bread

*Serving: 8 serving(s) | Prep: 10mins | Ready in:*

### Ingredients

- 3 (16 ounce) cans refrigerated biscuits
- 1 cup sugar
- 1 teaspoon cinnamon
- 1/2 cup margarine
- 1 cup of packed brown sugar

### Direction

- Separate biscuits; cut each biscuit into 4 pieces.
- Mix cinnamon and sugar in a bowl coat each piece of biscuit and pile into a Bundt or tube pan.
- Heat margarine and brown sugar until it is melted; pour over the biscuits.
- Bake at 350°F for about 20 minutes.
- When it has cooled, unmold onto plate.
- Pull apart to eat.

## Nutrition Information

- Calories: 896.2
- Protein: 11.5
- Sodium: 2188.4
- Sugar: 65.3
- Total Carbohydrate: 132.9

- Cholesterol: 0
- Total Fat: 36.4
- Saturated Fat: 8.3
- Fiber: 2.9

## 85. Cinnabutter Toast

*Serving: 1 slice, 1 serving(s) | Prep: 5mins | Ready in:*

### Ingredients

- 1 slice toast
- 2 teaspoons butter
- 1/4 teaspoon cinnamon
- 1/4 teaspoon sugar

### Direction

- Toast the bread and butter it.
- Combine cinnamon and sugar.
- Sprinkle the cinnamon-sugar over the butter.
- Say "Mmmmm."

### Nutrition Information

- Calories: 189.3
- Sugar: 1.8
- Cholesterol: 40.9
- Total Fat: 10.1
- Sodium: 253.9
- Protein: 4
- Saturated Fat: 5.4
- Fiber: 1.2
- Total Carbohydrate: 21

## 86. Cinnamon Apple Latkes

*Serving: 4-6 serving(s) | Prep: 10mins | Ready in:*

### Ingredients

- 2 eggs
- 3 tablespoons sugar
- 1 teaspoon salt
- 2 teaspoons cinnamon
- 1/3 cup water
- 3 cups cooking apples, chopped
- 3/4 cup flour, unsifted
- 1 teaspoon lemon peel, grated
- peanut oil
- 1/2 cup sugar

### Direction

- Beat eggs until light and foamy.
- Mix in 3 tablespoons sugar, salt, 1 teaspoons cinnamon, and water until well blended.
- Stir in chopped apple, flour and grated lemon peel; mix well.
- Heat the oil in skillet.
- Drop 1/4 cup apple mixture into hot oil. Flatten slightly. Fry on each side until golden brown.
- Drain on paper towels.
- Combine 1/2 cup sugar and cinnamon to make the topping.
- Sprinkle sugar-cinnamon mixture over hot latkes.
- Serve immediately.

### Nutrition Information

- Calories: 307.3
- Total Carbohydrate: 66.5
- Cholesterol: 105.8
- Total Fat: 2.9
- Sugar: 44.5
- Sodium: 618.5
- Fiber: 3.5
- Protein: 5.9
- Saturated Fat: 0.8

## 87. Cinnamony Carrots With Cream Cheese Dip

*Serving: 4-6 serving(s) | Prep: 5mins | Ready in:*

### Ingredients

- 1 (18 ounce) bag baby carrots
- water, for boiling
- salt, to taste
- 2 teaspoons dried onion flakes
- 1 tablespoon cinnamon
- 12 g sugar substitute (Splenda works best)
- 1 (8 ounce) package cream cheese, at room temperature (I use fat-free)

### Direction

- Boil carrots in water till tender or place in a microwave safe dish with water and microwave on high 12 minutes.
- Drain in large sieve, shaking constantly.
- while shaking, sprinkle first salt, then minced onion, cinnamon, and sugar substitute on the carrots, in that order.
- Let carrots sit in sieve 5 minutes to evaporate any leftover moisture.
- Serve with softened cream cheese for dip.

### Nutrition Information

- Calories: 259.9
- Total Fat: 20
- Saturated Fat: 12.5
- Cholesterol: 62.4
- Total Carbohydrate: 16.5
- Protein: 5.3
- Sodium: 267.9
- Fiber: 3.3
- Sugar: 8.8

## 88. Cocoa Krispies Squares

*Serving: 8-10 serving(s) | Prep: 10mins | Ready in:*

### Ingredients

- 6 ounces semi-sweet chocolate chips (1 cup)
- 1/3 cup peanut butter
- 4 cups COCOA KRISPIES® cereal

### Direction

- Melt chips and peanut butter in top of double boiler.
- Add to Cocoa Krispies.
- Press into a buttered pan; refrigerate and cut into squares, when ready to serve.

### Nutrition Information

- Calories: 243.7
- Saturated Fat: 5.3
- Total Fat: 12.4
- Sodium: 182.9
- Fiber: 2.3
- Sugar: 19.6
- Total Carbohydrate: 33.3
- Cholesterol: 0
- Protein: 4.7

## 89. Cocoa Peanut Logs

*Serving: 8 serving(s) | Prep: 8mins | Ready in:*

### Ingredients

- 1/3 cup peanut butter
- 4 cups COCOA KRISPIES® cereal
- 1 cup chocolate chips

### Direction

- Melt peanut butter and chips over low heat. Remove from heat.
- Add cocoa Krispies and pack into 8 x 8 inch buttered pan.
- Put into refrigerator, cut into squares when nearly firm. Keep refrigerated.

## Nutrition Information

- Calories: 242.5
- Total Fat: 12.3
- Saturated Fat: 5.2
- Sodium: 182.8
- Sugar: 19.4
- Protein: 4.7
- Fiber: 2.3
- Total Carbohydrate: 33.1
- Cholesterol: 0

## 90. Coconut Chocolate Tarts

*Serving: 8 Tarts | Prep: 10mins | Ready in:*

### Ingredients

- 2 egg whites
- 1/2 cup sugar
- 2 cups desiccated coconut
- FILLING
- 1 1/4 cups cream
- 300 g quality dark chocolate, chopped

### Direction

- Preheat oven to 350F (180C).
- Place the egg whites, sugar and coconut in a bowl and mix to combine them.
- With wetted hands or a spoon, press the coconut mixture into eight 3/4 cup (6 fl. oz.) capacity, deep muffin tins, covering the base and sides to make a shell.
- Place in a preheated oven and bake for 8-10 minutes or until the shells are just beginning to turn a light golden colour.
- Cool the shells for 1 minute, then gently remove them from the tin and place on a wire rack to cool.
- Make the filling while the bases are cooking.
- Place the cream in a saucepan over medium heat and heat until almost boiling.
- Remove the cream from heat.
- Add the chopped chocolate and stir through until the chocolate has melted and the filling is smooth.
- Pour the chocolate filling into the coconut tart shells and place in the freezer for 10 minutes or until the chocolate filling is set.
- Serve with coffee or berries as a dessert.

## Nutrition Information

- Calories: 467.3
- Cholesterol: 41.5
- Total Fat: 40.3
- Sugar: 21
- Total Carbohydrate: 35.5
- Protein: 7.9
- Saturated Fat: 26.6
- Sodium: 84.2
- Fiber: 8

## 91. Coconut Ghost Treats™

*Serving: 12 treats, 12 serving(s) | Prep: 20mins | Ready in:*

### Ingredients

- 3 tablespoons butter or 3 tablespoons margarine
- 1 (10 ounce) package large marshmallows, about 40 or 4 cups miniature marshmallows
- 6 cups kellogg's Rice Krispies
- flaked coconut
- canned frosting or decorating gel
- assorted candy

### Direction

- In large saucepan melt butter over low heat. Add marshmallows and stir until completely melted. Remove from heat.
- Add KELLOGG'S® RICE KRISPIES® cereal. Stir until well coated.

- Using 1/2-cup measuring cup coated with cooking spray divide warm cereal mixture into portions. Using buttered hands shape each portion into ghost shape. Cool. Decorate with coconut, frosting and/or candies. Best if served the same day.
- MICROWAVE DIRECTIONS.
- In microwave-safe bowl heat butter and marshmallows on HIGH for 3 minutes, stirring after 2 minutes. Stir until smooth. Follow steps 2 and 3 above. Microwave cooking times may vary.
- Note:
- For best results, use fresh marshmallows.
- 1 jar (7 oz.) marshmallow crème can be substituted for marshmallows.
- Diet, reduced calorie or tub margarine is not recommended.
- Store no more than two days at room temperature in airtight container. To freeze, place in layers separated by wax paper in airtight container. Freeze for up to 6 weeks. Let stand at room temperature for 15 minutes before serving.

## Nutrition Information

- Calories: 154.8
- Total Fat: 3.1
- Saturated Fat: 1.9
- Sodium: 172.3
- Total Carbohydrate: 31.2
- Protein: 1.4
- Fiber: 0.1
- Sugar: 14.9
- Cholesterol: 7.6

## 92. Coconut, Sultana Honey Loaf (Abm / Bread Machine)

*Serving: 11 serving(s) | Prep: 3mins | Ready in:*

## Ingredients

- 240 ml water (at room temerature)
- 350 g white bread flour
- 15 g honey
- 11 g desiccated coconut (About 1 1/2 Tablespoons)
- 1/4 teaspoon vitamin C powder (optional)
- 1 teaspoon salt
- 15 g nonfat dry milk powder (1 Tablespoon, heaped)
- 5 g butter (or for creamier taste just use 13g of Butter and omit the margarine)
- 8 g firm margarine
- 3 3/4 g bread machine yeast (1 Tsp slightly heaped)
- At Beep
- 65 g sultanas (or Raisins- untested)
- 1 dash cardamom (optional)

## Direction

- Weigh the main ingredients into the bread machine and select Raisin or Speciality Bread and preferred Crust type - I chose normal crust which worked nicely - and start the machine.
- At the beep, if you trust your machine not to mash up the fruit like mine always does, add the sultanas with just an incredibly light dusting of cardamom (or omit it if you don't like cardamom). For my machine I ignored the beep and waited until just over 3 minutes remained of the 2nd knead cycle and that worked great - guess it depends how squishy your sultanas are :).
- Cool on a wire rack.
- Makes a loaf just under 1 1/2 Lb which you won't be able to stop eating!
- Cooking time listed is the baking time for my machine.

## Nutrition Information

- Calories: 157
- Total Carbohydrate: 31.4
- Cholesterol: 1.2
- Protein: 4.2

- Total Fat: 1.6
- Sodium: 232.7
- Fiber: 1.2
- Sugar: 5.8
- Saturated Fat: 0.7

## 93. Copycat Keebler Pecan Sandies

*Serving: 48 cookies, 48 serving(s) | Prep: 15mins | Ready in:*

### Ingredients

- 1/2 cup vegetable shortening
- 1/2 cup white sugar
- 1/2 cup powdered sugar
- 1 egg, beaten
- 1/4 teaspoon salt
- 1/2 teaspoon cream of tartar
- 1/2 teaspoon baking soda
- 1 teaspoon vanilla
- 1 3/4 cups flour
- 1/2 cup finely chopped pecans

### Direction

- Preheat oven to 350 degrees.
- Measure flour, cream of tartar, and baking soda together and set aside.
- Cream vegetable shortening and sugars together until fluffy.
- Add vanilla, salt, and egg to sugar mixture and beat until smooth.
- Add flour mixture to sugar mixture 1/3 at a time, beating after each addition until completely mixed.
- Dough will seem a little thick.
- Stir pecans into dough with a strong spoon.
- Chill dough for 30- 45 minutes.
- Roll dough into 1- 1 1/4 inch balls and place on ungreased cookie sheet.
- Flatten balls to 1/4 inch thickness.
- Bake for 12- 15 minutes, until slightly golden.
- Remove to cooling rack.
- When completely cool, store in air-tight container.

### Nutrition Information

- Calories: 58.1
- Saturated Fat: 0.7
- Fiber: 0.2
- Total Carbohydrate: 7
- Protein: 0.7
- Total Fat: 3.1
- Sodium: 26.8
- Sugar: 3.4
- Cholesterol: 4.4

## 94. Corn Crackers

*Serving: 16 serving(s) | Prep: 10mins | Ready in:*

### Ingredients

- 1 cup cornmeal
- 1/2 teaspoon sea salt
- 1 teaspoon granulated sugar
- 1/8 teaspoon fresh ground pepper
- 2 tablespoons flour
- 1/2 teaspoon baking powder
- 1 cup boiling water
- 1 egg, beaten
- 2 tablespoons butter
- 2 tablespoons grated parmesan cheese

### Direction

- In a large bowl, mix first 6 ingredients.
- Pour boiling water over this and mix well.
- Then incorporate egg, butter, and cheese.
- Drop by tablespoon onto a parchment lined baking pan, spread thin w/ a flat knife and bake 325 for 20-25 minutes.
- Allow to cool 30 minutes.

### Nutrition Information

- Calories: 52.3
- Cholesterol: 17.6
- Protein: 1.4
- Total Fat: 2.2
- Sugar: 0.3
- Total Carbohydrate: 7
- Saturated Fat: 1.2
- Sodium: 111.2
- Fiber: 0.6

## 95. Cornflake Crunchies

*Serving: 36 crunchies | Prep: 10mins | Ready in:*

### Ingredients

- 2/3 cup sugar
- 1/2 cup vegetable shortening
- 1 egg
- 1 tablespoon milk
- 1 teaspoon orange extract
- 1 cup all-purpose flour
- 1 1/2 teaspoons baking powder
- 3 cups corn flakes cereal
- 1/2 cup walnuts, chopped

### Direction

- Preheat oven to 350 degrees F.
- Lightly grease cookie sheet.
- Beat sugar and shortening until creamy.
- Beat in egg, milk and orange extract.
- Stir in flour and baking powder.
- Add cereal and nuts; mix well.
- Drop by tablespoon onto prepared cookie sheet.
- Bake 10-12 minutes or until lightly browned.
- Let stand 1 minute before removing to racks to cool.

### Nutrition Information

- Calories: 74
- Total Fat: 4.1
- Saturated Fat: 1
- Sodium: 34.3
- Fiber: 0.3
- Protein: 0.9
- Sugar: 4
- Total Carbohydrate: 8.7
- Cholesterol: 5.9

## 96. Couscous For People Who Hate Couscous

*Serving: 2 serving(s) | Prep: 15mins | Ready in:*

### Ingredients

- 8 -10 inches celery, finely chopped
- 1 small white onion, finely chopped
- 5 -6 mushrooms, finely chopped
- 2 garlic cloves, minced
- 1 cup couscous
- 1 teaspoon ground coriander
- 1 teaspoon ground rosemary
- 1 teaspoon ground paprika
- 1 teaspoon ground turmeric
- 1 teaspoon ground cinnamon
- 1 teaspoon ground chili powder (optional)
- 1 cup chicken stock

### Direction

- Once you have chopped your vegetables and ground your spices, place the couscous in a large bowl, and add all of the ground spices.
- Using a vegetable peeler, shave some butter off the block and place in the bowl.
- Bring the chicken stock to a boil, and pour it over the couscous. Don't stir it. Place a plate over the bowl to cover it, and set aside.
- Melt some butter in a frypan with the garlic, and add the celery and onions. Fry until the onion starts to become soft.
- Add a little more butter to the frypan, and add the mushrooms. Fry for about 2 minutes over medium heat until the mushroom is soft.

- Remove the cover from the bowl of couscous, and stir it gently with a fork, being careful not to mash it.
- Add the contents of the frypan, and stir it through gently.
- Season with salt and pepper, if desired, and serve.

## Nutrition Information

- Calories: 412.6
- Saturated Fat: 0.6
- Fiber: 7.3
- Sugar: 4.4
- Total Carbohydrate: 80.4
- Cholesterol: 3.6
- Total Fat: 2.7
- Sodium: 188.9
- Protein: 16.4

## 97. Cowboy Energy Cookies

*Serving: 24-36 cookies | Prep: 0S | Ready in:*

### Ingredients

- 1 3/4 cups flour
- 1/2 cup butter
- 1 teaspoon baking soda
- 2 eggs
- 1/2 teaspoon salt
- 1 teaspoon vanilla extract
- 1 1/4 cups brown sugar
- 1 cup granulated sugar
- 1/2 cup chocolate, chips-semi sweet
- 1/3 cup raisins
- 1/4 cup dates
- 1/4 cup pecans
- 2 1/2 cups quick oats

### Direction

- In large bowl, cream together butter and sugars. Add eggs and vanilla.
- In separate bowl, mix flour, salt and soda.
- Gradually add dry ingredients with creamed mixture until dough forms.
- Fold in oats, chocolate chips, pecans, raisins, and dates one at a time.
- Roll into 1" balls and drop on lightly greased cookie sheet 2" apart.
- Bake 9-11 minutes at 375 degrees or until edges golden brown.
- Do not over bake. Cookies will firm as they cool.

## Nutrition Information

- Calories: 214.4
- Total Fat: 7.1
- Cholesterol: 27.8
- Protein: 3.4
- Saturated Fat: 3.6
- Sodium: 139.9
- Fiber: 1.9
- Sugar: 22
- Total Carbohydrate: 36.1

## 98. Cracker Sandwiches

*Serving: 2 serving(s) | Prep: 2mins | Ready in:*

### Ingredients

- 8 whole wheat crackers
- fruit spread
- cream cheese
- almond butter (optional)
- peanut butter (optional)

### Direction

- Spread condiments of choice on one cracker.
- Top with another cracker.
- Enjoy!

## Nutrition Information

- Calories: 70.9
- Fiber: 1.7
- Total Fat: 2.8
- Saturated Fat: 0.5
- Sodium: 105.4
- Sugar: 0.1
- Total Carbohydrate: 11
- Cholesterol: 0
- Protein: 1.4

## 99. Cream Cheese Bacon Croissants

*Serving: 32 croissants, 16 serving(s) | Prep: 15mins | Ready in:*

### Ingredients

- 8 ounces cream cheese (chive onion)
- 3 slices beef bacon, cooked and crumbled
- 2 (8 ounce) cans refrigerated crescent dinner rolls

### Direction

- Preheat oven to 375°F. Mix cream cheese and bacon in a small bowl until well blended.
- Separate each can of dough into 8 triangles. Cut each triangle in half lengthwise. Spread each triangle with 1 generous tsp of cream cheese mixture. Roll up, starting at shortest side of triangle and rolling to opposite point. Place point sides down on ungreased baking sheet.
- Bake 12 -15 minutes or until golden brown. Serve warm.

### Nutrition Information

- Calories: 136.5
- Total Fat: 6.8
- Sodium: 196.5
- Fiber: 1.1
- Saturated Fat: 3.6
- Sugar: 1.2
- Total Carbohydrate: 15.1
- Cholesterol: 29.8
- Protein: 3.8

## 100. Creamy Baked Brie With Strawberries, Pecans And Honey

*Serving: 8 serving(s) | Prep: 5mins | Ready in:*

### Ingredients

- 8 ounces brie cheese
- 2 tablespoons Dijon mustard
- 2 tablespoons toasted pecans, coarsely chopped
- 1 cup fresh strawberries, sliced
- 3 tablespoons honey
- toasted baguette, slices
- green apple, cored and thickly sliced
- pear, cored and thickly sliced

### Direction

- Preheat oven to 350 degrees.
- Spray shallow baking dish with no-stick cooking spray; place cheese in dish.
- Evenly spread the mustard over the top of the cheese; sprinkle with the toasted pecans.
- Bake uncovered for 5 - 6 minutes or until center feels soft when you push down with a spoon.
- Let sit for a minute or two; top with strawberries and drizzle with honey.
- Serve warm with toasted baguette slices and fresh slices of fruit.

### Nutrition Information

- Calories: 151.3
- Total Fat: 10.6
- Saturated Fat: 5.2
- Total Carbohydrate: 8.8
- Protein: 6.5

- Sodium: 220.8
- Fiber: 0.8
- Sugar: 7.7
- Cholesterol: 28.4

## 101. Creamy Jello Layers

*Serving: 6 serving(s) | Prep: 5mins | Ready in:*

### Ingredients

- 6 ounces gelatin, any flavor
- 3 cups boiling water
- 4 cups frozen Cool Whip
- sliced fresh fruit (optional)

### Direction

- Dissolve gelatin in water.
- Whisk in Cool Whip, reserving 1 cup to top each dish.
- Pour into individual dishes.
- Chill 30-60 minutes, then top with sliced fresh fruit and/or remaining Cool Whip.

### Nutrition Information

- Calories: 252.8
- Fiber: 0
- Sugar: 11.5
- Cholesterol: 0
- Protein: 24.6
- Total Fat: 12.7
- Saturated Fat: 10.9
- Sodium: 69.8
- Total Carbohydrate: 11.5

## 102. Crisco Party Snax

*Serving: 8 serving(s) | Prep: 5mins | Ready in:*

### Ingredients

- 1/3 cup shortening
- 1 tablespoon Worcestershire sauce
- 1/4 teaspoon salt
- 1/8 teaspoon garlic powder
- 2 cups pretzel sticks
- 2 cups bite-size cereal, squares (here in Canada, I'd use Shreddies)
- 1/2 cup pecans

### Direction

- Preheat oven to 300F.
- Place shortening in a 13x9 oblong pan, and place in oven until shortening melts; remove pan from oven.
- Stir Worcestershire sauce, salt and garlic powder into melted shortening, then add remaining ingredients and stir gently.
- Heat in oven, stirring gently several times, for 30 minutes.

### Nutrition Information

- Calories: 124
- Protein: 0.6
- Total Fat: 13.4
- Sodium: 93.5
- Total Carbohydrate: 1.4
- Cholesterol: 0
- Saturated Fat: 2.5
- Fiber: 0.7
- Sugar: 0.5

## 103. Crispy Guilt Free Pizza

*Serving: 2 serving(s) | Prep: 3mins | Ready in:*

### Ingredients

- 1 1/2 cups mozzarella cheese
- 1 cup pepperoni
- 1 large whole wheat tortilla
- 1/2 cup pizza sauce

### Direction

- Topping measurements are estimates, use as little or as much of the toppings you want. And if you prefer fresh mushrooms, or pineapple, etc. use that instead. You can also use Soy Cheese too. Taste fine either way.
- Spread your sauce over the tortilla. Next sprinkle on the cheese. Add your toppings and bake in the oven at 350 degrees on a cookie sheet that was sprayed with a non-stick spray and let it bake for about 10 minutes or until the cheese is melted. Enjoy!

### Nutrition Information

- Calories: 298.2
- Protein: 19.8
- Total Fat: 20.3
- Sodium: 827.3
- Fiber: 0.2
- Total Carbohydrate: 8.9
- Cholesterol: 66.4
- Saturated Fat: 11.2
- Sugar: 6.4

## 104. Crispy Peanut Butter Bars

*Serving: 24 serving(s) | Prep: 15mins | Ready in:*

### Ingredients

- CRUST
- 1 (18 ounce) package yellow cake mix
- 2 tablespoons peanut butter
- 1/2 cup butter or 1/2 cup margarine, softened
- 2 cups miniature marshmallows
- TOPPING
- 1/4 cup butter or 1/4 cup margarine
- 3/4 cup light corn syrup
- 1 (10 ounce) package peanut butter chips
- 2 cups cocktail peanuts
- 2 cups crisp rice cereal (Rice Krispies)

### Direction

- Preheat oven to 350F and grease a 9-inch by 13-inch baking pan.
- Mix together cake mix, peanut butter and butter until crumbly. Press into the bottom of prepared pan.
- Bake for 15 minutes or until lightly browned.
- Top with marshmallows and return to oven until marshmallows are melted and light brown. Remove from oven and set aside to cool.
- For topping, in a heavy saucepan, melt butter. Add corn syrup and PB chips and over low heat, stir until mixture comes to a slow boil.
- Remove from heat and quickly stir in peanuts and cereal.
- Dollop on top of marshmallow layer, spreading to cover. (A spoon or spatula sprayed with PAM makes this a little easier).
- Cool and cut into bars.

### Nutrition Information

- Calories: 334.1
- Total Fat: 18.5
- Sodium: 246.1
- Total Carbohydrate: 38
- Cholesterol: 15.7
- Saturated Fat: 6.5
- Fiber: 1.9
- Sugar: 19.9
- Protein: 6.9

## 105. Crock Pot Applesauce

*Serving: 6 cups | Prep: 25mins | Ready in:*

### Ingredients

- 4 lbs tart apples, cored and sliced thin
- 1/2 cup sugar
- 1/2 teaspoon cinnamon
- 1 cup water

- 1 tablespoon lemon juice

### Direction

- Mix apples (about 12 cups) with cinnamon and sugar and put into crock pot.
- Pour water and lemon juice over apples. Cook on low for 6 hours or high for 3 hours.

### Nutrition Information

- Calories: 222.8
- Sodium: 4.4
- Sugar: 48.1
- Cholesterol: 0
- Protein: 0.8
- Total Fat: 0.5
- Saturated Fat: 0.1
- Fiber: 7.4
- Total Carbohydrate: 58.8

## 106. Crunchy Banana Strawberry Parfaits

*Serving: 4 serving(s) | Prep: 15mins | Ready in:*

### Ingredients

- 3 (6 ounce) containersyoplait original 99% non-fat strawberry yogurt
- 2 cups Cocoa Puffs cereal
- 1/3 cup shelled unsalted sunflower seeds
- 2 bananas, sliced
- 4 strawberries

### Direction

- For each serving, spoon 1/4 cup yogurt into bottom of tall glass.
- Add 1/4 cup cereal.
- Top with 1 tablespoon sunflower seeds, several banana slices and 2 tablespoons yogurt.
- Repeat with cereal, banana slices and 2 tablespoons yogurt.
- Sprinkle with remaining sunflower seeds.
- Top each with strawberry.

### Nutrition Information

- Calories: 253.4
- Saturated Fat: 0.9
- Total Carbohydrate: 42.5
- Sugar: 25
- Cholesterol: 6.4
- Protein: 8.4
- Total Fat: 6.9
- Sodium: 144.2
- Fiber: 3.4

## 107. Crunchy Breakfast Biscuit Bites

*Serving: 32 snack bites, 16 serving(s) | Prep: 5mins | Ready in:*

### Ingredients

- 1 (10 ounce) canpillsbury golden layers refrigerated biscuits
- 2 tablespoons margarine or 2 tablespoons butter, melted
- 1 tablespoon cinnamon sugar (or more if desired)
- 3/4 cup Honey Nut Cheerios, finely crushed

### Direction

- Heat oven to 400°F.
- Spray large cookie sheet with nonstick cooking spray.
- Separate dough into 8 biscuits.
- Cut each biscuit into quarters.
- Place biscuit quarters in large bowl.
- Drizzle with margarine and sugar-cinnamon mixture; toss to coat.
- Add crushed cereal; toss to coat.
- Place biscuit quarters in single layer, sides not touching, on sprayed cookie sheet.

- Bake at 400°F for 7 to 9 minutes or until golden brown; serve warm.

## Nutrition Information

- Calories: 82.8
- Fiber: 0.4
- Sugar: 2.7
- Cholesterol: 0
- Protein: 1.3
- Total Fat: 4.1
- Saturated Fat: 0.9
- Sodium: 242.2
- Total Carbohydrate: 10.3

## 108. Crunchy Fudge Sandwiches

*Serving: 25 treats, 25 serving(s) | Prep: 20mins | Ready in:*

### Ingredients

- 1 cup butterscotch chips
- 1/2 cup peanut butter
- 4 cups Rice Krispies
- 1 (6 ounce) package semisweet chocolate morsels
- 1/2 cup powdered sugar
- 2 tablespoons butter or 2 tablespoons margarine, softened
- 1 tablespoon water

### Direction

- Melt butterscotch morsels with peanut butter in heavy saucepan over very low heat, stirring constantly until well blended. Remove from heat.
- Add KELLOGG'S® RICE KRISPIES® cereal to butterscotch mixture, stirring until well coated. Press half of cereal mixture into 8 x 8 x 2-inch pan coated with cooking spray. Chill in refrigerator while preparing filling. Set remaining cereal mixture aside.
- Combine chocolate morsels, powdered sugar, butter and water. Stir over very low heat until chocolate melts and mixture is well blended. Spread over chilled cereal mixture. Spread remaining cereal mixture evenly over top. Press in gently. Chill. Remove from refrigerator for about 10 minutes before cutting into squares.

## Nutrition Information

- Calories: 136.9
- Sodium: 79.1
- Fiber: 0.8
- Sugar: 11.4
- Total Carbohydrate: 16.3
- Cholesterol: 2.6
- Saturated Fat: 3.8
- Protein: 2
- Total Fat: 7.3

## 109. Deep Fried Sweet Potato Chips With Mozzarella

*Serving: 6-8 serving(s) | Prep: 15mins | Ready in:*

### Ingredients

- 5 lbs sweet potatoes or 5 lbs yams, peeled
- peanut oil (for deep frying, you can use vegetable oil in place of peanut oil)
- coarse salt
- black pepper (optional)
- 3 cups mozzarella cheese, shredded (or use any cheese for this)

### Direction

- Using a mandolin, slice the sweet potatoes into 1/16-inch thick slices, and pat them dry with paper towels.

- In a deep fryer heat enough oil to measure about 3 inches; heat oil to about 380 degrees (can be a little less).
- Fry the sweet potato slices in batches until they are golden brown.
- Transfer the chips to a paper towel to drain fat.
- Place on a baking sheet and sprinkle with coarse salt and black pepper if desired.
- Set oven to broil heat.
- Sprinkle the shredded cheese evenly on top of the fried sweet potatoes.
- Broil for about 4 minutes, or until the cheese melts.
- Place onto a serving dish.
- Delicious!

## Nutrition Information

- Calories: 493.4
- Cholesterol: 44.2
- Protein: 18.4
- Saturated Fat: 7.4
- Sodium: 559.2
- Fiber: 11.3
- Sugar: 16.4
- Total Carbohydrate: 77.3
- Total Fat: 12.7

## 110. Deli Cracker Dip

*Serving: 2 cups | Prep: 3mins | Ready in:*

## Ingredients

- 1 cup mayonnaise
- 1 cup grated cheddar cheese
- 1/2 cup bacon bits (real or soy)

## Direction

- Mix the ingredients.
- Refrigerate to meld the flavors.
- Serve at room temp with crackers
- OR spread a spoonful on a slice of toast or French bread broil for a minute.

## Nutrition Information

- Calories: 338.6
- Protein: 21.7
- Sodium: 824.4
- Fiber: 0
- Total Carbohydrate: 1
- Cholesterol: 81.9
- Total Fat: 27.3
- Saturated Fat: 14.7
- Sugar: 0.3

## 111. Dolly Parton's Green Tomato Cake

*Serving: 1 cake, 12 serving(s) | Prep: 20mins | Ready in:*

## Ingredients

- 1 cup raisins
- hot water
- 3 cups all-purpose flour
- 1 teaspoon salt
- 1 teaspoon baking powder
- 1 teaspoon ground cinnamon
- 1/2 teaspoon ground nutmeg
- 2 1/4 cups granulated sugar
- 1 cup butter, melted
- 3 eggs
- 2 teaspoons vanilla extract
- 1 cup chopped walnuts
- 1 1/4 lbs green tomatoes, cored, seeded, and diced small
- 1 cup unsweetened flaked coconut
- Cream Cheese Frosting
- 1 lb chilled cream cheese (two 8-oz packages)
- 8 tablespoons butter, at room temperature
- 1 tablespoon vanilla extract
- 4 cups powdered sugar, sifted
- 1 pinch ground cinnamon, to taste

## Direction

- Preheat oven to 350 degrees F. Butter two 9-inch cake pans and lightly dust them with flour.
- Place the raisins in a bowl and add hot water to cover; set aside. (Note from Julesong: you can use warm rum or other liquor, if you like.).
- Sift the flour into a medium bowl, then add the salt, baking powder, cinnamon, and nutmeg; stir to combine.
- In another large bowl, whisk together the sugar, melted butter, eggs, and vanilla. Gradually add the flour mixture, stirring, until a smooth batter forms.
- Drain the raisins in a sieve.
- Stir the walnuts, drained raisins, cored/diced tomatoes, and coconut flakes into the batter.
- Pour an equal amount of batter into each prepared cake pan and spread evenly with a spatula.
- Bake in preheated 350 degree F oven for about 60 minutes or until a toothpick inserted into center comes out clean. When done, remove from oven and let cake cool in pans on wire racks.
- When cake is cool to the touch, slide a knife or icing spatula around the inside rim of each pan to loosen edges and carefully flip the cake layers onto the wire racks to continue cooling. (You can use an inverted plate on top of the pan, flip, and carefully transfer to racks, if you like.).
- If you want to frost the cake, make the cream cheese frosting while layers are cooling.
- To make the frosting, in a medium bowl beat together the cream cheese and butter with an electric or hand mixer until well blended.
- Add the vanilla and beat until incorporated.
- Gradually add the powdered sugar while continuing to beat until smooth.
- Beat in cinnamon until incorporated. Use to frost the cake.
- To frost cake: when cake is completely cooled place one layer on serving plate and, using a spatula, frost all over with half the frosting. Place second layer on top. Frost second layer with remaining frosting.

## Nutrition Information

- Calories: 932.2
- Total Carbohydrate: 117.8
- Cholesterol: 155.5
- Protein: 10.8
- Total Fat: 48.9
- Saturated Fat: 28
- Sodium: 528.5
- Fiber: 3.8
- Sugar: 87

## 112. Dreamsicles

*Serving: 8 serving(s) | Prep: 10mins | Ready in:*

### Ingredients

- 1 (3 ounce) package Jello gelatin
- 1 cup hot water
- 1 (8 ounce) container Cool Whip or 1 pint softened ice cream

### Direction

- Dissolve Jell-O in 1 cup hot water.
- Add Cool Whip or ice cream.
- Pour into freezer cups.
- Freeze.

### Nutrition Information

- Calories: 130.6
- Protein: 1.2
- Total Fat: 7.2
- Saturated Fat: 6.2
- Sugar: 15.7
- Cholesterol: 0
- Sodium: 57.2
- Fiber: 0
- Total Carbohydrate: 16.1

## 113. Dry Diaper Surprise!

*Serving: 1 Happy Face, 1 serving(s) | Prep: 5mins | Ready in:*

### Ingredients

- 1 slice whole wheat bread, toasted
- 1/2 banana, smashed
- 1 grapes, halved
- 1 strawberry, sliced
- 2 slices apricots
- 8 raisins

### Direction

- Be sure bread is toasted or it will get soggy. Spread banana over toast and arrange fruit to make a smiley face on top. Use strawberry slices for hair, apricot slices for eyebrows, grape halves for eyes and raisins for the mouth.
- Encourage your little one to have fun eating the body parts!

### Nutrition Information

- Calories: 141.1
- Total Fat: 1.4
- Sugar: 12.6
- Total Carbohydrate: 31.5
- Cholesterol: 0
- Protein: 3.6
- Saturated Fat: 0.3
- Sodium: 148.8
- Fiber: 3.9

## 114. Easier French Fries Cold Oil Method (Cook's Illustrated)

*Serving: 4 serving(s) | Prep: 15mins | Ready in:*

### Ingredients

- 2 1/2 lbs yukon gold potatoes, scrubbed, dried, sides squared off, and cut length-wise in 1/4-inch batons (strips) (about 6 medium)
- 6 cups peanut oil, for frying
- kosher salt

### Direction

- Combine potatoes and oil in large Dutch oven. Cook over high heat until oil has reached a rolling boil, about 5 minutes. Continue to cook, without stirring, until potatoes are limp but exteriors are beginning to firm, about 12-15 minutes.
- Using tongs, stir potatoes, gently scraping up any that stick, and continue to cook, stirring occasionally, until golden and crisp, 5-10 minutes longer.
- Using skimmer or slotted spoon, transfer fries to thick paper bag or paper towels. Season with salt and serve immediately.

### Nutrition Information

- Calories: 3111
- Saturated Fat: 54.8
- Sodium: 11.3
- Fiber: 5.1
- Total Carbohydrate: 57.1
- Protein: 5.3
- Total Fat: 324.3
- Sugar: 2.5
- Cholesterol: 0

## 115. Easiest Banana Muffins Ever

*Serving: 12 large muffins | Prep: 5mins | Ready in:*

### Ingredients

- 2 -3 ripe bananas (to make 1 cup)
- 3/4 cup sugar

- 1 cup Miracle Whip
- 1 1/2 cups all-purpose flour
- 2/3 cup whole wheat flour
- 2 teaspoons baking soda
- 1/2 teaspoon salt

## Direction

- In medium size bowl beat bananas, sugar, and salad dressing. Stir in the flour, baking soda, and salt until it is just moistened. Fill muffin cups three quarters full. Bake at 350 degrees.

## Nutrition Information

- Calories: 145.4
- Total Fat: 0.3
- Saturated Fat: 0.1
- Cholesterol: 0
- Sodium: 307.5
- Fiber: 1.8
- Sugar: 15
- Total Carbohydrate: 33.8
- Protein: 2.7

## 116. Easy Apple Dip

*Serving: 1 cup | Prep: 5mins | Ready in:*

## Ingredients

- 8 ounces sour cream
- 4 teaspoons brown sugar
- 2 teaspoons cinnamon
- 6 apples

## Direction

- Mix everything but the apples until creamy.
- Serve with apple slices, I leave the skin on and use red and green apples with a bit of lemon juice on them to keep them from turning brown.

## Nutrition Information

- Calories: 1023.7
- Saturated Fat: 31.5
- Sodium: 143.4
- Fiber: 22.4
- Total Carbohydrate: 146.1
- Cholesterol: 105.2
- Total Fat: 51.7
- Sugar: 104.2
- Protein: 9.9

## 117. Easy Apple Pie Wontons

*Serving: 8-10 serving(s) | Prep: 30mins | Ready in:*

## Ingredients

- 1 (21 ounce) cancinnamon apple pie filling (or favorite flavor)
- 1 (16 ounce) package wonton wrappers
- oil (for frying)
- powdered sugar
- ice cream (optional)

## Direction

- Lay one wonton wrapper on work surface with one point towards you (diamond shape).
- Place 1 tablespoon apple pie filling in center.
- Moisten edges of wrapper on two sides closest to you.
- Fold wrapper in half, forming a triangle. Press to seal edges tightly.
- Repeat with remaining filling and wrappers.
- Heat oil in heavy skillet to 1/4-1/2 inch in depth.
- When hot, add wontons a few at a time.
- Brown on both sides and remove to paper toweling to drain.
- Sprinkle with powdered sugar and DEVOUR!

## Nutrition Information

- Calories: 240.8

- Total Fat: 0.9
- Fiber: 1.8
- Sugar: 10.3
- Total Carbohydrate: 52.5
- Cholesterol: 5.1
- Protein: 5.6
- Saturated Fat: 0.2
- Sodium: 357.3

- Sodium: 80.5
- Fiber: 1.9
- Sugar: 0.9
- Total Carbohydrate: 23.4
- Cholesterol: 4.4
- Total Fat: 12.4
- Saturated Fat: 2.4
- Protein: 4.3

## 118. Easy Baked Jo Jo Potatoes

*Serving: 25 pieces, 5 serving(s) | Prep: 5mins | Ready in:*

### Ingredients

- 3 large baking potatoes
- 1/4 cup extra light olive oil
- 1/4 cup flour
- 1/4 cup parmesan cheese
- 1/2 teaspoon ground black pepper
- 1/2 teaspoon onion salt
- 1/2 teaspoon garlic powder
- morton's hot salt (optional) or ground cayenne pepper (optional) or salt (optional)

### Direction

- Peel potatoes and place in cold water for at least 1 hour. Slice Potatoes into spears. Place on a heavy duty cookie sheet, poor Olive Oil over potatoes and toss. In a pie pan combine remaining ingredients (except hot salt) Press each potato wedge in flour Mixture. Place back on cookie sheet (Balance on skin part if possible) Sprinkle with Hot Salt now if desired. Bake in a 400 degree oven for approx. 45 minutes, or golden brown. Use spatula to remove from pan and serve with Ranch dressing and ketchup/salsa.

### Nutrition Information

- Calories: 219.3

## 119. Easy Greek Chips Omelette (Avga Omeleta Me Patates)

*Serving: 4 , 4 serving(s) | Prep: 5mins | Ready in:*

### Ingredients

- thin French fries (Shoestring fries, A big hand full)
- 4 eggs, beaten
- 1 tablespoon butter
- sea salt
- fresh ground black pepper

### Direction

- Bake shoestring fries according to package directions.
- Melt butter in a frying pan (I prefer cast iron). Sprinkle out cooked fries on top of the butter and pour in the beaten eggs.
- Sea salt and freshly grind black pepper to taste.
- Fold it over in half moon shape if you know how to do that without breaking!
- Cook until done to preference.
- Serve with pita bread as part of breakfast.

### Nutrition Information

- Calories: 99
- Saturated Fat: 3.4
- Total Carbohydrate: 0.4
- Cholesterol: 219.1

- Protein: 6.3
- Total Fat: 7.8
- Sodium: 90.5
- Fiber: 0
- Sugar: 0.4

## 120. Easy Low Fat Oven Roasted Peppered Potato Wedges

*Serving: 4 serving(s) | Prep: 10mins | Ready in:*

### Ingredients

- 2 lbs roasting potatoes
- 1 tablespoon olive oil
- fresh ground black pepper
- sea salt

### Direction

- Pre-heat oven to 220 C or 450°F.
- Wash and scrub your potatoes well - no need to peel them!
- Cut them into chunky wedges.
- Place in a Ziploc bag or plastic container and add the olive oil black pepper.
- Do NOT add the salt now as it encourages water!
- Shake the container or bag well - making sure every potato wedge has been covered in oil.
- Place peppered potatoes in a large and sturdy oven proof roasting tin - shake around to ensure they are in a single layer, more or less!
- Sprinkle on the sea salt and any herbs spices you may be using.
- Give another good twist of ground black pepper over the potato wedges and roast in the oven for about 45 - 60 minutes or until crispy and brown!
- Sprinkle over any fresh herbs, if you are using them for a garnish or just serve "au natural" as a vegetable accompaniment.

- I often serve these in paper cornets for a light lunch or supper time snack with vinegar sometimes, very naughty I KNOW, mayonnaise!

### Nutrition Information

- Calories: 204.6
- Total Fat: 3.6
- Sodium: 13.7
- Fiber: 5
- Sugar: 1.8
- Cholesterol: 0
- Protein: 4.6
- Saturated Fat: 0.5
- Total Carbohydrate: 39.7

## 121. Easy Microwave Popcorn

*Serving: 1 bag, 1 serving(s) | Prep: 1mins | Ready in:*

### Ingredients

- 1/4 cup popcorn
- 1 dash salt

### Direction

- Place popcorn in a lunch sized brown paper bag.
- Fold the open end once and staple with ONE staple. (ONE staple will not affect your microwave).
- Microwave until the popcorn slows down popping. My microwave takes 1:50.
- Open carefully and pour into a bowl.
- Top with your favorite toppings. I use spray margarine and garlic salt.

### Nutrition Information

- Calories: 0
- Protein: 0
- Sodium: 155

- Fiber: 0
- Cholesterol: 0
- Total Fat: 0
- Saturated Fat: 0
- Sugar: 0
- Total Carbohydrate: 0

## 122. Easy Moist Banana Blueberry Muffins

*Serving: 12 serving(s) | Prep: 10mins | Ready in:*

### Ingredients

- 3 large ripe bananas
- 3/4 cup sugar
- 1 egg, slightly beaten
- 1/3 cup melted butter
- 1 cup blueberries
- 1 teaspoon baking soda
- 1 teaspoon baking powder
- 1/2 teaspoon salt
- 1 1/2 cups flour

### Direction

- Mash bananas in a large mixing bowl.
- Add sugar and egg.
- Add butter and blueberries.
- Combine dry ingredients and gently stir into banana mixture.
- Pour into 12 well-greased muffin cups.
- Bake at 375 degrees for 20 minutes.

### Nutrition Information

- Calories: 193.9
- Fiber: 1.6
- Total Fat: 5.8
- Saturated Fat: 3.4
- Sodium: 283.8
- Protein: 2.6
- Sugar: 17.9
- Total Carbohydrate: 34.1

- Cholesterol: 29

## 123. Easy Party Mix

*Serving: 1/2 cup, 22 serving(s) | Prep: 10mins | Ready in:*

### Ingredients

- 4 cups honeycomb cereal or 4 cups Alpha-bits cereal
- 2 cups caramel popped popcorn
- 2 cups small pretzels
- 1 1/2 mini chips chocolate chip cookies
- 1 1/2 cups M's

### Direction

- MIX all ingredients in large bowl.
- STORE in tightly covered container at room temperature.

### Nutrition Information

- Calories: 90.7
- Sodium: 42
- Total Fat: 3.4
- Saturated Fat: 2
- Fiber: 0.5
- Sugar: 10.5
- Total Carbohydrate: 14.2
- Cholesterol: 2.3
- Protein: 0.9

## 124. Easy Rhubarb Upside Down Cake

*Serving: 1 9x13 cake, 12 serving(s) | Prep: 20mins | Ready in:*

### Ingredients

- 1 (18 ounce) package lemon cake mix or 1 (18 ounce) package white cake mix
- 3 eggs (or as called for by your cake mix) or 3 egg whites (or as called for by your cake mix)
- 1/3 cup oil (or as called for by your cake mix)
- 1 teaspoon lemon extract
- 1 1/3 cups water (or as called for by your cake mix)
- 4 cups rhubarb, cut up 1/2 inch pieces
- 6 teaspoons minute tapioca
- 1 1/2 cups sugar
- 1 (3 ounce) package strawberry Jell-O gelatin dessert or 1 (3 ounce) package raspberry Jell-O gelatin

### Direction

- Preheat oven to 350 degrees.
- Grease 9x13inch pan.
- Mix together Rhubarb, tapioca, sugar and package of DRY Jell-O (NO WATER) and pour into prepared pan.
- Prepare cake mix according to package directions (adding the lemon extract to the wet ingredients) and pour over Rhubarb mixture.
- Bake 1 hour.
- Serve with whipped cream or ice cream.

### Nutrition Information

- Calories: 396.2
- Total Fat: 12.3
- Sodium: 343.3
- Saturated Fat: 1.9
- Fiber: 1.2
- Sugar: 51.4
- Total Carbohydrate: 68.6
- Cholesterol: 47.4
- Protein: 4.4

## 125. Easy S'more Clusters Indoor S'mores

*Serving: 30 serving(s) | Prep: 10mins | Ready in:*

### Ingredients

- 6 (1 5/8 ounce) milk chocolate candy bars, broken into pieces
- 2 cups miniature marshmallows
- 8 graham crackers, coarsely chopped (about 1 3/4 cups)

### Direction

- Place candy pieces in medium microwave-safe bowl. Microwave at MEDIUM (50%) 1-1/2 to 2 minutes, or until chocolate is melted when mixture is stirred.
- Stir in marshmallows and graham cracker pieces until well coated.
- Drop by spoonfuls into miniature paper muffin cups (1-3/4 inches in diameter). Cover; refrigerate until firm. About 2-1/2 dozen snacks.

### Nutrition Information

- Calories: 65.9
- Total Fat: 2.8
- Sodium: 21
- Fiber: 0.4
- Sugar: 7.1
- Cholesterol: 2
- Protein: 0.9
- Saturated Fat: 1.3
- Total Carbohydrate: 9.4

## 126. Easy Shrimp And Crab Cakes

*Serving: 12 cakes, 6 serving(s) | Prep: 20mins | Ready in:*

### Ingredients

- 1/4 cup butter, room temperature
- 1 (5 ounce) jar Kraft Old English cheese spread
- 1 1/2 teaspoons mayonnaise
- 1/2 teaspoon garlic powder
- 1/2 jalapeno, seeded and chopped
- 1/2-1 teaspoon Old Bay Seasoning
- 2 (6 ounce) cans lump crabmeat, drained and chopped
- 1 (4 ounce) can shrimp, rinsed and chopped
- 6 English muffins, split (wheat is best, regular ones get soggy)
- For the sauce
- 1/2 cup mayonnaise
- 1 -2 tablespoon horseradish
- 2 tablespoons seafood cocktail sauce or 2 tablespoons ketchup
- 3/4 teaspoon chili-garlic sauce (optional)

## Direction

- Mix butter, cheese, mayo, garlic powder, jalapeno and Old Bay together.
- Add crab and shrimp.
- Spread onto muffins (I use quite a bit).
- Freeze on cookie sheet. When frozen put in zip-lock baggies.
- Bake frozen in 400 degree oven for 12 minutes.
- Broil on low for 3 to 5 minutes until browned on top.
- Cut into fourths, serve with my sauce, cocktail or tartar sauce.

## Nutrition Information

- Calories: 361.7
- Protein: 22
- Saturated Fat: 6.5
- Sodium: 709.1
- Fiber: 2.1
- Sugar: 3.6
- Cholesterol: 105.6
- Total Fat: 16.5
- Total Carbohydrate: 31.2

## 127.  Edmonds Scones

*Serving: 12 serving(s) | Prep: 10mins | Ready in:*

## Ingredients

- 3 cups plain flour
- 6 teaspoons baking powder
- 1/4 teaspoon salt
- 75 g butter
- 1 -1 1/2 cup milk
- extra milk

## Direction

- Sift flour, baking powder and salt into a bowl.
- Cut butter in until it resembles fine breadcrumbs.
- Add milk and mix quickly with a knife to a soft dough.
- Knead a few times.
- Lightly dust an oven tray with flour.
- Press scone dough out onto this.
- Cut into 12 even-sized pieces.
- Leave a 2 cm space between scones.
- Brush tops with milk.
- Bake at 220C for 10 minutes or until golden brown.

## Nutrition Information

- Calories: 172.5
- Total Fat: 6.1
- Saturated Fat: 3.7
- Fiber: 0.8
- Sodium: 284.9
- Sugar: 0.1
- Total Carbohydrate: 25.4
- Cholesterol: 16.2
- Protein: 4

## 128. Eggs And Toast With Marmite

*Serving: 1 serving(s) | Prep: 10mins | Ready in:*

### Ingredients

- 2 eggs
- marmite or vegemite
- 2 slices bread
- 1/4 cup butter
- salt and pepper

### Direction

- This can be prepared in one of three ways:
- Poach, scramble or soft boil your eggs according to how you prefer them to be made.
- Toast the bread and butter it.
- Spread with as much marmite as you like.
- Top with the eggs if poached or scrambled.
- If you have boiled your eggs, cut up the toast into "soldiers" and get dunking!

### Nutrition Information

- Calories: 686.9
- Sugar: 3
- Total Carbohydrate: 26.1
- Cholesterol: 545
- Fiber: 1.2
- Protein: 16.9
- Total Fat: 57.6
- Saturated Fat: 32.6
- Sodium: 807.4

## 129. Empanadas (Appetizer)

*Serving: 20 Empanadas | Prep: 20mins | Ready in:*

### Ingredients

- 1 (10 ounce) package frozen patty shells, thawed
- 1/2 lb lean ground beef
- 1/4 cup minced onion
- 3 tablespoons red chile salsa, hot or mild
- 1 teaspoon chili powder
- 1/2 teaspoon ground cumin
- 1/2 teaspoon garlic powder
- 1/2 teaspoon ground coriander
- salt and pepper

### Direction

- To make beef filling, crumble and saute beef and onion in a skillet until beef is cooked and onion is soft.
- Drain; stir in red chile salsa, chile powder, cumin, garlic powder, coriander, salt and pepper.
- Set aside.
- Place thawed patty shell dough on a floured board and roll out all in one piece to about 1/16 inch thickness.
- Cut dough into rounds with a 3 inch round cookie cutter or a large drinking glass.
- Put 2 teaspoons of filling on each dough circle.
- Fold each over into a half circle.
- Moisten edges with water and press edges together with a fork.
- Place empanadas slightly apart on an ungreased cookie sheet.
- Prick tops with a fork.
- Bake at 400 degrees for 15 to 20 minutes or until golden brown; serve hot.
- These may be wrapped carefully after baking and frozen.
- To reheat, bake frozen empanadas uncovered at 400 degrees for 5 to 8 minutes.

### Nutrition Information

- Calories: 64.4
- Total Fat: 1.8
- Sodium: 96.4
- Total Carbohydrate: 8
- Cholesterol: 7.4
- Protein: 3.8
- Saturated Fat: 0.6

- Fiber: 0.5
- Sugar: 1.1

## 130. Fantastic Microwaved Beet Chips

*Serving: 2 serving(s) | Prep: 5mins | Ready in:*

### Ingredients

- 1 -2 fresh beet, cleaned
- oil
- salt

### Direction

- Slice beets very thin. I use a mandolin set at the thinnest setting.
- Brush a thin layer of oil in the bottom of a microwave safe pan. I use my pampered chef stoneware.
- Lay the beet slices in the pan, slightly overlapping. They will shrink significantly, so no need to leave "breathing" room.
- Sprinkle LIGHTLY with salt. Since they shrink so much, the salt taste will be more concentrated when done.
- Microwave on high. My first pan takes 6 minutes. Each pan full after takes 5 - 5 1/2 minutes, since the pan's hot.
- There's no need to re-oil the pan after the first set.
- Feel free to experiment with different flavors on the chips.

### Nutrition Information

- Calories: 11
- Total Fat: 0.1
- Fiber: 0.5
- Cholesterol: 0
- Protein: 0.4
- Saturated Fat: 0
- Sodium: 19.2

- Sugar: 2
- Total Carbohydrate: 2.5

## 131. Farmhouse Cheddar Cheese And Cranberry Croque Monsieur Toasties

*Serving: 4 Toasties, 4 serving(s) | Prep: 3mins | Ready in:*

### Ingredients

- 8 thick slices white bread, crusts removed
- 50 g lightly-salted butter (2 ounces)
- 225 g west country farmhouse cheddar cheese, grated (8 ounces)
- 4 tablespoons cranberry jelly

### Direction

- Spread bread with half the butter in the normal way.
- Top 4 slices with the grated cheese and spoon on cranberry jelly. Top with the remaining bread (butter side down) to make 4 sandwiches.
- Gently fry the bread in the remaining butter until crisp and golden on both sides.
- Cut into triangles and serve whilst warm with fresh seasonal salad leaves.

### Nutrition Information

- Calories: 475.9
- Cholesterol: 86
- Protein: 18
- Total Fat: 30.5
- Saturated Fat: 18.7
- Sodium: 699.7
- Fiber: 1.4
- Sugar: 9
- Total Carbohydrate: 32.8

## 132. Ff Sf Pudding (Made With Yogurt)

*Serving: 4 1/2 cups, 4 serving(s) | Prep: 2mins | Ready in:*

### Ingredients

- 1 ounce fat-free sugar-free instant vanilla pudding mix
- 1 cup water
- 1 cup nonfat yogurt

### Direction

- Slowly poor pudding mixture into water while whisking (do not sub milk).
- Stir into yogurt.
- This keeps about 3 days due to the separation of yogurt.

### Nutrition Information

- Calories: 57.8
- Saturated Fat: 0.1
- Sodium: 342.8
- Fiber: 0.1
- Protein: 3.6
- Total Fat: 0.2
- Sugar: 4.8
- Total Carbohydrate: 10.2
- Cholesterol: 1.2

## 133. Fire Free S'more Treats

*Serving: 10 treats, 10 serving(s) | Prep: 5mins | Ready in:*

### Ingredients

- 5 jumbo marshmallows
- 5 full-sized graham crackers
- 1/2 cup chocolate frosting, preferably homemade
- cinnamon
- sugar

### Direction

- Break graham crackers in half.
- Smear each cracker half with a layer of frosting.
- Cut marshmallows in half length-wise, so that they have a curved side and a flat side.
- Place one marshmallow half onto one graham cracker half, curved side down. Repeat with the rest of the marshmallows.
- Mix cinnamon and sugar to desired ratio, and sprinkle on top of the marshmallows.
- Serve!

### Nutrition Information

- Calories: 91
- Total Carbohydrate: 15.9
- Cholesterol: 0
- Protein: 0.5
- Saturated Fat: 1
- Sodium: 54
- Fiber: 0.2
- Total Fat: 3.2
- Sugar: 12.6

## 134. Fish Finger Wraps Fish Stick Wraps (Usa)

*Serving: 4-6 serving(s) | Prep: 6mins | Ready in:*

### Ingredients

- 1 small onion, finely diced
- 410 g cream of mushroom soup, tin
- 1 tablespoon sweet chili sauce
- 140 g light sour cream
- 1/2 cup light cheese, grated
- 6 flour tortillas
- 12 frozen fish sticks (or fish fingers)
- 1/4 cup extra light cheese, grated

### Direction

- Preheat oven to 180°C.
- In a bowl combine onion, soup, sweet chilli sauce, sour cream and 1/2 cup grated cheese.
- Place two fish fingers down the centre of each tortilla and spoon over about 2 tbsps. sauce to cover fish fingers.
- Carefully roll up tortillas and place seam side down in a single layer in a baking dish.
- Spoon over remaining sauce and sprinkle with extra grated cheese.
- Bake for 15-20 mins until sauce is bubbling and tortillas golden.

Nutrition Information

- Calories: 491.6
- Total Fat: 24.4
- Sodium: 1326.4
- Fiber: 2.8
- Total Carbohydrate: 52
- Protein: 16
- Saturated Fat: 6.2
- Sugar: 5.3
- Cholesterol: 39.1

## 135. Flavor Packed Chicken Wraps

*Serving: 4 tortilla wraps | Prep: 10mins | Ready in:*

Ingredients

- 1/2 cup garlic herb spreadable cheese
- 4 (8 inch) flavored flour tortillas (your choice)
- 4 large lettuce leaves
- 2 plum tomatoes, thinly sliced
- 1 (8 ounce) package deli chicken, sliced
- 1 medium cucumber, thinly sliced
- 1/2 cup shredded carrot

Direction

- Spread about 2 tablespoons of cheese spread over EACH tortilla.
- Layer evenly with lettuce, tomatoes, chicken, cuke and carrots.
- Roll up tightly.
- That's it!

Nutrition Information

- Calories: 258.1
- Fiber: 3.2
- Cholesterol: 27.8
- Total Fat: 5.7
- Saturated Fat: 1.4
- Sodium: 1049
- Sugar: 4.8
- Total Carbohydrate: 36.1
- Protein: 16.2

## 136. Fleisch Perisky ( Meat Buns)

*Serving: 20 dozen | Prep: 5hours | Ready in:*

Ingredients

- Bun Dough
- 1 cup warm water
- 4 teaspoons granulated sugar
- 3 tablespoons fast rising yeast
- 1/2 cup melted margarine
- 1/2 cup melted lard
- 1 tablespoon salt
- 5 cups warm milk
- 1 egg
- 12 cups all-purpose flour (or more)
- Meat Filling
- 2 lbs lean ground beef
- 1/2 cup margarine
- 2 tablespoons all-purpose flour
- 2 cups water
- 2 envelopes Lipton Onion Soup Mix
- 1/2 package no-name onion soup mix
- 1 -2 cup fine dry breadcrumb

## Direction

- Brown ground beef in a large skillet.
- Melt 1/2 cup margarine in a separate saucepan over medium heat.
- Add 2 T. flour, stirring to incorporate.
- Add dry onion soup mixes and water to make a thick gravy.
- Bring to boil.
- Pour gravy over browned beef and simmer for about 1 hour. (I do this in my oven),
- Add fine dry bread crumbs just enough so mixture hold together. Do this just before you start forming your meat buns.
- In my Bosch mixing bowl mix the warm water, sugar and yeast.
- Warm the milk, margarine and lard in the Microwave about 3 - 4 minutes, until margarine and lard have melted.
- Add to yeast mixture, and add about 8 cups of flour.
- Allow this to proof, then add salt, egg and remaining flour, just enough to make a soft dough, allowing the machine to knead the dough.
- Place dough in a large bowl (I use my Tupperware fix-n-mix bowl). Let rise 10 - 15 minutes.
- Form perisky by pinching off pieces of dough the size of a walnut.
- Flatten the dough in your palm of hand and put about 1 tsp. filling on the dough. Pinch dough around the filling to seal well.
- Place on baking sheets and let rise. You can often starting baking the first pans before you are finished panning the remaining ones.
- Bake at 400 deg. for 10 - 12 minutes or golden brown.
- Enjoy!

## Nutrition Information

- Calories: 458
- Saturated Fat: 5.5
- Sugar: 1.2
- Total Fat: 13
- Sodium: 500.5
- Fiber: 2.3
- Total Carbohydrate: 63.4
- Cholesterol: 52.2
- Protein: 19.7

## 137. Football Dip

*Serving: 10 serving(s) | Prep: 5mins | Ready in:*

### Ingredients

- 12 ounces reduced-fat sausage (1 roll)
- 12 ounces chorizo sausage
- 6 ounces Velveeta cheese, cubed
- 5 ounces Campbell's cheddar cheese soup (about 1/2 of a can)

### Direction

- In a large saucepan, brown sausage and chorizo until fully cooked.
- On medium heat, add Velveeta, and stir until it begins to melt.
- Add cheddar cheese soup and stir until all the cheese melts and is well blended. The dip will start to look a little like chili.
- Let stand on low heat for 5 minutes.
- Stir and serve!

### Nutrition Information

- Calories: 211.2
- Total Carbohydrate: 2.6
- Saturated Fat: 7.5
- Sodium: 705.6
- Fiber: 0
- Sugar: 1.4
- Protein: 11.1
- Total Fat: 17.1
- Cholesterol: 44.4

## 138. French Toast Sandwich Fingers

*Serving: 4 serving(s) | Prep: 10mins | Ready in:*

### Ingredients

- 4 eggs
- 2 tablespoons orange juice or 2 tablespoons milk
- 1/2 teaspoon orange zest (omit if using milk)
- 1 pinch salt
- 1/2 cup strawberry jam
- 4 slices white bread
- 4 slices whole wheat bread
- cooking spray
- icing sugar (optional)
- maple syrup (optional)

### Direction

- Whisk eggs, juice, zest and salt together and set aside.
- Spread 2 Tbsps. jam on each slice of white bread. Top with whole wheat bread and trim off crusts. Cut each sandwich into 3 fingers.
- Spray a large non-stick pan with cooking spray and heat over medium heat.
- Dip fingers into egg mixture, coating both sides, and fry for 2 minutes per side or until golden brown.
- Serving suggestion: Dust with icing sugar and provide maple syrup for dipping.

### Nutrition Information

- Calories: 363.6
- Protein: 12.1
- Saturated Fat: 2
- Sodium: 387.4
- Fiber: 3.1
- Total Fat: 6.6
- Sugar: 30.1
- Total Carbohydrate: 63.3
- Cholesterol: 186

## 139. Fried Honey Buns

*Serving: 2 serving(s) | Prep: 5mins | Ready in:*

### Ingredients

- 2 honey buns
- 1 tablespoon butter

### Direction

- Heat a skillet on medium heat.
- When skillet is hot; add 1 tbsp. butter and let melt.
- When butter bubbles; add a honey bun and fry until lightly brown on both sides.
- Add other tbsp. of butter if needed.
- Enjoy!

### Nutrition Information

- Calories: 365.2
- Protein: 5
- Sodium: 307.7
- Fiber: 0.9
- Sugar: 18.5
- Total Carbohydrate: 34.6
- Cholesterol: 19.9
- Total Fat: 23.5
- Saturated Fat: 8.2

## 140. Frosted Pecans

*Serving: 1 pound pecans | Prep: 5mins | Ready in:*

### Ingredients

- 1 egg white
- 1 tablespoon cold water
- 1 lb pecans, halved (this is equivalent to 4-5 cups)
- 1 teaspoon salt
- 1 teaspoon cinnamon

- 1 cup sugar

### Direction

- Heat oven to 300 degrees.
- Liberally spray a baking sheet with cooking spray, such as Pam.
- Beat egg white and water until foamy, not stiff.
- Stir in pecans to coat.
- Mix salt, sugar and cinnamon together and add to coated pecans.
- Toss pecans until thoroughly coated.
- Place coated pecans on cookie sheet.
- Bake 30-35 minutes, TURNING EVERY 5-6 MINUTES (this is VERY important to the success of the recipe) Remove from oven and stir again before cooling.

### Nutrition Information

- Calories: 3931.4
- Total Carbohydrate: 264.9
- Cholesterol: 0
- Sodium: 2381.1
- Saturated Fat: 28.1
- Fiber: 44.8
- Sugar: 218.1
- Protein: 45.3
- Total Fat: 326.6

## 141. Frosty Strawberry Pops K

*Serving: 6 serving(s) | Prep: 15mins | Ready in:*

### Ingredients

- 1 quart ripe fresh strawberries, rinsed
- 1/3 cup tropical punch sugar- sweetened Kool-Aid drink mix

### Direction

- REMOVE tops from strawberries.
- Measure the soft drink mix using a dry measuring cup, leveling it with a straight-edged table knife.
- PLACE strawberries and drink mix in blender; cover.
- Blend on low speed 2 minute or until smooth.
- Pour evenly into six 5-oz. paper or plastic cups.
- Freeze 1 hour then INSERT wooden pop stick into center of each cup.
- Freeze an additional 3 hours or until pops are firm.
- Remove from freezer a few minutes before serving; let stand at room temperature to soften slightly.
- Peel off paper cups just before serving.

### Nutrition Information

- Calories: 30.7
- Saturated Fat: 0
- Fiber: 1.9
- Cholesterol: 0
- Protein: 0.6
- Total Fat: 0.3
- Sodium: 1
- Sugar: 4.5
- Total Carbohydrate: 7.4

## 142. Frozen JELLO Pops

*Serving: 12-24 serving(s) | Prep: 10mins | Ready in:*

### Ingredients

- 2 cups boiling water
- 1 package jell-o brand gelatin, any flavor (4-serving size)
- 1/2 cup sugar
- 2 cups cold water

### Direction

- Stir boiling water into gelatin and sugar in medium bowl at 2 minutes until completely dissolved.
- Stir in cold water.
- Pour into pops molds or plastic or paper cups.
- Freeze about 2 hours or until almost firm.
- Insert wooden spoon or stick or plastic spoon into each for handle.
- Freeze 8 hours or overnight until firm.
- Press firmly on bottom of mold to release pop.
- Store leftover pops in freezer.

## Nutrition Information

- Calories: 32.2
- Sugar: 8.3
- Total Carbohydrate: 8.3
- Cholesterol: 0
- Protein: 0
- Total Fat: 0
- Fiber: 0
- Saturated Fat: 0
- Sodium: 2.5

## 143. Frozen Fruit Pie Filling

*Serving: 1 9 inch pie | Prep: 15mins | Ready in:*

## Ingredients

- 3 lbs frozen fruit
- 1/3 cup flour
- 1/3 cup sugar, up to 1/2 c
- 1 pinch salt

## Direction

- Thaw fruit in a microwave oven in the fruit storage bag on the defrost cycle in 3 minute cycles, until the fruit is softened.
- Or submerge the bag of frozen fruit in tepid water 10-30 minutes, changing the water as it gets too cold.
- Drain the liquid from the bag and toss the fruit with flour, sugar and salt.
- Transfer to a prepared pie shell. Top with a crust or a crumb topping.
- Bake at 375 F until fruit is bubbly and crust in lightly browned, 25-35 minutes.

## Nutrition Information

- Calories: 409.3
- Saturated Fat: 0.1
- Sodium: 155.9
- Fiber: 1.1
- Sugar: 66.7
- Total Carbohydrate: 98.3
- Cholesterol: 0
- Total Fat: 0.4
- Protein: 4.3

## 144. Fruit Filled Spring Rolls

*Serving: 4-6 serving(s) | Prep: 10mins | Ready in:*

## Ingredients

- 2 bananas, sliced into thin rounds
- 8 medium strawberries, cut into small pieces lengthwise
- 12 large square sheets rice paper
- 200 g strawberry flavored vegan soy yogurt
- mint (to garnish) (optional)

## Direction

- Set up a wrapping 'station'. Have a large baking dish (big enough to completely submerge a rice paper sheet) filled with warm water.
- Next to that, have your package of rice paper, then your fruit, then your large plate, paper towels or a kitchen towel, then serving plate covered with plastic wrap.
- Place one rice paper sheet into water and press down softly to cover. Allow to sit 1 minute,

then pull out gently- don't tear it! Place it flat down on plate and place slices of banana and strawberry at the bottom corner.
- Fold up corner, then fold over. Wrap in the sides, then roll all the way up. It should look like a small egg roll. Best is 4 slices banana and a little over half a strawberry per roll.
- It's better to under fill than to overfill, as the paper will tear. Place on your serving plate and cover with the plastic wrap.
- Wipe off your rolling plate and repeat with remaining sheets and fruit, placing under plastic wrap after each one to keep from drying out.
- After all wraps are used up, uncover rolls and (with a very sharp knife), cut each in half on the diagonal. Arrange attractively on a serving plate and divide soy yogurt between 4 small dipping bowls (1 for each person). Garnish with a drizzle of sauce and a sprig of mint.
- Variations:
- * Try serving this on Asian plates with small dipping sauce bowls to match and eating with chopsticks.
- * Great with any fruit you would like. Great ones to try: Peaches, Pineapple, Coconut shreds, small Apple chunks, chopped Cherries, Mandarin orange segments (patted dry first), Mango, papaya, pear, etc.
- * A great sauce to try drizzled on bananas inside the roll: vegan chocolate melted with a bit of peanut butter- it's very easy to make these look elegant and taste delicious!
- * Try any dipping sauce you'd like. Blended fruit and applesauce is great, all different types of soy yogurt work, and a creamy dip made with coconut milk or coconut cream. (You can find it in Asian food stores in powdered form.) Shredded coconut, flavoring (like vanilla or almond extract, ginger or cinnamon) and vegan sugar or syrup simmered down is wonderful. Serve all the sauces cold and thick!

## Nutrition Information

- Calories: 60.2
- Protein: 0.8
- Total Fat: 0.3
- Sugar: 8.3
- Total Carbohydrate: 15.3
- Saturated Fat: 0.1
- Sodium: 0.8
- Fiber: 2
- Cholesterol: 0

## 145.     Fruit Roll Up

*Serving: 8 serving(s) | Prep: 4mins | Ready in:*

### Ingredients

- 2 quarts applesauce
- 1 (3 ounce) box sugar-free jello

### Direction

- Mix applesauce and Jell-O.
- Spread in food dehydrator, or a fruit leather tray, or a plastic wrapped tray.
- Dry by your dehydrator's manufacturer's instructions, until no wet spots are left.
- I have used all sorts of fruit puree not just apple sauce.
- Use your favorite flavor of Jell-O.

### Nutrition Information

- Calories: 228.8
- Total Fat: 0.5
- Fiber: 3
- Total Carbohydrate: 53.8
- Protein: 6.4
- Saturated Fat: 0.1
- Sodium: 365.4
- Sugar: 0
- Cholesterol: 0

## 146. Fruit Salsa With Cinnamon Sugar Tortillas

*Serving: 8 serving(s) | Prep: 15mins | Ready in:*

### Ingredients

- 2 medium granny smith apples, chopped
- 1 kiwi fruit, sliced and chopped
- 1 cup sliced fresh strawberries
- 2 tablespoons apple jelly
- 2 tablespoons brown sugar
- 1 orange, juice of
- 10 flour tortillas (1 package)
- cinnamon
- sugar

### Direction

- Combine fruits with jelly and brown sugar; squeeze juice of one sweet orange over salsa and stir gently.
- Brush tortillas with water and sprinkle with cinnamon and sugar.
- Bake tortillas at 350 for 5 minutes.
- Cut tortillas into pieces and serve with fruit salsa.

### Nutrition Information

- Calories: 178.3
- Saturated Fat: 0.7
- Sugar: 12.9
- Protein: 3.5
- Total Fat: 3.1
- Fiber: 2.7
- Total Carbohydrate: 34.9
- Cholesterol: 0
- Sodium: 242.3

## 147. Fruit Skewers For Children (And Adults Too!) Child Safe

*Serving: 8 fruit skewers, 4-8 serving(s) | Prep: 30mins | Ready in:*

### Ingredients

- 4 kiwi fruits, peeled and cut in half across the width
- 1/2 fresh pineapple, peeled and chopped (8 x 3cm wedges)
- 8 large strawberries
- 8 ice-cream sticks

### Direction

- Peel and chop fruit.
- Thread onto the ice-cream sticks. First the strawberries, then pineapple and lastly the kiwifruits.
- Use a small paring knife to cut a hole into the center of the fruits if they do not thread easily onto the ice-cream sticks.
- Refrigerate until needed.
- Suggestion - Serve with a yogurt as a dipping sauce.
- Variation - can use any fruits of your choice. They just need to be approx. 3 times wider than the ice cream stick.
- For older children you can use small wooden skewers.

### Nutrition Information

- Calories: 110.2
- Total Fat: 0.6
- Saturated Fat: 0
- Sodium: 3.6
- Protein: 1.6
- Fiber: 4.4
- Sugar: 19.1
- Total Carbohydrate: 27.7
- Cholesterol: 0

## 148. Fruit And Nut Chocolate Slice

*Serving: 16 pieces, 4-6 serving(s) | Prep: 10mins | Ready in:*

### Ingredients

- 100 g butter or 100 g margarine
- 1/2 cup sugar
- 1 egg
- 150 g nonfat yogurt
- 1 teaspoon vanilla essence
- 1 cup all-purpose flour
- 1/4 cup cocoa
- 1/2 teaspoon baking soda
- 1/4 cup almonds, finely chopped
- 1/4 cup walnuts, finely chopped
- 1/4 cup raisins
- 5 prunes, finely chopped
- 1/2 teaspoon lemon rind
- 1 tablespoon apple juice
- 1 tablespoon orange juice
- 1/2 teaspoon oil

### Direction

- Mix the almonds, walnuts, raisins, prunes, lemon rind, juices and oil in a medium bowl. Set aside.
- Grease and line a square microwave-safe cake tin with baking paper.
- Cream the butter and sugar together until pale and creamy.
- Stir in egg, yoghurt and vanilla until well combined.
- Sift together flour, cocoa and baking soda.
- Fold flour mixture lightly into butter mixture. Mixture will be firm.
- Fold fruit mixture inches.
- Spread cake into prepared cake tin, using the back of a spoon to smooth over.
- Cook at 600 watts (adjust according to your microwave e.g. for an 800 watt microwave, use 80 percent, for 1200 watts use 50%) for 7 minutes, until centre is just cooked. The centre should be damp on the surface and begin to shrink away from the sides of the dish. Test with a toothpick.
- If the cake isn't cooked yet, pop back in the microwave for another couple of minutes, but not too long.
- Leave in dish for 5 minutes before turning out. The crust will be soft, so turn out onto a clean tea towel placed on a cooking rack.
- Ice with your regular icing, although I prefer it un-iced. But only because I'm not really an icing sort of person.

### Nutrition Information

- Calories: 594.5
- Total Carbohydrate: 69.9
- Cholesterol: 107
- Total Fat: 32.5
- Saturated Fat: 14.6
- Sodium: 379.1
- Fiber: 5.1
- Sugar: 37.2
- Protein: 11.7

## 149. Fruit And Popcorn Balls

*Serving: 10-12 serving(s) | Prep: 30mins | Ready in:*

### Ingredients

- 10 cups popped popcorn
- 3/4 cup brown sugar
- 1/4 cup apple juice
- 3 tablespoons butter
- 2 tablespoons light corn syrup
- 1/4 teaspoon salt
- 2 cups raisins (nuts, may be substituted for part of the 2 cups of fruit. cashews, peanuts, shelled sunflower seeds) or 2 cups dried cranberries (nuts, may be substituted for part of the 2 cups of fruit. cashews, peanuts, shelled sunflower seeds) or 2 cups dried fruit (nuts,

may be substituted for part of the 2 cups of fruit. cashews, peanuts, shelled sunflower seeds)

## Direction

- Butter a very large bowl. Add popped popcorn and your selection of the 2 cups of fruit and/or nuts. I like 1 1/2 cups dried cranberries and 1/2 cup chopped cashews.
- Heat brown sugar, corn syrup, butter, salt, and juice until just boiling. Pour over dry ingredients in bowl.
- Butter hands with additional butter or cooking spray and form into tennis size balls. Compact lightly to get the mixture to hold a ball shape. Set aside. Wrap each popcorn ball in plastic wrap.
- Option: The balls can be drizzled with melted chocolate for gift giving. I like to use white chocolate on the cranberry/ cashew ones. After wrapping with plastic wrap, I tie with a burgundy colored ribbon.

## Nutrition Information

- Calories: 225.8
- Sodium: 95.8
- Fiber: 2.2
- Sugar: 35
- Protein: 2
- Saturated Fat: 2.3
- Total Carbohydrate: 49.4
- Cholesterol: 9.2
- Total Fat: 4

## 150. Fruit And Yogurt Breakfast Couscous

*Serving: 2 serving(s) | Prep: 5mins | Ready in:*

## Ingredients

- 3/4 cup couscous, uncooked (plain, unflavored)
- 1 1/2 cups water (substitute milk or soymilk if desired)
- 1/2 cup dried fruit
- 3 tablespoons honey, divided
- 6 ounces vanilla yogurt
- 1/2 teaspoon cinnamon (substitute or add extra spices of your choice)
- 1/4 cup almonds, chopped (substitute with any other nut)

## Direction

- Set aside two bowls and divide the dry couscous between them (pouring half in each).
- If using dried fruit, set aside a third bowl and fill with the fruit.
- Add the water and 1 tbsp. honey to a small saucepan. Bring the water to a boil and pour 1/2 cup boiling water over each bowl of couscous. Pour the remaining water over the dried fruit (this will allow the fruit to plump and become tender and even more delicious).
- Cover each bowl of couscous and let sit for 5-10 minutes until the water has been fully absorbed. Fluff with a fork.
- Drain the water from the bowl of fruit. Add half the yogurt to each bowl. Divide the fruit in half between the bowls. Divide the chopped almonds between the bowls. Drizzle each bowl with 1 tbsp. honey. Sprinkle 1/4 tsp cinnamon on each bowl. Mix, if desired. Enjoy, it's delicious!
- Notes: I love a combination of dried fruit with this dish. I have used dried apricots, pears, cherries, raisins, blueberries, Goji berries, currents and dates (not all at once, but hey why not?). Raisins are by far the easiest as they are a staple in many kitchens (and they're great in this dish).
- Notes (for serving an adult and a young child): Divide the dry couscous between two bowls: 1/2 cup and 1/4 cup. Make sure to chop the dried fruit into bite-sized pieces. When dividing the water between the bowls, add 5-oz boiling water to the adult portion and 3-oz

to the child portion (using a measuring cup makes this easy). Skip the nuts if your child hasn't been introduced to them yet or if the pieces are large enough to present a choking hazard. Also, make sure your child has gotten an OK from the doctor to eat honey (typically given at 1 year).

## Nutrition Information

- Calories: 626.2
- Fiber: 9.7
- Sugar: 30.7
- Total Carbohydrate: 118.6
- Cholesterol: 11.1
- Protein: 16.3
- Saturated Fat: 2.6
- Sodium: 120.7
- Total Fat: 12.4

## 151. Fruity Frosty Treat

*Serving: 3-4 serving(s) | Prep: 5mins | Ready in:*

### Ingredients

- 1/2 cup milk
- 1/2 banana, frozen
- 1 cup frozen blueberries
- 3/4 cup frozen peach slices
- plain yogurt
- honey, to taste

### Direction

- Put milk in a blender with frozen banana and 2-3 soup-spoonfuls of plain yogurt. Blend until liquefied, then keep adding other fruit little by little. You may need to stir in the ingredients before blending, because it gets pretty thick.
- Add the honey, and stir in if necessary.
- You should get a thick smoothie about the consistency of a Wendy's Frosty. Eat with a spoon.

- If you have any leftovers try making popsicles out of them: Fill a paper cup with the stuff, cover it with foil, then stick a straw or Popsicle stick in the center and freeze.

## Nutrition Information

- Calories: 132.9
- Sodium: 23.4
- Fiber: 3
- Total Carbohydrate: 30.4
- Saturated Fat: 1
- Sugar: 23.9
- Cholesterol: 5.7
- Protein: 2.2
- Total Fat: 1.7

## 152. Garbage Pickles

*Serving: 5-15 serving(s) | Prep: 15mins | Ready in:*

### Ingredients

- fresh red radish, by the bag
- 5 -10 garlic cloves
- Grandma Jennings all-purpose pickle brine
- 1 quart water, 1/4 C. vinegar, 1/4 C. pickling salt

### Direction

- Trim both ends of each radish and cut them into quarters. (If you leave the radishes whole you won't be able to pack the radishes in tightly and there will be too much room for brine in the jar. The pickles would then be far too salty).
- Pack the radishes as tightly as you can into a jar, spacing the garlic cloves evenly around. I recommend using a small-mouth pint jar, but a bag of radishes is not made to fit exactly into a jar of a particular size, so use your judgement on how many bags of radishes and jars you want to use. Cover the radishes with

brine and cap the jar. Turn it upside down and place it in the fridge for 3 weeks to pickle. You will notice that very quickly the vinegar starts to break down the red skin on the radishes, making the pickle juice and the radishes each uniformly pink.

- About that brine recipe. I make mine with a gallon of water, 1 cup salt and 1 cup vinegar as my Grandma taught me, but have cut the measurements down for folks who may not use so much. I keep this brine in a gallon jar and whenever I have something around that might be good to pickle (green tomatoes, string-beans, baby carrots, cauliflower etc.) I just grab a jar, pack it with veggies and seasoning (garlic, dill, curry, Italian seasonings etc.) and pour on the brine. I always have some very good pickles in my fridge! Makes a good gift as well, if you seal them.

## Nutrition Information

- Calories: 4.5
- Protein: 0.2
- Saturated Fat: 0
- Sodium: 6.2
- Sugar: 0
- Total Carbohydrate: 1
- Total Fat: 0
- Fiber: 0.1
- Cholesterol: 0

## 153. Gluten Free Sugar Free Brownie

*Serving: 12 bars | Prep: 20mins | Ready in:*

### Ingredients

- 4 tablespoons butter
- 2/3 cup xylitol sugar substitute
- 1/2 cup cold water
- 1 teaspoon vanilla
- 1 cup rice flour
- 4 tablespoons unsweetened cocoa powder
- 1 teaspoon baking powder
- 2 tablespoons shelled hemp seeds
- 2 tablespoons walnuts
- 1/2 cup sugar-free chocolate chips

### Direction

- Preheat oven to 350°.
- Melt butter and combine with xylitol sugar, water, and vanilla.
- Add flour, cocoa powder, baking powder, nuts, chips, Mix thoroughly.
- Coat the bottom of small baking pan with butter or non-stick spray and pour in batter.
- Bake for 20 minutes or until a toothpick inserted near the center comes out clean.
- Cool completely before cutting into bars.

## Nutrition Information

- Calories: 95.3
- Total Fat: 5.1
- Saturated Fat: 2.7
- Fiber: 1
- Total Carbohydrate: 11.9
- Sodium: 64.8
- Sugar: 0.1
- Cholesterol: 10.2
- Protein: 1.4

## 154. Golden Flapjacks

*Serving: 8 serving(s) | Prep: 5mins | Ready in:*

### Ingredients

- 100 g butter
- 100 g demerara sugar
- 100 g golden syrup
- 225 g porridge oats (rolled oats)

### Direction

- Preheat oven to 160 degrees Celsius grease and base line a 20cm round cake tin.
- To measure the golden syrup easier, measure the sugar first, keep it in the scales and pour the syrup on top to avoid sticking to plate.
- Put butter, syrup and sugar in a saucepan and heat gently until butter has melted and sugar dissolved.
- Remove from heat and stir in oats.
- Pour into lined tin and press down with back of a spoon until is surface is level.
- Bake in oven about 25-30 minutes until golden brown.
- Remove from oven and loosen from the sides of the tin with a palette knife and leave to cool for about 10 minutes.
- Tip out onto board, remove paper and cut into even wedges, leave to cool completely.

## Nutrition Information

- Calories: 284.4
- Sodium: 81.2
- Total Carbohydrate: 41.9
- Cholesterol: 26.7
- Total Fat: 11.9
- Saturated Fat: 6.7
- Fiber: 2.8
- Sugar: 16.6
- Protein: 4.6

## 155. Grammy's Rice Pudding

*Serving: 1 serving(s) | Prep: 5mins | Ready in:*

### Ingredients

- 3/4 cup cooked rice
- 3 tablespoons sugar
- 2 eggs
- 3/4 cup skim milk

### Direction

- Beat eggs, sugar, and milk together.
- Add rice and add cinnamon and raisins to taste; stir.
- Microwave for 10 minutes, stirring halfway through.

## Nutrition Information

- Calories: 550.3
- Sugar: 38.5
- Total Carbohydrate: 88.7
- Cholesterol: 426.7
- Protein: 23.2
- Total Fat: 10.7
- Saturated Fat: 3.5
- Sodium: 248.9
- Fiber: 0.4

## 156. Grandma's Popcorn Balls

*Serving: 12 balls, approx. | Prep: 2mins | Ready in:*

### Ingredients

- 1 cup sugar
- 1 cup Karo light corn syrup
- 2/3 cup vinegar
- 1 tablespoon butter, melted
- 4 quarts popped popcorn

### Direction

- In large pot mix well the sugar, Karo syrup, vinegar and bring to boil. Continue until mixture reaches the Hard Crack Stage on candy thermometer.
- Remove from heat and quickly stir in popped popcorn. Butter your hands and scoop enough coated mixture to form baseball sized balls.
- You have to work quickly as the coating will harden very fast. When cooled, wrap in wax paper, twisting to close.

- Preparation and cooking time does not include time to pop popcorn.
- Cooking time varies with weather conditions.

## Nutrition Information

- Calories: 197.1
- Total Fat: 1.5
- Saturated Fat: 0.7
- Sodium: 25.6
- Fiber: 1.6
- Total Carbohydrate: 46.8
- Cholesterol: 2.5
- Sugar: 24.4
- Protein: 1.4

## 157. Green Apple Monster

*Serving: 1 serving(s) | Prep: 5mins | Ready in:*

### Ingredients

- 2 slices granny smith apples, unpeeled (cut into about 1-inch slices)
- creamy peanut butter
- 2 large green seedless grapes
- 2 chocolate chips or 2 raisins
- lemon juice (optional)

### Direction

- Tip: If you wish, immediately after slicing the apples, you can squeeze a bit of lemon or orange juice to stop browning.
- MOUTH: Spread on some peanut butter on one slice of apple and place the other apple slice on top. It doesn't need to be perfect! You are trying to make it look like the monster has "ooze" coming out of its mouth! ;).
- EYES: Trim off one small end of each grape so that it's flat. Using a little bit of peanut butter attach the grapes to the top apple slice, creating the monster's eyeballs.
- Add another dollop of peanut butter to the top of the grapes and attach the chocolate chips (or raisins) creating the monster's pupils.
- Creature from the Black Lagoon still scares me!

## Nutrition Information

- Calories: 6.9
- Protein: 0.1
- Saturated Fat: 0
- Sodium: 0.2
- Fiber: 0.1
- Sugar: 1.6
- Cholesterol: 0
- Total Fat: 0
- Total Carbohydrate: 1.8

## 158. Halloween Spooky Spider Snacks (Fun For The Kids To Make)

*Serving: 24 serving(s) | Prep: 10mins | Ready in:*

### Ingredients

- 1/2 cup creamy peanut butter, plus
- 1 tablespoon creamy peanut butter
- 48 butter flavored crackers (Ritz)
- 1/2 cup chow mein noodles
- 1/4 cup raisins

### Direction

- Spread 1 tsp peanut butter on the tops of 24 crackers.
- Place three noodles on each side of cracker to look like three legs on each side (I know - not anatomically correct).
- Top with remaining crackers.
- Place small dot of peanut butter on two raisins per cracker and stick the raisins on the crackers to look like eyes.

## Nutrition Information

- Calories: 206.3
- Saturated Fat: 2.4
- Sugar: 3.8
- Total Carbohydrate: 22.6
- Protein: 3.8
- Total Fat: 11.6
- Sodium: 308.8
- Fiber: 1.1
- Cholesterol: 0

## 159. Ham Pineapple Scrolls

*Serving: 24 ham pineapple scrolls | Prep: 20mins | Ready in:*

### Ingredients

- 2 1/2 cups self-raising flour
- 1 teaspoon baking powder
- 1 pinch salt
- 55 g chilled butter
- 1 cup milk
- 1/2 cup pasta sauce
- 120 g shaved ham, shredded
- 440 g unsweetened crushed canned pineapple, well drained
- 1 cup grated cheddar cheese

### Direction

- Preheat the oven to 200°C and line a baking tray with non-stick baking paper.
- Sift the flour, baking powder and salt into a large bowl and rub the butter with your fingertips until the mixture resembles fine breadcrumbs; stir in the milk with a flat-bladed knife until the mixture comes together.
- Transfer the dough to a lightly floured surface and knead gently.
- Divide the dough in half and roll out each portion to a 15cm x 30cm rectangle.
- Spread each portion with pasta sauce, sprinkle with ham, pineapple and cheese and roll up from the longer side to enclose the filling.
- Trim the ends if necessary.
- Cut into 2cm wide pieces with a lightly floured serrated-edge knife and place the scrolls onto a lightly greased tray, allowing room for them spreading.
- Bake for 18-20 minutes or until puffed and golden.
- Serve warm or at room temperature.

## Nutrition Information

- Calories: 105.1
- Total Fat: 4.3
- Total Carbohydrate: 12.4
- Saturated Fat: 2.5
- Sodium: 335.3
- Fiber: 0.5
- Sugar: 1.9
- Cholesterol: 13.9
- Protein: 4.1

## 160. Ham And Spinach Quiche Make Ahead

*Serving: 1 9in quiche, 4-6 serving(s) | Prep: 30mins | Ready in:*

### Ingredients

- 8 ounces all-purpose flour
- 1 pinch salt
- 4 ounces chilled unsalted butter, cut into pieces
- 12 tablespoons chilled water
- Filling
- 1/2 ounce unsalted butter
- 4 scallions, finely chopped
- 10 ounces fresh spinach, washed
- 4 ounces roast ham, chopped
- 3 ounces sharp cheddar cheese, grated
- 2 large eggs

- 7 tablespoons milk
- salt  freshly ground black pepper

## Direction

- Sift the flour and salt into a large mixing bowl. Add the unsalted butter, rubbing it in with your fingertips until the mixture looks like fine breadcrumbs. Add the chilled water and mix it in with a round-bladed knife until the pastry clings together. Use your hand to form the dough into a ball – it should be firm enough to roll out without cracking. Wrap the pastry in plastic wrap and chill for 10 minutes.
- Preheat the oven to 400°F
- Roll out the pastry on a lightly floured surface and use it to line a 9 inch flan ring or flan dish. Line with a piece of crumpled foil or greaseproof paper and baking beans and bake 'blind' (i.e. without a filling) for 15 minutes.
- Take the flan from the oven and remove the foil or paper and baking beans. Reduce the oven temperature to 350°F
- To make the filling, melt the unsalted butter in a frying pan and fry the scallions for 3-4 minutes until soft. At the same time cook the spinach in a tiny amount of water for 2-3 minutes, until wilted. Drain well, squeezing out the excess moisture with the back of a spoon. Cool the scallions and the spinach.
- Scatter the cooked ham, scallions and spinach over the base of the flan and sprinkle the cheese on top. Beat the eggs and milk together with a little salt and pepper. Pour into the flan case, then bake for 30-35 minutes, until set.

## Nutrition Information

- Calories: 640.6
- Sugar: 1.1
- Saturated Fat: 22.9
- Sodium: 718.3
- Fiber: 3.6
- Protein: 24.3
- Total Fat: 38.9
- Total Carbohydrate: 49.3
- Cholesterol: 215.1

## 161.     Healthy Apple Shortcake Yoghurt

*Serving: 1 helping, 1 serving(s) | Prep: 2mins | Ready in:*

## Ingredients

- 135 g nonfat plain yogurt (about 1/2 a cup)
- 1 1/2 teaspoons applesauce
- 1/3 piece shortbread cookie (roughly crushed)
- 2 teaspoons granulated artificial sweetener, to taste
- 4 drops vanilla flavoring, to taste
- 1 dash cinnamon, to taste

## Direction

- Measure yoghurt into a clean, used individual yoghurt tub or other small plastic tub.  (I suggest plastic because it will keep the cold yoghurt cold).
- Add a few of drops of vanilla flavouring.
- Add a couple of teaspoons sweetener to taste. Please don't use sugar unless preparing and chilling well in advance and holding back the shortbread (to save it going soggy) because the sugar will take ages to dissolve.
- Add the roughly crushed piece of shortbread/shortcake cookie.  (Around a teaspoonful is about right.).
- Add a generous teaspoon and a half of a nice chunky applesauce.
- Sprinkle a generous dash of ground cinnamon.
- Stir well.
- SERVE.
- For a delicious ultra-healthy variant, substitute half a teaspoon oat bran for the shortbread.
- Can be made very quickly into a larger bowl in bigger quantities for several servings.

## Nutrition Information

- Calories: 82.5

- Saturated Fat: 0.2
- Sodium: 106.2
- Fiber: 0.2
- Sugar: 10.4
- Total Carbohydrate: 12.1
- Total Fat: 0.3
- Cholesterol: 2.7
- Protein: 7.8

## 162. Healthy Banana Bran Muffins

*Serving: 12 muffins | Prep: 5mins | Ready in:*

### Ingredients

- 1 1/2 cups bran flakes
- 1 cup mashed ripe banana (3 medium)
- 1/2 cup milk (i used skim)
- 1 egg
- 3 tablespoons vegetable oil
- 1 cup flour
- 1/4 cup sugar (i used 4 packages of Splenda)
- 2 teaspoons baking powder
- 1/2 teaspoon baking soda
- 1/8 teaspoon ground nutmeg (i used a little nutmeg and 1/4 t cinnamon)
- 1/4 cup chopped walnuts (i added, but it's optional)

### Direction

- Preheat oven to 400 degrees. Grease or paper line muffin cups (I sprayed).
- Combine cereal, bananas, milk, egg and oil in bowl; mix well. Let stand 5 minutes; stir to break up cereal.
- Combine flour, sugar (sweetener), baking powder, baking soda, spices and nuts (if using) in separate bowl.
- Add flour mixture all at once to cereal mixture, stirring just until moistened.
- Divide evenly among prepared muffin cups, which comes to about a heaping tablespoon per muffin.
- Bake 20-25 minutes or until tester inserted in centre comes out clean.
- Serve warm (room temp is OK too).

### Nutrition Information

- Calories: 139.7
- Cholesterol: 19.1
- Fiber: 1.6
- Sugar: 6.6
- Saturated Fat: 1
- Sodium: 158.7
- Total Carbohydrate: 19.8
- Protein: 2.9
- Total Fat: 6

## 163. Healthy Bean Bars

*Serving: 16 squares, 16 serving(s) | Prep: 15mins | Ready in:*

### Ingredients

- 2 cups cooked beans
- 2/3 cup powdered milk
- 1 cup wheat flour
- 2/3 cup applesauce
- 1 teaspoon baking soda
- 2 egg whites, beaten
- 1 teaspoon ground cinnamon
- 1/2 cup molasses
- 1/2 teaspoon ground cloves
- 1/3 cup olive oil
- 1/2 teaspoon ground nutmeg
- 1 cup raisins
- 1/2 teaspoon ground allspice

### Direction

- Mash the beans into a paste consistency.
- Add the rest of the ingredients to the paste.

- Stir mixture thoroughly.
- Pour into 8 x 8 baking pan.
- Bake in a preheated 350 degrees oven for 40 minutes.
- Optional:
- The use of pears, or other fruit can be used to replace the applesauce.

## Nutrition Information

- Calories: 160.7
- Sugar: 13.3
- Total Carbohydrate: 24.9
- Protein: 3.2
- Saturated Fat: 1.6
- Sodium: 113.7
- Fiber: 1.4
- Total Fat: 6.2
- Cholesterol: 5.2

## 164. Healthy Peanut Butter Balls

*Serving: 30 serving(s) | Prep: 10mins | Ready in:*

### Ingredients

- 1/3 cup crunchy peanut butter
- 1/2 cup nonfat dry milk powder
- 2 tablespoons wheat germ
- 1 tablespoon honey

### Direction

- Place ingredients into food blender in the order listed.
- Turn on and blend until mixture is evenly mixed and crumbly looking.
- Use a small melon ball scoop to make the peanut butter balls. Push the peanut butter mixture in there so it's nice and compact like brown sugar.
- Put onto a plate or in a container and put in the fridge. You can eat them right away but they are really good after they've sat in the fridge for a little while. Enjoy!
- You can also use creamy peanut butter, but I'm a crunchy kinda gal. Also you can roll the balls in additional wheat germ for an even crunchier ball.

## Nutrition Information

- Calories: 28
- Sodium: 24.7
- Fiber: 0.3
- Total Carbohydrate: 2.5
- Cholesterol: 0.4
- Total Fat: 1.5
- Sugar: 1.9
- Protein: 1.5
- Saturated Fat: 0.2

## 165. Heavenly Oat Bars

*Serving: 24 bars | Prep: 15mins | Ready in:*

### Ingredients

- 1/2 cup margarine, softened
- 1/2 cup brown sugar, packed
- 1/2 cup corn syrup
- 1 teaspoon vanilla
- 3 cups oats, uncooked (quick or old fashioned)
- 1 cup semi-sweet chocolate chips
- 1/2 cup peanut butter, creamy

### Direction

- Beat the first four items with a mixer on medium speed until smooth and well-blended.
- Stir in oats.
- Spread in a greased 9" square baking pan and bake at 350 degrees, for 25 minutes (center should be just firm).
- Cool slightly.

- In the microwave, heat the chocolate chips in a dry, microwavable bowl, for 1 minute, stir, then heat 1 more minute, stir until smooth.
- Stir in the peanut butter.
- Spread over warm (not hot) bars.
- Cool on a wire rack, completely.

## Nutrition Information

- Calories: 210.7
- Total Fat: 9.9
- Saturated Fat: 2.7
- Fiber: 2.8
- Sugar: 10.4
- Total Carbohydrate: 27.8
- Sodium: 72.1
- Cholesterol: 0
- Protein: 5

## 166. Herb Potato Chips

*Serving: 2 serving(s) | Prep: 5mins | Ready in:*

### Ingredients

- 1 russet potato (or Idaho if desired)
- 1-2 tablespoon butter, melted (or more if needed)
- fresh dill (or other fresh herbs)

### Direction

- Preheat oven to 350°F.
- Peel potato and slice it paper-thin with a mandolin.
- Line a baking sheet with parchment paper and spray with cooking spray.
- Place the potato slices flat on the sheet. Brush the potatoes with melted butter, then place fresh dill spring on each slice.
- Place another potato slice on top of each herb-potato slice (Try to use a slice of similar size/shape - you can use kitchen scissors to trim it if necessary).
- Spray the potatoes with cooking spray and cover with another sheet of parchment paper.
- Place a baking sheet on top of the parchment paper.
- Bake at 350 for 20 minutes.
- Eat as a snack or garnish your favorite soup with these chips.

## Nutrition Information

- Calories: 132.9
- Sodium: 57.1
- Fiber: 2.3
- Sugar: 0.8
- Total Carbohydrate: 18.6
- Cholesterol: 15.3
- Total Fat: 5.8
- Saturated Fat: 3.7
- Protein: 2.2

## 167. Holly Leaves (No Bake)

*Serving: 14 serving(s) | Prep: 15mins | Ready in:*

### Ingredients

- 5 tablespoons margarine
- 20 large marshmallows
- 2 cups corn flakes
- 1/2 teaspoon green food coloring
- red cinnamon candies
- wax paper

### Direction

- In a double boiler, melt margarine.
- Add marshmallows a few at a time.
- Stir until marshmallows are completely melted.
- Add green food coloring and remove from heat.
- Stir in corn flakes gently.
- Drop by spoonful on waxed paper.

- Put 3 red hots on each spoonful to resemble holly berries.

## Nutrition Information

- Calories: 82.5
- Total Fat: 4.1
- Saturated Fat: 0.7
- Sodium: 84.4
- Sugar: 6.2
- Protein: 0.5
- Fiber: 0.1
- Total Carbohydrate: 11.7
- Cholesterol: 0

## 168. Homemade Microwave Popcorn

*Serving: 6-8 cups | Prep: 2mins | Ready in:*

## Ingredients

- 1/3 cup popcorn
- 2 -3 tablespoons melted butter
- salt

## Direction

- Pour kernels into a small paper bag (standard lunch size is fine) and fold the top of the bag over twice to close (each fold should be 1/2 inch deep; remember the kernels need room to pop).
- Seal the bag with 2 staples placed 2 to 3 inches apart. (Editor's Note: Using metal staples in a microwave can be hazardous, please consider an alternate method).
- Place bag in microwave on carousel. Cook on high 2-3 minutes, or until the pops are 5 seconds apart. Pour in melted butter and salt and shake the bag to distribute.

## Nutrition Information

- Calories: 35.7
- Fiber: 0.1
- Sugar: 0
- Total Fat: 3.9
- Sodium: 33.8
- Protein: 0.1
- Saturated Fat: 2.4
- Total Carbohydrate: 0.3
- Cholesterol: 10.2

## 169. Homemade Nutella Better Than The Real Thing!

*Serving: 2 cups | Prep: 10mins | Ready in:*

## Ingredients

- 1 1/2 cups chopped hazelnuts
- 1/2 cup dark chocolate chips or 1/2 cup semi-sweet chocolate chips
- 1 -2 tablespoon canola oil (I use sunflower oil)

## Direction

- Place the hazelnuts in a dry skillet and toast over medium heat 2 to 4 minutes or until just starting to brown.
- Place the hazelnuts and the chocolate chips in the work bowl of a food processor fitted with a metal blade. Process for 3 to 5 minutes until the mixture starts to become smooth.
- Drizzle in one tablespoon of oil while continuing to process. If necessary, add another tablespoon of oil until the mixture becomes smooth and spreadable.
- Store in the fridge in a clean jar or lidded container for up to 2 weeks. You will probably need to mix the spread before each use as the oil can separate.

## Nutrition Information

- Calories: 898.9
- Sodium: 4.6

- Sugar: 27.3
- Total Carbohydrate: 43.4
- Cholesterol: 0
- Protein: 16.9
- Saturated Fat: 12.5
- Fiber: 12.3
- Total Fat: 81.1

## 170. Homemade Pop Tarts

*Serving: 12 pop tarts | Prep: 15mins | Ready in:*

### Ingredients

- For Pie Crust
- 1 1/2 cups flour
- 1/2 teaspoon salt
- 1/4 cup shortening
- 1/4 cup butter, softened
- 3 tablespoons cold water
- For Filling
- 1/2 cup jam (your choice)
- For Glaze
- 1 cup powdered sugar
- 3 ounces milk, to thin
- candy sprinkles

### Direction

- Preheat oven to 450°F
- Combine flour and salt in a large bowl. Add shortening and butter and blend with a fork, pastry cutter, or your hands. Blend until mixture is fairly coarse. Add water, 1 tablespoons at a time, gently mixing dough after each addition until dough forms a ball.
- Place dough on a lightly floured surface and roll into a square/rectangle. To about 1/8 thickness. Cut out long strips about 2 inches wide and 3 inches long. Repeat until dough runs out.
- Take one pie crust rectangle and lace 1 teaspoons of jam on top. Cover with another piece of pie crust and crimp all four edges. Repeat with the rest of dough. Place Pop-tarts on a baking sheet with parchment paper, and bake for 7-8 minutes.
- While pop-tarts are baking, make glaze. Place powdered sugar in a bowl. Pour milk slowing until it has a consistency of really thick syrup. 1/2 a tablespoons to 1 tablespoons might be enough.
- Once pop-tarts are done and cooled, top with glaze. Sprinkle and decorate with colorful sprinkle.

## Nutrition Information

- Calories: 209.3
- Sodium: 132.6
- Fiber: 0.6
- Sugar: 16.3
- Total Carbohydrate: 31.4
- Cholesterol: 11.2
- Protein: 1.9
- Total Fat: 8.6
- Saturated Fat: 3.7

## 171. Homemade Sweet Dill Yum Yum Pickles

*Serving: 2 (32-ounce) jars pickles | Prep: 48hours | Ready in:*

### Ingredients

- 2 (32 ounce) jarslarge-size garlic dill pickles (drained and washed under cold water)
- 4 cups white sugar, divided (measured exactly)
- 1/2 cup white vinegar
- 1/2 cup water
- 1 tablespoon pickling spices

### Direction

- Slice the washed pickles into about 1/4 to 1/3-inch slices, then place in a medium bowl.

- Pour 2 cups sugar over the slices and toss/stir to coat with the pickle slices.
- Allow to sit out at room temperature for 24 hours tossing several times with a spoon during the 24 hours (I just leave a spoon in the bowl, juice will gather in the bowl, do not drain!).
- After the 24 hours (do not drain the juice in the bowl) in a medium saucepan combine 2 cups sugar, vinegar, water, pickling spice; bring to a boil over medium heat stirring until the sugar is dissolved (about 2 minutes).
- Make certain that the bowl is Pyrex or heat-proof or it might crack when you pour the boiling water into it -- pour the water mixture over the sugared pickles and the sugar juice that has gathered in the bowl; mix very well with a spoon.
- Allow the mixture to stand at room temperature for about 8 hours or overnight.
- Drain pickles (you don't have to completely drain).
- Transfer pickles to clean glass jars and store covered or uncovered in refrigerator.
- Serve cold.

## Nutrition Information

- Calories: 1725.1
- Total Fat: 1.7
- Saturated Fat: 0.4
- Cholesterol: 0
- Protein: 5.7
- Sodium: 11725.3
- Fiber: 11
- Sugar: 432
- Total Carbohydrate: 438.1

## 172. Hot Fried Non Nudist Peanuts

*Serving: 4-8 serving(s) | Prep: 15mins | Ready in:*

## Ingredients

- 1/2 lb non-nudist peanuts (you know, the kind with their clothes still on!)
- sea salt, finely ground, to taste
- cayenne pepper, ground, to taste
- 1 cinnamon stick, optional
- 6 whole cloves (optional)
- oil (for deep frying, NOT peanut oil – they don't like being cooked in their own kind!)

## Direction

- Take off the peanuts' clothes – do this after the kids have gone to bed so that they are not aware of any indecent behaviour in your house.
- Throw their clothes in the trash – they won't ever be needing them again.
- Deep-fry the now-naked nuts, for only a minute or two, in a wire basket in oil that's as hot as a Chinese fire-cracker on the 4th of July.
- Drain the now-not-so-naked but badly-sunburned nuts for just a few seconds in the wire basket – don't be a woos and use anything absorbent for this purpose.
- While they are still very warm and oily, sprinkle them with sea salt and cayenne pepper, and shake them up so that they all get coated.
- Store them in sterile or very clean glass jars with tight-fitting lids.
- Optional – pop a stick of cinnamon or a few whole cloves in each jar.
- Optional – fool your family and/or guests by putting them in an empty Planter's (or other brand) peanuts jar that is labelled "Honey-roasted" and then watch their faces as they munch on something that tastes nothing like what they expected!
- Serve with cocktails or ice-cold beer.

## Nutrition Information

- Calories: 321.5
- Fiber: 4.8
- Sugar: 2.2

- Total Carbohydrate: 9.2
- Cholesterol: 0
- Total Fat: 27.9
- Saturated Fat: 3.9
- Sodium: 10.2
- Protein: 14.6

## 173. Iced Chocolate

*Serving: 2 serving(s) | Prep: 5mins | Ready in:*

### Ingredients

- 2 tablespoons cocoa
- 2 teaspoons cornflour
- 1/4 cup sugar
- 2 cups milk

### Direction

- In a saucepan combine first 3 ingredients with a small bit of the milk, to form a lump free paste.
- Add rest of the milk and bring to boil.
- Remove and let cool.
- Refrigerate until chilled.
- Serve in a large glass with ice cream and whipped cream sprinkled with grated chocolate.
- Can easily be double, tripled, etc.

### Nutrition Information

- Calories: 281.7
- Saturated Fat: 5.6
- Total Carbohydrate: 41.2
- Total Fat: 9.5
- Sodium: 119.9
- Fiber: 1.2
- Sugar: 25
- Cholesterol: 34.2
- Protein: 9.2

## 174. Indian Yam Fritters / Classic Crunch Patties

*Serving: 30 crunch patties, 2 serving(s) | Prep: 40mins | Ready in:*

### Ingredients

- 1 1/2 lbs fresh yams (or one 15-oz can yams, rinsed and drained)
- 1/2 cup besan (also called gram, chickpea flour)
- 1 teaspoon garam masala
- 1/2 teaspoon curry powder
- 1/2 teaspoon sea salt
- 1/4 cup olive oil, for frying

### Direction

- Wash and peel the yams. Boil until tender, about 20 minutes.
- Drain the yams thoroughly and puree in the food processor with the flour. A thick and sticky mixture should result.
- Add the seasonings and pulse again.
- Form little discs with your hands (I hope you washed them) about the size of half-dollars. (50p coins to those across the pond.).
- Shallow pan fry in olive oil, blot on paper towels.
- Serve with tamarind date sauce or a good chutney (many fine chutney recipes on the zaar!).

### Nutrition Information

- Calories: 724.3
- Sodium: 624.1
- Total Carbohydrate: 107.5
- Cholesterol: 0
- Protein: 10.3
- Total Fat: 29.1
- Saturated Fat: 4
- Fiber: 15.9
- Sugar: 4.2

## 175. Italian Bagel Bites

*Serving: 25 pieces, 25 serving(s) | Prep: 10mins | Ready in:*

### Ingredients

- 1 (17 ounce) package miniature bagels (found in the freezer section "or" just buy a bunch of different varieties of bagels)
- 1 (8 ounce) package cream cheese, softened
- 1 (2/3 ounce) package dried Italian salad dressing mix

### Direction

- Cut the bagels in half, lengthwise, toast in the oven on broil.
- Mix softened cream cheese with the salad dressing mix.
- Spread cream cheese mixture on the toasted bagel halves.
- Place on platter and refrigerate until ready to serve.

### Nutrition Information

- Calories: 31.7
- Sodium: 26.9
- Fiber: 0
- Total Carbohydrate: 0.2
- Cholesterol: 10
- Total Fat: 3.2
- Saturated Fat: 2
- Sugar: 0
- Protein: 0.7

## 176. Jello Jigglers Fusion

*Serving: 24 1-inch squares | Prep: 3mins | Ready in:*

### Ingredients

- 1 (6 ounce) boxjello strawberry-banana gelatin
- 1 (6 ounce) boxjello blackberry gelatin
- 2 1/2 cups boiling water

### Direction

- Combine the two packages in a large bowl.
- Stir boiling water into the gelatin for 3 minutes until powder is dissolved.
- Pour into a 13x9-inch pan sprayed with cooking spray and refrigerate until firm (about 3 hours.).
- To loosen Jell-O from pan, dip bottom of pan in warm water about 15 seconds.
- Cut into 1-inch squares (or use cookie cutters to make shapes).
- Lift from pan and place on serving tray.

### Nutrition Information

- Calories: 54
- Saturated Fat: 0
- Sodium: 66.5
- Fiber: 0
- Sugar: 12.2
- Cholesterol: 0
- Total Fat: 0
- Total Carbohydrate: 12.8
- Protein: 1.1

## 177. Joe's Corn O' The Kettle

*Serving: 5-6 cups | Prep: 10mins | Ready in:*

### Ingredients

- 1/3 cup popcorn (or enough to cover bottom of pan in single layer)
- oil (for frying)
- 1/3 cup granulated sugar (I use unbleached sugar)
- 1/4 cup real butter
- salt

## Direction

- In 10" cast-iron skillet on medium heat, pour enough oil to a depth of 1/8". Heat until hot, but not smoking.
- Place one corn kernel in pan. If it starts to sizzle, then the popcorn kernels are ready to be placed in the skillet.
- Pour kernels, sugar and butter into skillet, stir then carefully move skillet back and forth over burner to distribute popcorn kernels and to avoid burning.
- Eventually, (usually about 5 minutes), the kernels will begin to pop. Cover and keep cooking and moving skillet back and forth. From time to time use a fork to stir the popcorn/sugar mixture. The last minute of cooking, increase heat to medium-high. Take skillet off heat promptly when the majority of kernels have popped. Remove skillet lid carefully.
- Place popped corn in a serving bowl. Set the old maids aside for me. Season with salt. Stir well.
- Serve.

## Nutrition Information

- Calories: 132.9
- Total Fat: 9.2
- Saturated Fat: 5.8
- Sugar: 13.3
- Total Carbohydrate: 13.3
- Cholesterol: 24.4
- Sodium: 65.4
- Fiber: 0
- Protein: 0.1

---

**178.    Joyce's Unbeatable Banana Bread**

---

*Serving: 1 regular loaf, 4 serving(s) | Prep: 15mins | Ready in:*

## Ingredients

- 1 1/2 cups flour
- 1 cup sugar
- 1/2 teaspoon salt
- 1 teaspoon baking soda
- 1/2 cup shortening
- 2 eggs
- 2 bananas (very, very ripe and I mean the blacker the better!!)

## Direction

- Grease and flour one regular loaf pan or two small loaf pans.
- Preheat oven to 350 degrees Fahrenheit.
- Combine flour, sugar, salt, baking soda, and shortening. Cut shortening in as for pie crust (I use a pastry blender.).
- In a separate bowl, beat eggs and sliced bananas until mixed well.
- Add banana mixture to shortening mixture and mix well.
- Place batter in prepared pan(s).
- Bake approximately 30 minutes.
- Tip: I usually use the toothpick test, but the toothpick should not come out completely clean. This is a very moist recipe, so look for the toothpick or knife to be mostly clean. When the bread is done, it will be a dark brown and should have a slight crack down the middle.

## Nutrition Information

- Calories: 678.9
- Sugar: 57.3
- Total Carbohydrate: 99.4
- Cholesterol: 93
- Protein: 8.6
- Total Fat: 28.7
- Saturated Fat: 7.3
- Sodium: 642.9
- Fiber: 2.8

## 179. Julie's Seedy Bars

*Serving: 2 pie plates | Prep: 5mins | Ready in:*

### Ingredients

- 1 cup steel cut oats
- 1/3 cup dried cranberries or 1/3 cup blueberries
- 1/2 cup pumpkin seeds
- 1/2 cup sunflower seeds
- 1/2 cup raisins
- 1/4 cup prune, chopped
- 1/4 cup psyllium, husk
- 1/4 cup flax seed meal (ground flax seeds)
- 1 teaspoon cinnamon
- 1 cup nut butter
- 1/2 cup liquid honey or 1/2 cup maple syrup

### Direction

- Combine first ten ingredients and then stir in nut butter and honey or syrup. Mix well.
- Press into two glass pie plates (or a pan with that holds a similar amount) which have been coated with olive oil.
- Bake at 325 F for approximately 20 minutes. Cut when cooled or crumble into granola.

### Nutrition Information

- Calories: 1197.3
- Saturated Fat: 6.4
- Fiber: 21.6
- Sugar: 101.3
- Protein: 34.3
- Total Fat: 45.2
- Total Carbohydrate: 183.6
- Cholesterol: 0
- Sodium: 21.5

## 180. Just Peachy Yogurt

*Serving: 1 serving(s) | Prep: 5mins | Ready in:*

### Ingredients

- 3/4 cup low-fat vanilla yogurt or 3/4 cup non-fat vanilla yogurt
- 1 dash cinnamon (more if you wish)
- 1 medium peach (I used half of a really big peach)

### Direction

- Sprinkle cinnamon over yogurt and stir. (I did this part before leaving home and packed the peach to cut and add later so it would be fresh).
- Cut the peach into bite-sized pieces. (Peel if you wish--I was on my lunch break and didn't have time!).
- Add peach pieces to yogurt and gently stir.
- Top with additional toppings if desired (see recipe description) and enjoy!

### Nutrition Information

- Calories: 194.7
- Saturated Fat: 1.5
- Total Carbohydrate: 34.8
- Protein: 10
- Total Fat: 2.5
- Fiber: 1.5
- Sugar: 33.6
- Cholesterol: 9.2
- Sodium: 121.3

## 181. Kaha's Delicious Lunch Box Kiwi Salsa

*Serving: 2 serving(s) | Prep: 20mins | Ready in:*

### Ingredients

- 2 green kiwi fruits (or a combo) or 2 gold kiwi fruits (or a combo)
- 1 small tomatoes, seeded and diced
- 2 tablespoons thinly sliced green onions

- 1 tablespoon chopped cilantro or 1 tablespoon parsley
- 1 teaspoon lemon juice
- 1 cup tortilla chips

## Direction

- Peel and dice the kiwifruit.
- Combine with the tomato, onion, cilantro, and the lemon juice.
- Enjoy as a light snack or pack as part of a healthy school lunch for your child.

## Nutrition Information

- Calories: 57.2
- Sugar: 8.2
- Cholesterol: 0
- Saturated Fat: 0
- Fiber: 3
- Total Carbohydrate: 13.6
- Protein: 1.4
- Total Fat: 0.5
- Sodium: 5.8

## 182. Khachapuri (Georgian Cheese Bread)

*Serving: 4 serving(s) | Prep: 50mins | Ready in:*

## Ingredients

- The Dough
- 1 1/4 cups full fat yogurt
- 1 egg
- 1/4 teaspoon baking powder
- 1/4 teaspoon salt
- 3 1/2 cups whole wheat flour
- The Filling
- 9 ounces buffalo mozzarella cheese
- 9 ounces cream cheese
- 1 egg
- 1 1/2 tablespoons butter
- salt, to taste
- butter, for frying

## Direction

- Make a smooth dough out of the dough ingredients. Use as much flour as needed to keep dough light without it sticking to your hands.
- Leave the dough to rest for 30 minutes.
- Prepare the filling. Grate the mozzarella and then mix with the cream cheese. Add the egg and butter and process into a smooth, glutinous mixture using either a hand mixer or a wooden spoon.
- Season with salt, if needed, and divide into 4 balls.
- Shape the dough into 4 balls also and roll these out to form 8 inch circles.
- Put the cheese filling balls into each dough circle and bring the edges of the dough circle up and over to seal. (Example: like an omelet or a calzone) Press firmly to seal.
- Carefully press the dough flat into a circular shape until each will fill a large skillet.
- Fry individually in hot butter, covered, before turning them and frying the other side, uncovered.
- Cut each flat loaf into 4 portions and serve hot.

## Nutrition Information

- Calories: 888
- Saturated Fat: 26.3
- Sodium: 884.6
- Fiber: 11.2
- Cholesterol: 235.2
- Total Fat: 48
- Sugar: 6.8
- Total Carbohydrate: 83.4
- Protein: 37.7

## 183. Khinkali (Ground Meat Filled Pasta Pockets)

*Serving: 6-8 serving(s) | Prep: 30mins | Ready in:*

### Ingredients

- Filling 1
- 1 3/4 lbs ground lamb
- salt, to taste
- black pepper, to taste
- 3 large onions, minced
- 1 bunch cilantro, minced
- Filling 2
- 12 ounces ground beef
- 12 ounces ground pork
- 4 tablespoons cilantro, minced
- 1 teaspoon dried fenugreek leaves
- 1/2 teaspoon crushed red chili pepper flakes
- 3 small yellow onions, minced
- Dough
- 4 1/2 cups all-purpose flour
- 2/3 cup lukewarm salt water

### Direction

- Knead together the filling you have chosen and about 7 tbsp. lukewarm water.
- Prepare a smooth dough from the flour and the salted water. Roll it out thinly and cut out 6 inch circles using a plate.
- Place about 2 tbsp. filling in center of round, and fold edges of dough over filling, creating pleats in dough as you go, until filling is covered.
- Holding dumpling in the palm of one hand, grasp top of dumpling where pleats meet and twist to seal pleats and form a knot at top of dumpling. Repeat with remaining dough rounds and filling.
- Put the khinkali in a large pan with boiling, lightly salted water and simmer gently, gently agitating them with a wooden spoon now and again.
- When the khinkali float to the surface, continue to simmer for about 6 more minutes. Total time should be about 8 minutes.
- Remove from the water with a wire skimmer, sprinkle black pepper over each and serve hot with cold beer.

### Nutrition Information

- Calories: 1032.2
- Saturated Fat: 21.5
- Fiber: 4.6
- Total Carbohydrate: 82.1
- Cholesterol: 176.2
- Total Fat: 52.7
- Sodium: 160
- Sugar: 5
- Protein: 53.1

## 184. Kid Friendly Thai Grilled Chicken

*Serving: 4-6 serving(s) | Prep: 5mins | Ready in:*

### Ingredients

- 2 kg chicken pieces, my kids love the legs
- marinade
- 2 tablespoons sweet chili sauce
- 2 tablespoons peanut oil
- 2 tablespoons reduced sodium soy sauce
- 1 tablespoon fish sauce
- 1 tablespoon lime juice

### Direction

- Mix all the marinade ingredients together (a large zip lock bag saves washing up!).
- Toss chicken in marinade for 2 hrs. (or more-or less) grill -- great for bbq -- even work great in the oven.
- Prepare in 5 mins (excluding time while marinating).

### Nutrition Information

- Calories: 1150.6

- Saturated Fat: 22.8
- Sodium: 1047.3
- Fiber: 0.3
- Sugar: 0.5
- Total Carbohydrate: 2.4
- Protein: 94
- Total Fat: 82.4
- Cholesterol: 375.6

## 185. Kidney Bean Burritos

*Serving: 10 serving(s) | Prep: 20mins | Ready in:*

### Ingredients

- 2 1/4 lbs cooked kidney beans
- 5 ounces onions, chopped
- 1 teaspoon soy sauce
- 5 ounces ready-made salsa
- 1 garlic clove, crushed
- 1/2 tablespoon ground cumin
- 1 jalapeno pepper, diced
- 1/2 red pepper, diced
- 1/2 bunch cilantro, chopped
- 1 teaspoon ground coriander
- 1/2 teaspoon paprika
- 10 soft flour tortillas
- salad leaves, to serve

### Direction

- Preheat the oven to 350°F
- Place all the ingredients for the filling together in a blender and whiz to a puree.
- Divide the filling between the tortilla wraps and spread evenly. Roll up and lay in a baking dish.
- Bake for 10 minutes. Serve with salad leaves.

### Nutrition Information

- Calories: 192.5
- Fiber: 6.1
- Protein: 8.5
- Saturated Fat: 0.7
- Sodium: 621.5
- Cholesterol: 0
- Total Fat: 3.1
- Sugar: 3.9
- Total Carbohydrate: 33.5

## 186. Kids Favorite Veggie Dip

*Serving: 1 bowl | Prep: 15mins | Ready in:*

### Ingredients

- 2/3 cup mayonnaise
- 2/3 cup sour cream
- 1 tablespoon onion soup mix (dry)
- 1 tablespoon parsley
- 1 tablespoon chives
- 1/2 teaspoon Worcestershire sauce
- 1/2 teaspoon Accent seasoning

### Direction

- Mix all ingredients well and refrigerate.
- Serve with assorted fresh veggies.

### Nutrition Information

- Calories: 948
- Total Fat: 84.9
- Fiber: 0.2
- Sugar: 10.7
- Total Carbohydrate: 45.1
- Cholesterol: 108.7
- Protein: 6.5
- Saturated Fat: 27.8
- Sodium: 1231.1

## 187. Kids Snack Mix

*Serving: 10 serving(s) | Prep: 5mins | Ready in:*

Ingredients

- 1 (15 ounce) bag small pretzels
- 1 (15 ounce) bag plain Doritos
- 0.5 (15 ounce) box Cap'n Crunch cereal
- 1 (15 ounce) bag Cheetos cheese curls
- 1 (15 ounce) bag chedder cheese flavored popped popcorn

Direction

- Mix all the ingredients together and enjoy. Store leftovers in an air tight container.

Nutrition Information

- Calories: 462.9
- Total Carbohydrate: 77.8
- Cholesterol: 1.3
- Protein: 8.7
- Sodium: 997.9
- Fiber: 3.8
- Sugar: 12.1
- Total Fat: 13.4
- Saturated Fat: 2.2

## 188. Kids' Fondue

Serving: 1 serving(s) | Prep: 1mins | Ready in:

Ingredients

- 10 -20 semi-sweet chocolate chips
- 1 teaspoon peanut butter
- Chex cereal

Direction

- Put the peanut butter and chocolate chips in a microwave safe bowl.
- Heat for 20 seconds than stir. Heat 20 more seconds than stir. Heat for 15 more seconds than stir. Heat ten last seconds and --
- Dip your Chex into the chocolate goo and enjoy!

Nutrition Information

- Calories: 54.6
- Sugar: 3.1
- Cholesterol: 0
- Protein: 1.6
- Fiber: 0.6
- Sodium: 25.5
- Total Carbohydrate: 4
- Total Fat: 4.2
- Saturated Fat: 1.4

## 189. Kissables Crunch

Serving: 4 cups, 32-36 serving(s) | Prep: 5mins | Ready in:

Ingredients

- 2 cups miniature pretzels
- 1 cup Hershey kissables
- 1 cup miniature marshmallow
- 1/2 cup banana chips (from the Health Food Store, at least that's where I found them, also, try in your supermarket fruit)

Direction

- Stir together pretzels, candies, marshmallows and banana chips.
- Store in airtight container in cool, dry place.

Nutrition Information

- Calories: 5
- Saturated Fat: 0
- Sugar: 0.9
- Total Carbohydrate: 1.3
- Protein: 0
- Total Fat: 0
- Sodium: 1.2
- Fiber: 0
- Cholesterol: 0

## 190. Kittencal's Chinese Chicken Balls With Sweet And Sour Sauce

*Serving: 8 serving(s) | Prep: 25mins | Ready in:*

### Ingredients

- SWEET AND SOUR SAUCE
- 1/2 cup ketchup
- 1 teaspoon soy sauce
- 1/3 cup white vinegar
- 1/2 cup brown sugar, lightly packed
- 1 cup white sugar (can reduce a 2-3 tablespoons for a less sweeter taste)
- 3/4 cup cold water (or can use unsweetened pineapple juice or half each, I prefer the pineapple juice)
- 3 tablespoons cornstarch (for a thinner sauce reduce to 2 tablespoons, if you want an very thick sauce use 4 tablespoons)
- CHICKEN BALL BATTER
- 1 cup all-purpose flour
- 1 cup cornstarch
- 2 teaspoons baking powder
- 2 teaspoons baking soda
- 1/2 teaspoon garlic powder (garlic lovers add 1 teaspoon)
- 2 teaspoons sugar
- 1 1/3 cups cold water (if you are reducing to half a recipe use 1/2 cup plus 2-1/2 tablespoons water)
- 1 -2 teaspoon sesame oil (optional but good to add)
- oil (for frying)
- 8 chicken breasts, cut into bite-size pieces
- seasoning salt (optional)

### Direction

- To make the sweet and sour sauce; in a saucepan combine the first 5 ingredients until combined.
- In a cup or bowl whisk the cold water or pineapple juice with cornstarch until smooth and well blended, then whisk vigorously into the ketchup mixture; bring to a boil stirring or whisking constantly over medium-high heat until bubbly.
- Reduce the heat to medium-low and continue simmering and mixing until thickened (be patient the sauce takes a few minutes to thicken up) remove from heat and allow to sit at room temperature while making the chicken balls or you may cool to room temperature then refrigerate until ready to use (I prefer the sauce at room temperature).
- To make the chicken balls: in a large bowl combine flour, cornstarch, baking powder, baking soda, garlic powder; add in water and sesame oil; whisk vigorously until smooth.
- Add in chicken pieces; using clean hands and mix until well coated.
- Heat oil in a deep-fryer or Dutch oven to 375 degrees.
- Carefully dip the battered chicken pieces in hot oil and fry until golden brown (about 3-4 minutes).
- Remove to a paper towel.
- Sprinkle with seasoning salt immediately after frying if desired.
- Serve immediately with sweet and sour sauce.
- Delicious!

### Nutrition Information

- Calories: 555
- Total Carbohydrate: 73.1
- Cholesterol: 92.8
- Total Fat: 14.2
- Fiber: 0.7
- Sugar: 42.9
- Protein: 32.3
- Saturated Fat: 4
- Sodium: 714.4

## 191. Krispymallow Treats

*Serving: 1 Square, 25 serving(s) | Prep: 8mins | Ready in:*

### Ingredients

- 3 tablespoons light butter
- 3 cups miniature marshmallows
- 2 cups Fiber One cereal
- 5 cups Kashi (7 whole grain puffs) or 5 cups puffed wheat cereal

### Direction

- Melt butter spread in a large saucepan over low heat. Add marshmallows and stir until completely melted.
- Remove from heat. Add both cereals. Stir until well coated.
- Using a spatula, press mixture evenly into a baking pan coated with nonstick cooking spray. Allow to cool. Cut into 25 squares.

### Nutrition Information

- Calories: 67.4
- Fiber: 3.1
- Protein: 1.3
- Total Carbohydrate: 15.7
- Cholesterol: 1.8
- Total Fat: 1.3
- Saturated Fat: 0.7
- Sodium: 52.9
- Sugar: 5.6

## 192. Large Batch Banana Nut Bread

*Serving: 60 loaves, 640 serving(s) | Prep: 1hours30mins | Ready in:*

### Ingredients

- 25 lbs all-purpose flour
- 7 7/8 ounces baking soda
- 2 5/8 ounces salt
- 20 lbs sugar
- 3 1/2 lbs eggs
- 13 lbs vegetable oil
- 2 1/2 lbs milk
- 30 lbs bananas, mashed (about two large)
- 12 lbs chopped nuts

### Direction

- Mix flour, soda, salt and sugar.
- Blend in eggs, oil and milk.
- Stir in banana and nuts.
- Pour into greased loaf pans and bake at 350 degrees approximately one hour.
- ALTERNATELY: Pour batter into pans and freeze before baking. When you're ready to bake, allow to thaw at room temp for 30 minutes and then bake as directed.

### Nutrition Information

- Calories: 275.4
- Total Fat: 14.2
- Saturated Fat: 1.9
- Sodium: 202.2
- Total Carbohydrate: 34.9
- Fiber: 1.8
- Sugar: 17.2
- Cholesterol: 10.8
- Protein: 3.9

## 193. Leanne Remy's Easy Garlic Study Bread

*Serving: 4 Pieces, 2 serving(s) | Prep: 5mins | Ready in:*

### Ingredients

- 4 hamburger buns
- 1/16 cup butter
- 1 tablespoon garlic salt

### Direction

- Butter all buns and add small amount of garlic salt.
- Toast until crispy and all butter has been melted.
- Best eaten with chocolate milk and a study buddy.

## Nutrition Information

- Calories: 290.4
- Fiber: 1.8
- Sugar: 5.4
- Total Carbohydrate: 42.5
- Protein: 8.2
- Saturated Fat: 4.5
- Cholesterol: 15.1
- Total Fat: 9.4
- Sodium: 452.5

## 194. Lemon (Or Lime) Rice Krispies Treats

*Serving: 15-20 serving(s) | Prep: 20mins | Ready in:*

## Ingredients

- 6 cups Rice Krispies
- 10 ounces miniature marshmallows
- 2 lemons (or 3 limes)
- 3 tablespoons margarine
- yellow food coloring (optional)

## Direction

- Put a piece of parchment or wax paper into the bottom of a 13x9 inch pan.
- Add margarine to a medium saucepan on low, but make sure that the margarine isn't melting too fast.
- Use a microplane or zester to zest both lemons (and all 3 limes). Make sure to get all the zest off of the lemons.
- Catching the seeds in your hands, squeeze the juice of one lemon (or 1 1/2 limes) into the butter and zest.
- Add the 10 oz. bag of marshmallows and stir continuously. It will take a while for the marshmallows to melt but don't turn the heat up too high or the marshmallows will burn.
- Add in a few drops of yellow food colouring. Green food colouring is best for lime flavour.
- Once the marshmallows have completely melted, gently stir them into the cereal and make sure to get them evenly coated.
- Spread them out into the pan and when they have cooled, it's time to eat!

## Nutrition Information

- Calories: 126.6
- Saturated Fat: 0.5
- Total Carbohydrate: 26.5
- Protein: 1.2
- Total Fat: 2.5
- Sodium: 148.6
- Fiber: 0.8
- Sugar: 11.9
- Cholesterol: 0

## 195. Lemon Garlic Pita Chips

*Serving: 4 serving(s) | Prep: 5mins | Ready in:*

## Ingredients

- 3 (6 inch) pita bread rounds, split in half horizontally
- 2 teaspoons olive oil
- 1 1/2 teaspoons lemon pepper
- 1/4 teaspoon garlic powder

## Direction

- Preheat oven to 400°.
- Cut each pita half into 4 wedges; place on a baking sheet. Drizzle oil evenly over wedges.

- Combine lemon pepper and garlic powder; sprinkle evenly over wedges. Bake at 400° for 5 minutes or until crisp.

## Nutrition Information

- Calories: 134.7
- Total Fat: 2.8
- Saturated Fat: 0.4
- Sodium: 222.7
- Fiber: 0.9
- Sugar: 0.6
- Total Carbohydrate: 23.3
- Cholesterol: 0
- Protein: 3.8

### 196. Littlemafia's Parmesan Sticks

*Serving: 96 sticks, 8 serving(s) | Prep: 10mins | Ready in:*

## Ingredients

- 12 slices white bread
- 1/8 cup margarine, melted
- 1/4 cup parmesan cheese, grated
- 2 tablespoons sesame seeds

## Direction

- Cut each slice of bread into 8 sticks, and arrange on ungreased baking sheets.
- Brush bread stick lightly with margarine.
- Sprinkle evenly with Parmesan cheese and sesame seeds
- Bake at 350 degs for 10-15 mins or until golden brown.

## Nutrition Information

- Calories: 151.5
- Protein: 4.5
- Total Fat: 6.1
- Saturated Fat: 1.5

- Sugar: 1.6
- Total Carbohydrate: 19.7
- Cholesterol: 2.8
- Sodium: 336.6
- Fiber: 1.2

### 197. Low Fat Dried Fruit Granola

*Serving: 1/2 cup, 22 serving(s) | Prep: 10mins | Ready in:*

## Ingredients

- 18 ounces rolled oats
- 8 ounces almonds, slivered
- 1 tablespoon cinnamon
- 1 cup honey
- 1/2 cup water
- 5 egg whites
- 8 ounces dried blueberries
- 8 ounces dried cherries
- 8 ounces dried cranberries

## Direction

- Preheat oven to 300 degrees.
- Combine oats, almonds, and apple pie spice.
- In a separate bowl combine honey, water, and eggs whites.
- Pour honey mixture over oats and stir to combine.
- Set aside for 15 minutes.
- Place granola on a wax paper lined baking sheet and place in oven for 60-90 minutes. Stir every 10-15 minutes.
- Remove granola from oven when it is dry and crunchy.
- When granola is completely cool stir in dried fruit.
- Store in an airtight container.

## Nutrition Information

- Calories: 210.6

- Cholesterol: 0
- Total Fat: 7.3
- Saturated Fat: 0.7
- Fiber: 4.2
- Sugar: 14
- Total Carbohydrate: 31.9
- Sodium: 51.4
- Protein: 7

## Nutrition Information

- Calories: 89
- Fiber: 1.3
- Saturated Fat: 0.2
- Sodium: 125.3
- Cholesterol: 19.2
- Protein: 2.1
- Total Fat: 0.7
- Sugar: 8.8
- Total Carbohydrate: 19.5

### 198. Low Fat (But You Wouldn't Know It) Banana Bread

*Serving: 22 slices | Prep: 15mins | Ready in:*

## Ingredients

- 3/4 cup white sugar
- 1/2 cup unsweetened applesauce
- 2 eggs, beaten
- 3 bananas, mashed
- 1 cup all-purpose flour
- 1 cup whole wheat flour
- 1 teaspoon baking soda
- 1/2 teaspoon salt
- 1/2 teaspoon baking powder

## Direction

- Beat the sugar and applesauce together.
- Add eggs and mashed banana and beat well.
- In another bowl combine both flours, baking soda, baking powder and salt. Add this to the banana mixture and mix well.
- Pour the batter into a greased and floured 9x5x21/2" loaf pan.
- Bake at 350oF for about 1 hour. If a wooden tester inserted into the center of the bread comes out clean the bread is done. Turn the bread out of the loaf pan and allow cake to cool on a wire rack. Wrap the bread in tin foil and store overnight before slicing.
- Enjoy!

### 199. Low Fat Banana Nut Bread

*Serving: 2 loafs, 24 serving(s) | Prep: 10mins | Ready in:*

## Ingredients

- 1 3/4 cups all-purpose flour
- 2 teaspoons baking powder
- 1/4 teaspoon baking soda
- 1/2 teaspoon salt
- 1 cup Splenda sugar substitute
- 1/2 cup chopped pecans (walnuts for substitute)
- 2 eggs
- 2 mashed bananas
- 1 small chopped banana
- 1/2 cup vegetable oil
- 1 teaspoon vanilla extract

## Direction

- Preheat oven to 350 degrees F (175 degrees C). Grease and flour two 8x4 inch loaf pans. Set aside.
- Sift together flour, baking powder, baking soda, salt, and Splenda. Stir in nuts, eggs, mashed bananas, oil, and vanilla extract. Before you pour into pans, chop your last banana into mini chunks, and lightly fold into mixture. Pour into prepared pans. Bake for 45 to 55 minutes. Cool on wire rack for 10 minutes before removing from pans.

- Enjoy!
- NUTRITION INFORMATION: serving size = 1in. slice, calories 146, 3g fat, sodium 180mg, total carbs 26.2g.

## Nutrition Information

- Calories: 108.3
- Sodium: 98
- Fiber: 0.8
- Total Carbohydrate: 10.6
- Protein: 1.8
- Saturated Fat: 0.9
- Sugar: 1.9
- Cholesterol: 17.6
- Total Fat: 6.7

### 200. Low Fat Chocolate Chip Banana Muffins

*Serving: 12 muffins, 12 serving(s) | Prep: 10mins | Ready in:*

## Ingredients

- 3 ripe bananas
- 3/4 cup flour
- 3/4 cup whole wheat flour
- 1/2 cup sugar
- 4 tablespoons unsweetened applesauce
- 1 egg
- 1 teaspoon vanilla extract
- 1 teaspoon baking soda
- 1/2 teaspoon baking powder
- 1/2-3/4 cup chocolate chips

## Direction

- Mash bananas.
- Add remaining ingredients except chocolate chips and mix.
- Add chocolate chips and stir (I start with the 1/2 c and add more if it looks like too little.).
- Pour into greased muffin tins and bake at 350 for approx. 15-20 minutes (until toothpick comes out clean).

## Nutrition Information

- Calories: 155.2
- Saturated Fat: 1.4
- Total Carbohydrate: 31.6
- Cholesterol: 15.5
- Protein: 3
- Total Fat: 2.9
- Sodium: 127.5
- Fiber: 2.2
- Sugar: 16.3

### 201. Low Fat Milk Pudding

*Serving: 1-2 serving(s) | Prep: 1mins | Ready in:*

## Ingredients

- 1 -1 1/2 cup skim milk
- 3 egg whites
- 1/2 egg yolk
- 1/2 teaspoon cornflour
- artificial sweetener or sugar

## Direction

- Put all ingredients into a bowl.
- Blend with electric hand mixer.
- Put in microwave for 1.5 minutes on high.
- Take out and blend till smooth.
- Put in microwave for 30 second.
- Take out and blend till smooth.
- Repeat steps 56 until thick and creamy
- Allow 1-2 minutes to set.
- Enjoy!

## Nutrition Information

- Calories: 181.4
- Total Carbohydrate: 15.6

- Cholesterol: 87.9
- Saturated Fat: 1.1
- Sodium: 313.2
- Sugar: 0.8
- Total Fat: 2.9
- Fiber: 0.1
- Protein: 21.8

## 202. Low Gi Creamy Scrambled Eggs

*Serving: 1 serving(s) | Prep: 5mins | Ready in:*

### Ingredients

- 2 eggs
- 1 teaspoon butter or 1 teaspoon margarine
- 2 tablespoons low-fat cream cheese
- 1 slice grain bread (granary bread)

### Direction

- Toast the granary bread to your desired brownness.
- In a sauce pan heat the butter until foamy.
- Whisk the eggs with a fork to combine and then place in pan.
- Stir the eggs until just setting and then add the cream cheese.
- Continue to stir until the eggs have a porridge consistency.
- Serve over the dry toast.

### Nutrition Information

- Calories: 248.4
- Total Fat: 19.8
- Saturated Fat: 9.2
- Sodium: 270.3
- Fiber: 0
- Protein: 15.2
- Sugar: 1.3
- Total Carbohydrate: 1.7
- Cholesterol: 403.1

## 203. Low Low Fat Southwestern Egg Rolls

*Serving: 8 eggrolls, 8 serving(s) | Prep: 15mins | Ready in:*

### Ingredients

- 8 egg roll wraps
- 0.5 (14 ounce) package firm tofu
- 1/2 cup frozen spinach (defrosted and drained)
- 3 slices fat-free cheddar cheese (or any other cheese)
- 1 onion
- 1/2 cup white rice
- 1/2 cup fresh cilantro
- 1/2 cup fat-free vegetarian refried beans
- 1/4 cup chopped chipotle peppers or 1/4 cup dried crushed red pepper flakes

### Direction

- Cut tofu into moderate chunks and pan fry with onions until golden brown on all sides.
- Pan fry rice in a sauce pan until golden and then add a cup of water to cook (frying will make the texture of the rice a little firmer).
- Preheat oven to 400 degrees.
- After tofu and rice is cooked, begin to make your egg rolls; there are directions on the package on how to roll them and also pictures in case you get confused.
- Place wrap in front of you in a diamond shape and spread beans in the middle of it. Add peppers, cilantro, spinach, tofu and onions, rice, then finally top with thin pieces of the cheese slices.
- Be careful not to add too much cheese because it will melt out of the wrapper.
- Finally fold the piece closest to you over the insides and tuck tightly. Fold the outer corners in then roll to form the egg roll.
- Place onto cookie sheet and bake for 10 minutes or until golden brown (I spray 9

calorie butter spray casually to make them crispier).
- Take out, cool, and enjoy.

## Nutrition Information

- Calories: 177.7
- Cholesterol: 3.8
- Protein: 8.4
- Total Fat: 1.8
- Saturated Fat: 0.4
- Sugar: 2.1
- Total Carbohydrate: 32.1
- Sodium: 316.3
- Fiber: 2

## 204. Mac And Cheese Quesadillas

*Serving: 2 serving(s) | Prep: 2mins | Ready in:*

### Ingredients

- 2 tortillas (I prefer the wheat style ones but the white ones work just fine)
- 1/2 cup prepared macaroni and cheese (leftovers work fine)
- 1 slice cheese, if you like it extra gooey use (optional)

### Direction

- Microwave Directions:
- Place 1 of the tortilla shells on a microwave plate.
- Place the Mac and Cheese (and the sliced cheese if desired) on top of the shell.
- Place the 2nd shell over the Mac and Cheese.
- Cook for 1 minute and 45 seconds or until cheese is melted.
- Cut into quarters and let cool for about 1 minute.
- Yum Yum Eat It Up.
- Stove Top Directions.
- Place Mac and Cheese (and extra cheese desired put it closer to the bottom) on 1 of the shells.
- Place Mac and Cheese covered shell in warm pan over medium heat.
- Cook about 3 minutes, or until the cheese gets gooey.
- Place 2nd shell on top of the Mac and Cheese.
- Flip over and cook for another 2 to 3 minutes.

## Nutrition Information

- Calories: 218.4
- Cholesterol: 0
- Protein: 5.8
- Total Fat: 5.4
- Sodium: 445.2
- Total Carbohydrate: 36
- Saturated Fat: 1.3
- Fiber: 2.2
- Sugar: 1.3

## 205. Macaroni And Cheese Chowder

*Serving: 4-6 serving(s) | Prep: 10mins | Ready in:*

### Ingredients

- 1 cup uncooked macaroni (I use elbow)
- 2 tablespoons butter
- 1/4 cup onion, coarsely chopped
- 2 carrots, coarsely chopped
- 2 stalks celery, coarsely chopped
- 1/4 cup all-purpose flour
- 1/2 teaspoon dry mustard
- 1/4 teaspoon salt
- 3 cups milk
- 1 cup chicken broth
- 2 cups shredded American cheese (I use pepper jack also)

### Direction

- Cook macaroni according to directions, Drain and set aside.
- In a large saucepan, melt butter, add onion, carrots and celery.
- Cook over medium heat, stirring occasionally until vegetables are crisp tender (3-5 minutes).
- Stir in flour, mustard and salt, Continue cooking until bubbly (about 1 minute).
- Stir in milk and broth.
- Continue cooking, stirring occasionally, until mixture comes to a full boil (8-12 minutes) Boil 1 minute.
- Stir in macaroni and then cheese, continue stirring occasionally until cheese melts (1-2 minutes).

## Nutrition Information

- Calories: 324.9
- Cholesterol: 40.9
- Protein: 12.1
- Sodium: 505.5
- Fiber: 2.4
- Total Carbohydrate: 39
- Total Fat: 13.5
- Saturated Fat: 8
- Sugar: 2.9

## 206. Mama Zuquinis Pizza Margherita

*Serving: 4-8 serving(s) | Prep: 5mins | Ready in:*

### Ingredients

- 1 (12 inch) pizza crusts
- 3 plum tomatoes, thinly sliced
- 1/3 cup pesto sauce
- 1 1/2 cups mozzarella cheese, shredded
- 1/2 teaspoon crushed red pepper flakes

### Direction

- Preheat oven to 450 degrees F. Place pizza crust on baking sheet.
- Spread pesto over pizza crust. Arrange tomatoes over pesto. Sprinkle with cheese and crushed red pepper.
- Bake for 10 to 12 minutes or until cheese is melted and crust is golden brown. Cut into wedges.

## Nutrition Information

- Calories: 134.7
- Saturated Fat: 5.5
- Fiber: 0.6
- Sugar: 1.7
- Cholesterol: 33.2
- Protein: 9.7
- Total Fat: 9.5
- Sodium: 265.8
- Total Carbohydrate: 2.8

## 207. Mango And Feta Quesadilla

*Serving: 1 serving(s) | Prep: 5mins | Ready in:*

### Ingredients

- 1 (8 inch) whole wheat tortillas
- 1/8 cup mango chutney (I use mango salsa)
- 2 slices deli ham
- 1/8 cup feta cheese (crumbled)
- 1 tablespoon scallion (chopped)

### Direction

- Spread tortilla with mango chutney (or mango salsa).
- Add deli ham, feta cheese, and scallion.
- Fold in half and grill 2 to 3 minutes on each side.
- Cut into quarters and serve.

## Nutrition Information

- Calories: 142.7
- Protein: 12.1
- Total Fat: 8.8
- Saturated Fat: 4.5
- Fiber: 0.9
- Total Carbohydrate: 3.4
- Sodium: 940.5
- Sugar: 0.9
- Cholesterol: 48.6

## 208. Marbled P B Sheet Cake

*Serving: 18 serving(s) | Prep: 1hours20mins | Ready in:*

### Ingredients

- Cake Ingredients
- 2 1/4 cups all-purpose flour
- 1 1/2 cups sugar
- 1/2 cup peanut butter
- 1 1/4 cups milk
- 3 1/2 teaspoons baking powder
- 1 teaspoon salt
- 1 teaspoon vanilla
- 3 eggs
- 3 tablespoons cocoa, sifted
- 1/8 teaspoon baking soda
- Icing Ingredients
- 1/4 cup chocolate fudge topping
- 3 cups icing sugar, sifted
- 1/3 cup butter, softened
- 1 1/2 teaspoons vanilla
- 1/4 cup milk
- 1/4 cup peanut butter

### Direction

- Preheat oven to 350 degrees F.
- Spray bottom and sides of 13" x 9" pan with cooking spray.
- Mix flour, sugar, 1/2 cup peanut butter, milk, baking powder, salt, vanilla and eggs with electric mixer on low speed for 30 seconds until well blended.
- Make sure to scrape the sides and bottom of bowl so everything is mixed.
- Beat on high speed 3 minutes, scraping sides of bowl occasionally.
- Spread about three cups of batter evenly in prepared pan.
- Mix the cocoa and baking soda into remaining batter until well blended.
- Drop heaping tablespoons of the chocolate batter randomly on the peanut butter batter.
- Marble the batters by pulling a knife through the batters in S shaped curves in one direction, then turn and do S shaped curves across the lines done previously.
- Bake for 40 to 45 minutes or until done.
- Cool completely in pan on wire rack.
- About 1 hour.
- Stir together icing sugar and 1/3 cup butter in medium bowl.
- Stir in vanilla, milk and 1/4 cup peanut butter.
- Beat until smooth and spreadable.
- Spread the icing mixture evenly on the cake.
- Either drizzle the chocolate topping evenly over the top of the icing or put it on in stripes or teaspoonfuls and marble it using a knife drawn through the icing, first in one direction at 1" intervals and then in the other.

## Nutrition Information

- Calories: 336.7
- Cholesterol: 47.2
- Total Fat: 11.1
- Saturated Fat: 4.2
- Sodium: 319.1
- Sugar: 38.8
- Protein: 6.4
- Fiber: 1.5
- Total Carbohydrate: 55.1

## 209. Melon And Strawberry Lassi

*Serving: 2 serving(s) | Prep: 3mins | Ready in:*

### Ingredients

- 1/4 small pineapple, peeled, chopped
- 1/8 small cantaloupe, peeled, chopped
- 125 g strawberries, hulled
- 1/4 cup low-fat yogurt
- 1/2 cup unsweetened pineapple juice
- 1/4 teaspoon ground cardamom
- 2 cups ice cubes
- mint sprig, to serve

### Direction

- Combine fruit in a blender. Blend until smooth.
- Add yoghurt, pineapple juice, cardamom and ice. Blend until creamy and smooth. Pour into glasses. Garnish with mint sprigs and serve.

### Nutrition Information

- Calories: 110.9
- Fiber: 2.5
- Sugar: 18.9
- Total Carbohydrate: 24.9
- Cholesterol: 1.8
- Protein: 2.8
- Total Fat: 0.9
- Saturated Fat: 0.3
- Sodium: 30.9

## 210. Mexican Chicken Wrap * Chicken Fajita * Applebee's Copycat

*Serving: 4 tortillas, 4 serving(s) | Prep: 5mins | Ready in:*

### Ingredients

- 3/4 cup salsa (mild or hot)
- 1/2 cup mayonnaise (softened) or 1/2 cup sour cream (softened) or 1/2 cup cream cheese (softened)
- 4 (10 inch) flour tortillas
- 1 1/2 cups grated cheddar cheese
- 1 tablespoon oil
- 2 cups chicken meat
- 1 1/2 teaspoons hot sauce (you decide)
- salt, to taste
- 2 cups finely chopped iceberg lettuce
- 1 cup chopped tomato

### Direction

- In a small bowl, mix salsa and mayo; set aside.
- Preheat oven to 350; arrange tortillas on two baking sheets; sprinkle with cheese; bake for five minutes (cheese melts).
- While that's cooking, warm oil in large skillet on medium-high; add chicken, sauce and salt and stir-fry until cooked through.
- Place tortillas on counter, top with lettuce, chicken, tomatoes; roll up, cut in half and serve with the mayo-salsa dip.
- OPTIONS: Black or green olives.
- SUBSTITUTIONS: Crab or shrimp instead of chicken, romaine lettuce for the iceberg, Monterey Jack for the Cheddar, corn instead of flour tortillas.

### Nutrition Information

- Calories: 560.2
- Protein: 18.1
- Sodium: 1261
- Fiber: 3.9
- Sugar: 6.8
- Cholesterol: 52.1
- Total Fat: 32.9
- Saturated Fat: 12.2
- Total Carbohydrate: 49.4

## 211. Microwave Buckaroo Bars (chocolate, Peanut Butter Oatmeal)

*Serving: 1 9x13" pan, 16 serving(s) | Prep: 7mins | Ready in:*

### Ingredients

- 4 cups quick oatmeal, dry
- 3/4 cup brown sugar
- 2/3 cup margarine, softened
- 1/2 cup white syrup
- 1 egg
- 3/4 cup chunky peanut butter
- 6 ounces chocolate chips

### Direction

- Mix first five ingredients and put in a 9x13 inch glass pan.
- Microwave 3 1/2- 4 minutes on high, turning every minute or bake for 15 minutes at 350F in the oven.
- Allow to cool.
- Melt peanut butter and chocolate chips together in the microwave, and spread the mixture on top of the oatmeal.
- Refrigerate.
- Cut into bars.

### Nutrition Information

- Calories: 319.9
- Sodium: 159.8
- Sugar: 17.9
- Cholesterol: 13.2
- Protein: 7.1
- Total Fat: 18.4
- Saturated Fat: 4.5
- Fiber: 3.6
- Total Carbohydrate: 35.4

## 212. Microwaveable Quick Muffins

*Serving: 6 muffins, 6 serving(s) | Prep: 5mins | Ready in:*

### Ingredients

- 1 cup sifted buttermilk biscuit mix
- 1 tablespoon vegetable oil
- 1 egg
- 3/8 cup milk
- 2 tablespoons sugar

### Direction

- Combine milk, sugar, and egg and oil in a small mixing bowl, blend well.
- Add biscuit mix to milk mixture and blend vigorously until all the flour is moistened.
- Divide mixture into a six-pan muffin pan.
- Heat in microwave on power level 7 for 3 to 4 minutes.

### Nutrition Information

- Calories: 143.9
- Total Fat: 6.7
- Fiber: 0.4
- Sugar: 6.6
- Protein: 3.1
- Saturated Fat: 1.7
- Sodium: 274.3
- Total Carbohydrate: 17.6
- Cholesterol: 37.8

## 213. Mini Flaky Pizza

*Serving: 16 mini pizza's, 4-6 serving(s) | Prep: 35mins | Ready in:*

### Ingredients

- 1 (8 ounce) can Pillsbury Refrigerated Crescent Dinner Rolls
- 1/3 cup pizza sauce

- 1/4 cup grated parmesan cheese
- 1 ounce pepperoni slice (16 slices)
- 1 1/2 ounces shredded mozzarella cheese

## Direction

- Heat oven to 375°F Spray cookie sheet with nonstick cooking spray. Unroll dough into 1 large rectangle; press perforations to seal.
- Spread pizza sauce evenly over rectangle to within 1 inch of edges. Sprinkle with Parmesan cheese. Starting at short side, roll up rectangle, jelly-roll fashion. With sharp knife, cut into 16 slices. Place cut side down on sprayed cookie sheet.
- Top each slice with 1 pepperoni slice and about 1 teaspoon mozzarella cheese.
- Bake at 375°F for 9 to 11 minutes or until edges are golden brown and cheese is melted. (Bottoms will be very deep golden brown.).

## Nutrition Information

- Calories: 280.5
- Total Carbohydrate: 32.1
- Cholesterol: 50.5
- Total Fat: 11.2
- Saturated Fat: 4.5
- Sodium: 579.6
- Fiber: 2.5
- Sugar: 3
- Protein: 12.2

## 214. Mini Phyllo Roasted Red Pepper Spinach Bites

*Serving: 12 bites | Prep: 25mins | Ready in:*

## Ingredients

- 4 sheets phyllo dough
- 1 red pepper
- 1/2 white onion
- 1 -2 garlic clove, mashed
- oregano
- basil
- rosemary (or use italian seasoning in place of all)
- 20 ounces fresh spinach, stems removed
- feta (optional)

## Direction

- Roast red pepper whole in a 450*F oven for 20-40 until charred to liking.
- Wrap in foil and set aside Adjust oven to 350*F.
- In Dutch oven, sweat onion, garlic, and a little of the spices over medium-low heat.
- Meanwhile, fold each sheet in half long-ways and cut into 3 even pieces.
- Place in muffin cups and place in oven for 10 minutes, then remove and turn around to the other side and leave in until crispy.
- Dump in spinach into onions and garlic and cook down. Season to taste.
- Once pepper has cooled, unwrap and peel (should come right off).
- Cut off top and take out seeds. Discard.
- Finely dice remaining pepper. Once spinach has cooked down, turn off heat.
- Drain liquid and stir in crumbled feta, if desired.
- Divide red pepper among the muffin cups and place in phyllo.
- Divide spinach mixture and place in phyllo.
- Serve hot, warm, or at room temperature.
- Warning: Phyllo will soften and/or get soggy later, so put back in a 350*F for a few minutes to crisp it back up.
- For Vegan omit the Feta cheese.

## Nutrition Information

- Calories: 35.8
- Saturated Fat: 0.1
- Fiber: 1.5
- Total Carbohydrate: 6.4
- Total Fat: 0.6
- Cholesterol: 0

- Protein: 2.1
- Sodium: 72.1
- Sugar: 0.8

## 215. Mini Pizzas For School Lunches

*Serving: 10 pizzas | Prep: 15mins | Ready in:*

### Ingredients

- 1 (7 1/2 ounce) package refrigerated buttermilk biscuits (10 biscuits)
- 1/4 cup tomato sauce
- 1 teaspoon italian seasoning
- 10 slices pepperoni
- 3/4 cup shredded mozzarella cheese

### Direction

- Preheat oven to 425 degrees.
- Flatten each biscuit into a 3-inch circle and press into a greased muffin cup.
- Combine the tomato sauce and Italian seasoning; spoon 1 teaspoonful into each cup. Top each with a slice of pepperoni and about 1 tablespoon of cheese.
- Bake for 10-15 minutes or until golden brown.
- Serve immediately or store in refrigerator.

### Nutrition Information

- Calories: 103.8
- Total Carbohydrate: 10
- Sugar: 2.1
- Cholesterol: 8.9
- Protein: 3.6
- Total Fat: 5.5
- Saturated Fat: 2.1
- Sodium: 354.5
- Fiber: 0.4

## 216. Mini Snack Pizzas

*Serving: 8 pizzas, 8 serving(s) | Prep: 10mins | Ready in:*

### Ingredients

- 1 (8 ounce) canpillsbury refrigerated dinner rolls
- 1 (8 ounce) jar pizza sauce
- 4 slices mozzarella cheese
- 16 pepperoni or 8 pieces Canadian bacon

### Direction

- Preheat oven to 375.
- Place rolls on ungreased baking sheet try to flatten rolls so they resemble flat circles.
- Take a spoonful of sauce and spread on top of each rolls.
- Then cut up cheese into small bits and garnish.
- Add meat on top of cheese and then place remaining cheese on top of meat.
- Cook for about 15 min of until rolls are golden.

### Nutrition Information

- Calories: 345
- Sodium: 670.1
- Fiber: 2.3
- Sugar: 5.4
- Protein: 14.1
- Total Fat: 10.9
- Total Carbohydrate: 47.5
- Cholesterol: 19.9
- Saturated Fat: 3.8

## 217. Mmm Good Yogurt Dip For Fruit!

*Serving: 1 cup, 4 serving(s) | Prep: 5mins | Ready in:*

### Ingredients

- 1 cup yogurt, adjust to need (I use plain yogurt, but flavored is fine)
- 1/4 cup applesauce
- 1 tablespoon cinnamon-sugar mixture
- 2 cups fresh fruit, cut

## Direction

- Mix together the first 3 ingredients in the serving bowl.
- Serve with fruit (apples, oranges, bananas, strawberries, etc.)
- VARIATIONS: Squeeze a little orange juice in place of applesauce, or any kind of fruit juice.

## Nutrition Information

- Calories: 49.5
- Sugar: 2.9
- Total Carbohydrate: 6
- Cholesterol: 8
- Saturated Fat: 1.3
- Sodium: 32.6
- Fiber: 0.2
- Total Fat: 2
- Protein: 2.1

## 218. Molasses Glazed Chicken Wings

*Serving: 20 wings | Prep: 5mins | Ready in:*

## Ingredients

- 20 chicken wings
- 1/4 cup vegetable oil
- Molasses Rub (use 1 cup)
- 1 cup packed brown sugar
- 2 tablespoons molasses
- 2 teaspoons paprika
- 2 teaspoons dried thyme
- 1 teaspoon garlic powder
- 1 1/2 teaspoons salt
- 1 1/2 teaspoons fresh ground black pepper

## Direction

- Preheat oven to 180.C.
- In a food processor or blender, combine the ingredients for the rub and process until mixture is well blended.
- In a large bowl, toss the chicken wings in the oil until the wings are completely coated, add the molasses rub and toss again until all the wings are coated.
- Place the seasoned wings in a large roasting pan bake for 35-40 mins or until wings are cooked through.

## Nutrition Information

- Calories: 182
- Total Fat: 10.6
- Sugar: 11.8
- Protein: 9.1
- Cholesterol: 37.7
- Saturated Fat: 2.6
- Sodium: 215.5
- Fiber: 0.2
- Total Carbohydrate: 12.6

## 219. Mom's Holiday Veggie Dip

*Serving: 6-8 serving(s) | Prep: 5mins | Ready in:*

## Ingredients

- 1 ounce hidden valley ranch dressing mix (buttermilk style)
- 1 cup mayonnaise
- 1 (8 ounce) container small curd cottage cheese
- 1 dash of lawry's garlic salt (you can omit this and use garlic powder if you don't want too much salt in your dip)

## Direction

- Place 1 cup of mayonnaise into bowl. (Use spoon or fork to mix).
- Mix in the package of dressing.
- Then add the cottage cheese.
- Mix well until blended.
- Sprinkle in garlic salt.
- Surround with veggies of your choice and stand back.
- This goes fast!

## Nutrition Information

- Calories: 189.8
- Cholesterol: 16.6
- Total Fat: 14.7
- Saturated Fat: 2.6
- Sodium: 415.6
- Protein: 4.5
- Fiber: 0
- Sugar: 3.5
- Total Carbohydrate: 10.7

## 220. Mom's Mini Chocolate Chip Pancakes

*Serving: 48 mini pancakes, 12 serving(s) | Prep: 5mins | Ready in:*

## Ingredients

- 1 1/4 cups self-rising flour
- 2 tablespoons white sugar
- 1 cup milk
- 2 tablespoons vegetable oil
- 1 egg
- 1 cup chocolate chips

## Direction

- Preheat lightly greased skillet or griddle to medium heat.
- *NOTE: My mother always uses regular canola non-stick spray, but I use olive oil non-stick spray, and the pancakes come out lighter and fluffier.*.
- In large bowl, combine flour and sugar. Add milk, oil and egg and mix with wire whisk until well combined.
- Stir in chocolate chips.
- Pour onto hot surface by tablespoonfuls and cook until golden brown on both sides. (Watch for top surface to get very bubbly before flipping first time.).
- Enjoy!

## Nutrition Information

- Calories: 160.5
- Total Fat: 7.8
- Fiber: 1.2
- Cholesterol: 20.5
- Protein: 3.1
- Saturated Fat: 3.4
- Sodium: 182.7
- Sugar: 9.8
- Total Carbohydrate: 21.6

## 221. More Than Just Gorp!

*Serving: 1 container, 12 serving(s) | Prep: 1mins | Ready in:*

## Ingredients

- 2 cups dry roasted peanuts, salted
- 2 cups plain M's
- 2 cups raisins
- 1 cup red-hot candies

## Direction

- Mix all ingredients together and store in an airtight container!

## Nutrition Information

- Calories: 463.9

- Protein: 11.2
- Saturated Fat: 7.2
- Sodium: 331.1
- Sugar: 38
- Total Carbohydrate: 52
- Total Fat: 26.2
- Fiber: 4.8
- Cholesterol: 4.8

## 222. Mozzarella Chorizo Omelet For One

*Serving: 1 serving(s) | Prep: 5mins | Ready in:*

### Ingredients

- 3 eggs
- 3 1/2 ounces mozzarella cheese
- 3 1/2 ounces chorizo sausage, sliced
- 2 ounces cheddar cheese
- 1 tablespoon chives, chopped
- 1/2 red pepper, sliced
- cayenne pepper
- milk
- olive oil

### Direction

- Fry the chorizo and peppers in olive oil in a hot pan for 4 minutes.
- Whisk the eggs until light and frothy then add a dash of milk, some salt and pepper and half the chives.
- Add the egg to the hot pan with the pepper and chorizo and cook for two minutes.
- Slice the mozzarella and place over one half the omelet. Fold the other half over to cover the cheese and cook for 1-2 minutes, flipping to make sure both sides are cooked.
- Grate some cheddar over the top and place under a hot broiler for 30 seconds to a minute.
- Scatter over the rest of the chives and serve.

### Nutrition Information

- Calories: 1214.5
- Saturated Fat: 44
- Fiber: 1.3
- Total Carbohydrate: 9.6
- Protein: 79.6
- Total Fat: 94
- Sodium: 2411
- Sugar: 5
- Cholesterol: 859.8

## 223. Mozzarella Cheese Sticks With Sauce

*Serving: 10 mozzarella sticks, 5-10 serving(s) | Prep: 5mins | Ready in:*

### Ingredients

- 10 string cheese sticks
- 2 cups flour
- 2 cups cornmeal
- 2 eggs
- 1 cup olive oil (or veggie oil, it doesn't matter)
- 1 1/2 cups of any kind tomato sauce
- 2 tablespoons milk

### Direction

- Pour in the oil into the skillet and put heat at low to medium heat, leave skillet uncovered.
- Get one bowl and put in the 2 cups of flour, set it aside.
- Get another bowl and put in the 2 cups of corn meal, set that aside.
- Get the one more bowl and beat the 2 eggs and the 2 tablespoons of milk in it then set that aside.
- Start peeling' off those wrappers from the string cheese.
- Cover string cheese in flour.
- Dip in the flour covered string cheese into the egg and milk mixture.
- Cover the egg and milk, flour covered string cheese with the corn meal.

- Put 5 of the string cheese into skillet then cover.
- Leave the string cheese there for 5 minutes covered, then flip and cover again for another 5 minutes.
- Place the cooked now mozzarella sticks onto the platter or plate.
- Repeat steps 9, 10, and 11 with the remaining cheese sticks.
- Heat up the tomato sauce in small bowl using microwave for 2 minutes, stirring each 30 seconds.
- Place bowl of tomato sauce onto platter or plate.
- Eat and enjoy!

## Nutrition Information

- Calories: 797.4
- Total Fat: 47.8
- Sugar: 3.7
- Saturated Fat: 7.1
- Sodium: 435.1
- Fiber: 6
- Total Carbohydrate: 81.5
- Cholesterol: 85.5
- Protein: 12.8

## 224. Mr. Breakfast's Boo Nana ( Tasty Dish )

*Serving: 1 serving(s) | Prep: 15mins | Ready in:*

## Ingredients

- 1 firm banana
- 3/4 teaspoon peanut butter
- 1 green grape, cut in half
- 1 dried cherries (original recipe used 1 M M ) or 1 dried cranberries (original recipe used 1 M M )
- 1 -2 tablespoon chocolate syrup

## Direction

- Note: Be sure to read the intro for special instructions.
- Peel a banana half way down.
- Add a dab of peanut butter where the eyes would go and attach each grape half.
- Attach the dried cherry (or cranberry) in where the nose goes by pushing in carefully using your finger.
- Push in the vitamin (or piece of fruit) to make the mouth.
- Carefully spoon the chocolate sauce down the top of the banana head to create the scary boo-nana hair!

## Nutrition Information

- Calories: 197.7
- Total Carbohydrate: 40.4
- Total Fat: 4.1
- Sodium: 84.5
- Sugar: 21.8
- Saturated Fat: 1.3
- Fiber: 3.9
- Cholesterol: 0.4
- Protein: 3.2

## 225. Mrs. Truman's Martian Cookies

*Serving: 24 cookies, 24 serving(s) | Prep: 15mins | Ready in:*

## Ingredients

- 1 cup butter
- 1 cup brown sugar
- 1/2 teaspoon salt
- 1 teaspoon baking soda (dissolved in water)
- 1/4 cup boiling water
- 1 teaspoon vanilla
- 2 cups flour
- 2 cups instant oats
- 2 tablespoons milk, for dipping fork in

## Direction

- Pre-heat oven to 375 degrees. Mix all dry ingredients in a bowl. Dissolve baking soda in water cream together butter and sugar, add vanilla, then add water and flour alternating. Make into small balls. On cookie sheet Press flat with fork dipped in milk. Cook for 7-9 minutes till just turning brown on edges.

## Nutrition Information

- Calories: 167.5
- Cholesterol: 20.5
- Saturated Fat: 5
- Sodium: 160.1
- Fiber: 0.9
- Sugar: 9
- Total Fat: 8.2
- Total Carbohydrate: 21.5
- Protein: 2.3

### 226. Mum's Simple Economy Scones

*Serving: 12 scones | Prep: 10mins | Ready in:*

## Ingredients

- 2 cups self rising flour
- 1/4 teaspoon salt
- 30 g butter
- 250 ml milk

## Direction

- Preheat your oven to 250C
- Sift flour and salt in a bowl.
- Rub in the butter with your fingertips, until it resembles breadcrumbs.
- Make a well, and add almost all of the milk.
- (Reserve about a tbsp.) With a butter knife, quickly work in the milk to the flour, making a dough.
- On a lightly floured surface, knead the dough very lightly.
- Flatten gently with your hands to 1.5cm thick
- Use a round cutter to cut out discs.
- On a buttered tray place scones next to each other.
- Brush with reserved milk.
- Bake for 10 minutes, or until scones sound hollow when tapped.
- Serve with tea, whipped cream and strawberry jam and you have Devonshire tea. Or add herbs/grated cheese for savory scones to serve with soups and casseroles.

## Nutrition Information

- Calories: 104.6
- Total Fat: 3
- Saturated Fat: 1.8
- Protein: 2.8
- Sodium: 337.3
- Fiber: 0.6
- Sugar: 0.1
- Total Carbohydrate: 16.4
- Cholesterol: 8.2

### 227. Murray's Fried Spaghetti

*Serving: 4 serving(s) | Prep: 10mins | Ready in:*

## Ingredients

- 2 tablespoons olive oil
- 1 tablespoon butter
- 12 ounces cooked ham, cubed (leftovers you can also use are hot dogs or bologna or even chicken about 1.5 cups)
- 1 small onion, chopped
- 4 cups cooked spaghetti
- 1/2 teaspoon salt (to taste)
- 1/2 teaspoon black pepper (to taste)

## Direction

- In large skillet heat oil and butter over medium-high heat. Add meat and onions and sauté for 2-3 minutes.
- Add cooked spaghetti, salt and pepper. Using side of spatula, chop up spaghetti while mixing ingredients.
- Toss and sauté until hot. Serve immediately.

## Nutrition Information

- Calories: 546.4
- Fiber: 2.8
- Total Carbohydrate: 45.1
- Sugar: 1.5
- Cholesterol: 87.5
- Protein: 31.1
- Total Fat: 25.9
- Saturated Fat: 8.5
- Sodium: 364.3

## 228. My Best Ever Deviled Eggs!

*Serving: 6 serving(s) | Prep: 15mins | Ready in:*

### Ingredients

- 6 hard-cooked eggs
- 1/4 cup mayonnaise
- 1 teaspoon vinegar
- 1/2 teaspoon Worcestershire sauce
- 1/4 teaspoon salt
- 1/2 teaspoon dry mustard
- 1 tablespoon sweet pickle relish (optional)
- 1 teaspoon paprika (to garnish)

### Direction

- To cook perfect hard boiled eggs: Place eggs in a pot of water seasoned with salt, enough to cover the eggs. Bring the water to a rolling boil. Cover the eggs, turn off heat completely and set the timer for 12 minutes. The eggs should be perfectly yellow in the center!
- To make the deviled eggs: Slice eggs in half lengthwise; and carefully remove yolks. Using a fork, mash the yolk with the mayonnaise. Add remaining ingredients (I never use relish, but I know some people like it!) except relish and paprika. Using an electric mixer, start on low speed, then increase to high speed to reach a creamy consistency. Use two spoons to fill each egg with the yolk mixture. Sprinkle a little paprika on each egg, then let set in the refrigerator for about 15 minutes. Eat and enjoy! I often make twelve eggs and double the ingredients.

## Nutrition Information

- Calories: 118.1
- Saturated Fat: 2.1
- Sodium: 233.4
- Sugar: 1.3
- Total Carbohydrate: 3.2
- Protein: 6.5
- Total Fat: 8.7
- Fiber: 0.1
- Cholesterol: 189.1

## 229. My Best Friend's Best Granola Bars

*Serving: 24 bars, 24 serving(s) | Prep: 5mins | Ready in:*

### Ingredients

- 3 cups quick-cooking oats
- 1 (14 ounce) can sweetened condensed milk
- 2 tablespoons butter, melted
- 1 cup flaked coconut
- 1 cup sliced almonds
- 1 cup miniature semisweet chocolate chips
- 1/2 cup dried sweetened cranberries

### Direction

- Preheat oven to 350 degrees F (175 degrees C). Grease a 9x13 inch pan.
- In a large bowl, mix together the oats, sweetened condensed milk, butter, coconut, almonds, chocolate chips and cranberries with your hands until well blended. Grease a spatula and press it hard into the pan.
- Bake for 20 to 25 minutes in the preheated oven, depending on how crunchy you want them. Lightly browned just around the edges will give you moist, chewy bars. Let cool for 5 minutes, cut into squares then let cool completely before serving.

## Nutrition Information

- Calories: 179.4
- Total Fat: 8.2
- Saturated Fat: 3.9
- Sodium: 37
- Fiber: 2.1
- Sugar: 16.2
- Total Carbohydrate: 24.6
- Cholesterol: 8.2
- Protein: 4.2

## 230. Nacho Cucumbers!

*Serving: 4-6 serving(s) | Prep: 5mins | Ready in:*

## Ingredients

- 1 cucumber (sliced)
- 4 ounces salsa
- 4 ounces pre-shredded fat-free cheddar cheese

## Direction

- Peel and slice cucumber.
- Put 1 teaspoon salsa on each slice of cucumber.
- Top with shredded cheese.
- Put slices on paper towel and microwave for approximately 15 seconds or until cheese begins to melt slightly.
- Very delicious, quick, and delicious!

## Nutrition Information

- Calories: 61.6
- Total Fat: 0.4
- Saturated Fat: 0.2
- Fiber: 0.9
- Total Carbohydrate: 8.5
- Cholesterol: 3.1
- Protein: 7.3
- Sodium: 621.2
- Sugar: 5

## 231. Nancy Black's School Brownies

*Serving: 16 serving(s) | Prep: 10mins | Ready in:*

## Ingredients

- 1/2 cup margarine, at room temperature
- 1 cup sugar
- 1 large egg
- 1 cup presifted all-purpose flour
- 1/2 teaspoon baking soda
- 1 1/2 teaspoons baking powder
- 1/2 teaspoon ground cinnamon
- 1/4 teaspoon ground nutmeg
- 1 large rome beauty apple (Came out very soft and juicy using MacIntosh Apple; Excellent)
- 3/4 cup chopped walnuts
- 1 teaspoon vanilla extract

## Direction

- Preheat oven to 350 degree.
- Grease and flour 8"x8" baking dish.
- Cream together the margarine and sugar in a medium-size bowl.
- Beat in the egg.
- In another bowl, mix together the flour, baking soda, baking powder, and spices.
- Stir into the batter.

- Peel, core, and dice the apple.
- Add to the batter with the chopped walnuts and vanilla extract.
- Stir to combine.
- Pour into the baking dish and bake for 30 minutes or until a skewer inserted in the middle comes out clean.
- Cool in the pan on a wire rack.
- Slice into squares.

## Nutrition Information

- Calories: 176.2
- Sodium: 144.7
- Sugar: 14.1
- Total Fat: 9.7
- Saturated Fat: 1.4
- Total Carbohydrate: 21.3
- Cholesterol: 13.2
- Protein: 2.1
- Fiber: 0.9

## 232. Nene's Amazing Avocado Dip

*Serving: 4-6 serving(s) | Prep: 2mins | Ready in:*

### Ingredients

- 1 cup parsley
- 2 green onions
- 4 avocados
- 3 tablespoons lemon juice
- 1 cup Hellmann's mayonnaise
- 1 teaspoon beef bouillon
- 1/8 teaspoon Tabasco sauce
- 1 cup sour cream
- 1/2 teaspoon dill
- 3/4 teaspoon salt

### Direction

- Just blitz all ingredients in a food processor or mix by hand. That's it! Serve with your favourite tortilla chips or anything you'd like. If there are leftovers just squeeze a bit of lemon juice on top and place plastic wrap right on the dip to prevent browning.

## Nutrition Information

- Calories: 684.6
- Saturated Fat: 14.7
- Fiber: 14.2
- Sugar: 5.8
- Total Carbohydrate: 36.1
- Sodium: 915.9
- Cholesterol: 40.6
- Protein: 7
- Total Fat: 61.3

## 233. Nine Layer Mexican Dip

*Serving: 12 serving(s) | Prep: 15mins | Ready in:*

### Ingredients

- 1 (9 ounce) canspicy bean dip
- 3/4 cup guacamole
- 1/2 cup sour cream
- 1 (4 ounce) can diced green chilies
- 1 (4 ounce) candiced jalapenos (optional)
- 1 (4 ounce) cansliced black olives
- 1/4 cup green onions with top, sliced
- 1 large tomatoes, diced small
- 2 cups shredded cheddar cheese

### Direction

- Spread bean dip in an even layer on a medium sized serving platter.
- Spread guacamole over the bean dip.
- Spread the sour cream over the guacamole.
- Sprinkle the chilies, jalapeños, olives, onions, and tomatoes over the sour cream.
- Sprinkle the cheese over the entire dip covering all the ingredients beneath.
- Serve with chips.

- Note: If desired, you could turn this into a wonderful taco salad by making this in individual taco salad tortilla bowls and adding seasoned ground beef and shredded lettuce.

## Nutrition Information

- Calories: 112.7
- Saturated Fat: 5.4
- Total Carbohydrate: 2.5
- Protein: 5.3
- Fiber: 0.7
- Sugar: 0.9
- Cholesterol: 24
- Total Fat: 9.3
- Sodium: 317.2

## 234. No Bake Breakfast Cookies

*Serving: 24 cookies, 24 serving(s) | Prep: 10mins | Ready in:*

### Ingredients

- 1/2 cup light corn syrup
- 1/2 cup instant non-fat powdered milk
- 1/2 cup raisins
- 1/2 cup peanut butter
- 2 1/2 cups coarsely crushed corn flakes cereal

### Direction

- Heat corn syrup (or honey) and peanut butter in a medium saucepan over low heat. Stir until blended.
- Remove from heat; stir in dry milk.
- Fold in cereal and raisins.
- Drop by heaping tablespoonfuls onto waxed paper to form mounds.
- Cool to room temperature; Store in refrigerator.

## Nutrition Information

- Calories: 80.3
- Protein: 2.5
- Total Fat: 2.8
- Sodium: 63.9
- Sugar: 5.8
- Total Carbohydrate: 12.7
- Cholesterol: 0.5
- Saturated Fat: 0.6
- Fiber: 0.5

## 235. No Sugar Lite Vanilla Yogurt

*Serving: 6 serving(s) | Prep: 20mins | Ready in:*

### Ingredients

- 4 cups milk (your choice whole-skim)
- 1/2 cup powdered dry milk
- 1 tablespoon vanilla extract
- 5 packets Splenda sugar substitute
- 1/2 cup yogurt starter (unflavored plain yogurt with active cultures)

### Direction

- Set 1/2 yogurt starter out to warm to room temperature.
- (I usually buy a large container of plain active culture plain whole milk yogurt-no gelatin and freeze in baby food jars for starters).
- Heat the milk to almost a boil.
- (I like to microwave in a glass bowl for 5 minutes on high then 2 minutes on medium) Cool the milk (to a "barely warm"/ babies bath temperature cool water bath works well).
- Add Dry Milk, Vanilla and Sweetener of your choice.
- Stir well.
- Stir in yogurt starter (do not whip but mix very well!).
- "Cook "the yogurt using your preferred method and time (longer makes a firmer, more

tart yogurt. I like to cook about 12 hours) Chill 4 hours before eating.

## Nutrition Information

- Calories: 166
- Total Carbohydrate: 12.7
- Total Fat: 8.8
- Saturated Fat: 5.5
- Sodium: 119.5
- Fiber: 0
- Sugar: 5
- Cholesterol: 33.1
- Protein: 8.1

## 236. No Sugar, Low Fat "fruity" Oatmeal Cookies

*Serving: 35 cookies | Prep: 15mins | Ready in:*

### Ingredients

- 6 tablespoons organic yogurt (flavoring is your choice, but I use the Vanana from Trader Joe's)
- 3 organic bananas (I used very ripe ones, like the type you'd use for banana bread. I find they have great flavor)
- 2 organic eggs
- 1/4 cup organic milk (I use low fat)
- 4 tablespoons honey
- 1 2/3 cups whole wheat flour
- 2 teaspoons baking powder
- 1/4 teaspoon baking soda
- 1 1/2 cups oats
- 1/2 cup organic raisins

### Direction

- Preheat the oven to 400 degrees.
- Cream together the yogurt and bananas in a large bowl.
- Gradually work the egg, milk, honey, flour, baking powder and soda, and oats into the mixture.
- Stir in the raisins.
- Drop batter by tablespoonfuls onto parchment lined baking sheet (get as many as you can on the sheet. These cookies don't spread out).
- Bake for 7 minutes at 400 degrees.
- Remove from the oven and cool.

## Nutrition Information

- Calories: 74.9
- Protein: 2.6
- Sodium: 36.6
- Sugar: 4.6
- Total Carbohydrate: 14.8
- Fiber: 1.8
- Cholesterol: 12.7
- Total Fat: 1
- Saturated Fat: 0.3

## 237. Norwegian Pancakes

*Serving: 30 serving(s) | Prep: 5mins | Ready in:*

### Ingredients

- 4 eggs
- 2 cups all-purpose flour
- 2 cups milk (any kind)
- 1/2 cup sugar (optional)
- 1/2-1 cup butter
- 2 drops vanilla extract

### Direction

- Melt butter into a mixer than add ingredients in order as listed.
- It should become like a pancake constancy.
- Pour into a medium heated pan.
- Fill up whole pan with mix, then pour out extra mix back into the bowl.
- Flip over pancake when it becomes golden brown on the bottom.
- Serve hot and sprinkle with sugar or jelly.
- Roll up and eat!

## Nutrition Information

- Calories: 77.7
- Protein: 2.3
- Total Fat: 4.4
- Saturated Fat: 2.5
- Sodium: 39.3
- Fiber: 0.2
- Cholesterol: 38.6
- Sugar: 0.1
- Total Carbohydrate: 7.2

## 238. Nut And Egg Free Cookies

*Serving: 36-48 cookies | Prep: 5mins | Ready in:*

### Ingredients

- 1 cup margarine
- 3/4 cup brown sugar
- 1 tablespoon corn syrup
- 2 cups flour
- 1 teaspoon vanilla
- 3/4 cup sugar
- 2 teaspoons baking soda
- 2 cups oatmeal
- 1 cup chocolate chips
- 1/3 cup boiling water

### Direction

- Combine margarine, sugars, syrup, and vanilla. Beat until creamy. Add in flour, and baking soda. Mix well. Add boiling water and oatmeal. Stir until well blended. Mix in chocolate chips.
- Drop by teaspoonfuls onto a cookie sheet.

### Nutrition Information

- Calories: 145.2
- Sodium: 131.7
- Total Carbohydrate: 20.4
- Total Fat: 6.8
- Saturated Fat: 1.8
- Protein: 1.7
- Fiber: 0.9
- Sugar: 11.3
- Cholesterol: 0

## 239. Nutella S'mores

*Serving: 2-4 serving(s) | Prep: 5mins | Ready in:*

### Ingredients

- 4 graham cracker squares
- 4 teaspoons nutella
- 4 large marshmallows or 36 mini marshmallows

### Direction

- Heat broiler.
- Break each graham cracker square in half and spread about a teaspoons (or more!) Nutella on 4 of the halves.
- Top the halves with the Nutella each with either a large marshmallow or about 9 minis. Set other 4 squares aside.
- Place assembled s'mores on a sheet and place under broiler. Be sure to keep an eye on it as it really won't take long to start browning and then you will want to turn your sheet to evenly brown each one.
- When browned to desired amount take out and top each with the remaining graham cracker halves.
- Enjoy!

### Nutrition Information

- Calories: 229.7
- Total Fat: 6.5
- Saturated Fat: 3.9
- Sodium: 149.8

- Fiber: 1.5
- Sugar: 23.4
- Total Carbohydrate: 40.5
- Cholesterol: 0
- Protein: 2.9

## 240. Nutty Pineapple Nibbles ( Stuffed Celery)

*Serving: 6 serving(s) | Prep: 10mins | Ready in:*

### Ingredients

- 6 celery ribs
- 1/4 cup canned crushed pineapple, drained
- 1/2 cup soft light cream cheese
- 2 tablespoons creamy peanut butter
- 1 tablespoon honey
- 1/4 cup dried fruit
- 1/4 cup dry-roasted nuts, finely crushed

### Direction

- Rinse the celery, them trim off the leafy parts, and cut into 10-inch pieces.
- In a medium-sized bowl, combine the drained pineapple, cream cheese, peanut butter, and honey.
- Stir with a rubber spatula until well mixed.
- Stir in the raisins or fruit bits and hot sauce, if desired.
- Using a table knife, fill the groove of each celery stalk with the cheese mixture.
- Sprinkle the crushed nuts over the stalks.

### Nutrition Information

- Calories: 155.6
- Saturated Fat: 3.8
- Sodium: 171.9
- Fiber: 2.3
- Sugar: 5.1
- Total Carbohydrate: 13.7
- Total Fat: 10.2

- Protein: 4.8
- Cholesterol: 14.4

## 241. Nutty Popcorn

*Serving: 8 serving(s) | Prep: 5mins | Ready in:*

### Ingredients

- 1 bag microwave popcorn, popped
- 1/2 cup light corn syrup
- 1/4 cup creamy peanut butter or 1/4 cup chunky peanut butter
- 1 teaspoon vanilla
- 1 cup miniature M baking bits
- 1/4 cup nuts

### Direction

- Shake bag of popcorn to settle unpopped kernels; pour popcorn into large bowl.
- In a small saucepan, melt corn syrup, peanut butter and vanilla over medium heat until warm and syrupy; DO NOT ALLOW TO BOIL!
- Pour syrup mixture over popcorn and toss until well coated.
- Add mini M's and nuts; toss together and serve warm.

### Nutrition Information

- Calories: 306.1
- Cholesterol: 0
- Total Fat: 8.3
- Sodium: 82.5
- Fiber: 7.3
- Total Carbohydrate: 53.5
- Protein: 8.5
- Saturated Fat: 1.4
- Sugar: 7.1

## 242. OAMC Chicken Nuggets

*Serving: 48 nuggets, 4-6 serving(s) | Prep: 15mins | Ready in:*

### Ingredients

- 2 lbs boneless skinless chicken breasts
- 1 teaspoon seasoning salt
- 1/3 cup hot sauce
- 3/4 cup buttermilk
- 1 cup all-purpose flour
- 1/4 cup cornstarch
- 1/4 cup cornflour
- 1 tablespoon paprika
- 1 teaspoon salt
- 1 teaspoon black pepper
- 1/4 teaspoon garlic powder
- 1/4 teaspoon onion powder
- 1/4 teaspoon ground sage
- oil (for frying)

### Direction

- In a gallon size zip lock bag combine buttermilk, hot sauce, and seasoning salt.
- Cut chicken breasts lengthwise into three strips. Cut strips into bite sized pieces for nuggets or cut strips in half for chicken fingers.
- Add the chicken to the buttermilk mixture and refrigerate for AT LEAST 4 hours. Overnight is best.
- In a large bowl combine flour, cornstarch, corn flour, paprika, salt, pepper, garlic powder, onion powder, and sage. Stir with a whisk until well combined.
- Remove chicken pieces from buttermilk and dredge in the flour mixture.
- Fry in 350-360 degree oil until light golden brown. Remove from oil and drain on paper towels while you fry the rest of the chicken.
- When you've fried it all put the drained pieces on a baking sheet and freeze. Put frozen chicken nuggets/fingers in bags and label. These will keep for 2 or 3 months in the freezer.
- To serve, preheat oven to 350 degrees and bake for 10 to 15 minutes or until heated through and crispy. I like to serve mine with buffalo ranch dipping sauce. Combine 1/4 cup ranch dressing and 2 teaspoons of hot sauce in a small bowl or ramekin.

### Nutrition Information

- Calories: 452.4
- Sodium: 1276.6
- Fiber: 1.9
- Sugar: 2.8
- Cholesterol: 133.5
- Protein: 57.7
- Saturated Fat: 1.1
- Total Fat: 3.9
- Total Carbohydrate: 42.6

## 243. Oatmeal Banana Muffins

*Serving: 18 muffins | Prep: 10mins | Ready in:*

### Ingredients

- 1/2 cup margarine, softened
- 1/2 cup sugar
- 2 eggs
- 1 cup mashed ripe banana
- 3/4 cup honey
- 1 1/2 cups flour
- 1 cup quick-cooking oats
- 1 teaspoon baking powder
- 1 teaspoon baking soda
- 3/4 teaspoon salt

### Direction

- Cream margarine and sugar in mixing bowl.
- Add eggs, bananas and honey; mix well.
- In separate bowl, combine dry ingredients; stir into creamed mixture just until moistened.
- Line muffin tins with paper cups or grease tins.

- Fill cups 2/3 full.
- Bake in preheated 350 degree oven for 18-20 minutes.
- Cool in pan 10 minutes before removing to wire rack.

## Nutrition Information

- Calories: 180.4
- Sugar: 18.3
- Total Fat: 6
- Sodium: 254.9
- Fiber: 1
- Total Carbohydrate: 30.2
- Cholesterol: 23.5
- Protein: 2.7
- Saturated Fat: 1.1

## 244. Oh So Good Homemade Tortilla Chips

*Serving: 10 large handfuls, 10 serving(s) | Prep: 5mins | Ready in:*

### Ingredients

- 10 tortillas (white or yellow flour OR corn)
- vegetable oil cooking spray
- popcorn salt (optional)

### Direction

- Preheat the oven to 350 or 375.
- Lay the tortillas on the counter top, side by side, very close together.
- Spray tortillas generously with the oil spritzer; sprinkle with optional salt.
- If using the pizza cutter AND in a hurry, stack tortillas in piles of 3 or 5 and slice up quickly into triangles (make five to six cuts to get uniform sizes).
- If using cookie cutters, don't pile up the tortillas--it's too thick and aggravating!
- Lay the "chips" on the cookie sheets and pop them into the oven---bake ONLY until a very light brown.
- Cool slightly and THEN--dive in!
- You might as well double the recipe, because you're going to wish you did as soon as you take your first bite!

## Nutrition Information

- Calories: 218.4
- Sodium: 445.2
- Sugar: 1.3
- Protein: 5.8
- Saturated Fat: 1.3
- Fiber: 2.2
- Total Carbohydrate: 36
- Cholesterol: 0
- Total Fat: 5.4

## 245. Old Fashioned Red Candied Apples

*Serving: 6 serving(s) | Prep: 10mins | Ready in:*

### Ingredients

- 2 cups sugar
- 1 cup water
- 1/4 teaspoon cream of tartar
- red food coloring
- apple

### Direction

- Mix 1st 3 ingredients in saucepan.
- Put on high heat with candy thermometer positioned in center of fluid level.
- While it is boiling, thoroughly wash and dry your apples, and spear with the sticks.
- Boil mixture until reaches hard crack (300°F), then immediately add red food coloring and stir.

- Quickly immediately dip the apples, twisting to cover, and set on a greased cookie sheet.

## Nutrition Information

- Calories: 258.3
- Sugar: 66.5
- Total Carbohydrate: 66.7
- Cholesterol: 0
- Protein: 0
- Saturated Fat: 0
- Sodium: 1.9
- Fiber: 0
- Total Fat: 0

## 246. Olive Garden Summer Pizza

*Serving: 6 serving(s) | Prep: 20mins | Ready in:*

## Ingredients

- 2 (6 inch) prepared pizza crust
- Toppings
- 4 green onions, cut into 3 pieces
- 1 red pepper
- 1 yellow pepper
- 1 (10 ounce) jar marinara sauce (your favorite)
- 1/2 lb mozzarella cheese, grated
- 10 slices pepperoni
- 16 black olives, pitted and cut into halves
- 1 tablespoon dried oregano (garnish)
- 2 basil leaves, chopped (garnish)

## Direction

- Place washed green onion, yellow and red pepper onto grill. Allow to grill for approximately 5 minutes or until grill marks are visible. Remove from grill and set aside. Once peppers are cool enough to handle, remove skin and cut into 1" pieces.
- Prepare toppings and divide in half. Spread half of marinara sauce on each crust. Sprinkle green onions, peppers, olives and pepperoni over crusts. Top with mozzarella and Parmesan. Sprinkle tops with oregano and basil.
- Bake in a 375F oven for 8 to 10 minutes until filling is hot and cheese has melted. Cut each pizza into 6 wedges.

## Nutrition Information

- Calories: 198.9
- Saturated Fat: 5.9
- Sodium: 650.2
- Sugar: 6.1
- Protein: 10.9
- Fiber: 1.8
- Total Carbohydrate: 11.8
- Cholesterol: 33.7
- Total Fat: 12.4

## 247. Orange Ginger Oatmeal Porridge Delight

*Serving: 1 serving(s) | Prep: 1mins | Ready in:*

## Ingredients

- 57 g porridge oats or 4 tablespoons porridge oats
- vanilla flavoring, to taste
- 1/3 teaspoon ground ginger (or to taste)
- 1/3 teaspoon caraway seed (optional or to taste)
- 4 teaspoons Splenda sugar substitute (R) or 4 teaspoons sugar or 4 teaspoons artificial sweetener, to taste
- 1 teaspoon marmalade (chunky style orange marmalade, with rind)
- 1 1/2 teaspoons low-fat yogurt or 1 1/2 teaspoons single cream
- 345 ml water or 1 1/2 cups water

## Direction

- It helps to quickly make the topping first.
- Take a small pot such as a small washed empty yogurt pot or egg cup and put in about a medium teaspoon of chunky orange marmalade. Add a bit of boiling or hot water and stir to make a medium thick paste.
- Porridge:
- Measure the porridge oats - I suggest 57g as a good sized portion into a saucepan. I tested this to work out to be pretty much exactly 4 Tablespoons extremely well heaped (- or about 1/4 cup apparently). I'm on a calorie-controlled diet and this is just enough for me to enjoy without feeling either underfed or too heavy - but you may prefer more or less and adjust the other ingredients accordingly.
- Add 345ml water (about 1 1/2 cups) - or enough to be absorbed to your satisfaction. Water weighs 1g per ml so you can weigh in 345g if you have electronic scales.
- Add just a couple of small drops vanilla flavouring - I prefer the artificial one as it's got a much stronger flavour - if you use real vanilla essence you may need about 1/3 Teaspoon because it's so much weaker. (Note: calorie wise, artificial vanilla has 50 Kcal/100ml versus 600 Kcal/100ml for real vanilla essence!).
- Add about 1/3 teaspoon of Ground Ginger (to taste) - quite a lot is really good! - But breakfast time cravings vary about as much as personal tastes :).
- Add about 1/3 teaspoon caraway seeds (to taste - or leave them out if you don't really like caraway seeds).
- Place on stove and boil and simmer until just the consistency you like.
- When just about thick enough, add 2 medium teaspoons of Splenda(R), or granulated sweetener or sugar (or as much/little as suits your taste) and stir it in well.
- Pour into breakfast bowl and top with about 1 1/2 to 1 1/2 teaspoons natural (plain) yogurt (ideally fat-free/low-fat) or single cream if you're not counting calories.

- Sprinkle the top, in particular the yogurt with a teaspoon or two of Splenda (R) (or granulated sweetener or sugar).
- Add the prepared, diluted marmalade over the yogurt.
- SERVE.
- NOTES:
- Don't go too mad with the yogurt or cream! It actually tastes better if you don't drown it in yogurt or cream - probably because the porridge itself tastes so wonderful.
- SUGGESTIONS FOR ALTERNATIVE TOPPINGS:
- As an alternative to orange marmalade you might try a couple of teaspoons of orange or lemon juice, or crushed hazelnuts, or ginger jam/conserve, or pieces of crystallized ginger or slices of ginger preserved in sugar syrup, or maybe just honey. You might like to sometimes put a teaspoon of raisins in with the topping (or in with the porridge :) for a special treat. Incidentally I'm currently using 'Streamline' 'Zest' Reduced Sugar, High-Fruit (55% fruit) Orange Grapefruit marmalade which is to die for if you can get it!
- SWEETENERS:
- If using a different granulated sweetener it's worth knowing that aspartame becomes unstable and loses its sweetness above 85 degrees centigrade hence the suggestion to use Splenda(R) which is fine above 100 centigrade and can be boiled no problem. Some granulated sweeteners contain acesulfame-K in addition to aspartame. Acesulfame-K stays sweet above 100 centigrade but some people think it doesn't taste so nice :) If in doubt, maybe spoil yourself and use sugar!
- CALORIC VALUES:
- I calculate calories per serving using sweetener and low-fat yoghurt to max out at around 265 calories depending on make and types of ingredients used. If you use sugar you can add another 70 calories for the suggested quantity here. For Cream add another 30 or more calories. Mine usually works out about 245 calories maximum but I use low sugar marmalade, fat-free yogurt etc.

### Nutrition Information

- Calories: 244.2
- Saturated Fat: 0.7
- Fiber: 6
- Protein: 9.7
- Total Fat: 3.9
- Sugar: 5.3
- Total Carbohydrate: 43.9
- Cholesterol: 0.5
- Sodium: 18.4

## 248. Oregon Trail Mix

*Serving: 9 cups | Prep: 10mins | Ready in:*

### Ingredients

- 1 cup chocolate chips (dark or milk-dark my choice)
- 1 cup roasted hazelnuts
- 1 cup roasted walnut
- 1 cup roasted pepitas
- 1 cup roasted whole almond
- 1 cup roasted sunflower seeds
- 1 cup dried peaches, cut into small pieces
- 1 cup raisins
- 1 cup dried cranberries

### Direction

- Note: all ingredient amounts are estimated. Please feel free to adjust the proportions to your preference. The ingredient's list is merely a basic guideline.
- In a large bowl combine all ingredients and mix well.
- Transfer to an airtight container.
- Prep time does not include roasting the seeds/nuts.

### Nutrition Information

- Calories: 621.1
- Sugar: 22.4
- Total Carbohydrate: 50.1
- Protein: 16.1
- Sodium: 8.9
- Fiber: 8.6
- Total Fat: 45.6
- Saturated Fat: 7.5
- Cholesterol: 0

## 249. Pan Fried Spinach Ravioli

*Serving: 4 serving(s) | Prep: 25mins | Ready in:*

### Ingredients

- 16 ounces spinach
- 5 tablespoons extra virgin olive oil
- 1 onion, finely chopped
- 4 ounces chive onion cream cheese or 4 ounces cream cheese, softened
- 1/2 cup finely grated parmesan cheese, plus more for serving
- salt and pepper
- 1 -2 pinch crushed red pepper flakes (optional)
- 48 wonton wrappers (from a 12-ounce package)
- 1 1/2 cups store-bought tomato sauce mushrooms, warmed, for serving
- chopped parsley, for sprinkling

### Direction

- In a large skillet, bring 1 cup water to a simmer over medium heat.
- Add the spinach and cook until wilted, about 3 minutes; drain, rinse until cool, then squeeze dry.
- Chop and transfer to a medium bowl.
- Using the same skillet, add 1 tablespoon olive oil the onion crushed red pepper flakes (if using) and cook, stirring, over medium high heat until softened, about 5 minutes.
- Stir into the spinach, along with the cream cheese, parmesan and 1/2 teaspoon pepper.

- Lay 12 wonton wrappers on a work surface; place 1 tablespoon of the spinach filling in the center of each.
- Working with 1 at a time, moisten the edges with water and lay another wrapper on top; seal the edges, pressing out any air.
- Repeat with the remaining wrappers and spinach filling.
- Using the same skillet, bring 3/4 cup water, 2 tablespoons olive oil and a pinch of salt to a boil.
- Add 12 ravioli, cover and cook until tender, about 3 minutes; transfer to a platter.
- Repeat with the remaining ravioli, 2 tablespoons olive oil, more water and another pinch of salt.
- Spoon the tomato sauce over the ravioli and sprinkle with parsley and parmesan.

## Nutrition Information

- Calories: 619
- Sodium: 915.1
- Fiber: 4.6
- Sugar: 1.8
- Total Carbohydrate: 63.8
- Cholesterol: 50.8
- Protein: 19.9
- Saturated Fat: 11.1
- Total Fat: 32.2

## 250. Pasta With Crunchy Crumbs And Feta For One

*Serving: 1 serving(s) | Prep: 5mins | Ready in:*

## Ingredients

- 3 ounces tagliatelle pasta noodles or 3 ounces spaghetti
- 1 ounce butter
- 6 tablespoons white breadcrumbs (day old or from the freezer)
- 1/2 lemon
- 2 ounces feta cheese, cubed
- chopped parsley, a good handful
- salt freshly ground black pepper
- olive oil, for drizzling

## Direction

- Pour boiling water into a large pan, add some salt and the pasta and cook according to the pack instructions.
- Meanwhile, heat the butter in a small saucepan and when sizzling add the breadcrumbs and cook for about 5 mins, stirring occasionally until crisp and golden. Use a zester (or grater) to grate the lemon zest into the crumbs. Cut the lemon half into two wedges and set aside.
- Drain the pasta, put it back in the pan, toss in the crumb mixture, add the feta cheese chunks, parsley and seasoning.
- Serve in a large warm bowl drizzled with olive oil and with the lemon wedges on the side. Squeeze lemon juice over as you eat the pasta to bring out the flavour.

## Nutrition Information

- Calories: 800.8
- Sodium: 1109
- Sugar: 5.7
- Total Carbohydrate: 88.2
- Cholesterol: 186.3
- Protein: 24.4
- Total Fat: 41
- Saturated Fat: 24.9
- Fiber: 6.3

## 251. Paula's Fried Biscuits And Honey Butter

*Serving: 10 biscuits, 10 serving(s) | Prep: 5mins | Ready in:*

## Ingredients

- Biscuits
- 3-4 cups vegetable oil
- 1 (12 ounce) can refrigerated biscuits
- Honey butter
- 1 lb squeeze margarine (in the bottle) or 1 lb squeeze butter (in the bottle)
- 1/4 cup honey, to taste

### Direction

- In a heavy deep skillet or deep fryer, heat the oil over medium high.
- When oil is hot, carefully add in the biscuits and cook about 2 to 3 minutes per side until golden brown (don't do too many biscuits at once, or the oil will lose temperature too quickly).
- Remove biscuits from oil and drain on paper towels; repeat steps until all biscuits are done.
- Make the honey "butter": remove about 1/4 of the squeeze margarine from the bottle and store for later use; add the honey and stir with a long teaspoon (like the ones for ice cream shakes), a wooden skewer, or the handle of a wooden spoon.
- Serve the biscuits with the honey butter.

### Nutrition Information

- Calories: 1050.3
- Total Fat: 107.1
- Sodium: 796.5
- Saturated Fat: 17.4
- Fiber: 0.3
- Sugar: 9.7
- Total Carbohydrate: 23.3
- Cholesterol: 0.3
- Protein: 3

## 252. Pb Fruit Pita Pockets

*Serving: 4 serving(s) | Prep: 10mins | Ready in:*

### Ingredients

- 1 apple, peeled, cored and finely diced
- 1 medium bartlett pear, peeled, cored and finely diced
- 1 1/2 tablespoons raisins
- 2 teaspoons orange juice
- 3 tablespoons chunky peanut butter
- 4 large lettuce leaves or 8 large spinach leaves
- 2 (6 inch) whole wheat pita bread

### Direction

- Combine diced apples, pears and raisins with orange juice and hold for 5 minutes.
- Add peanut butter and mix well.
- Wash and dry lettuce or spinach leaves on absorbent paper towels.
- Tear lettuce into pita size pieces.
- Warm pita in toaster on lowest color setting.
- Cut pita in half, and carefully open each half to make a pocket.
- Line each pocket with lettuce or spinach leaves and spoon in equal portions of fruit and peanut butter mixture.
- Serve and enjoy.
- Serves 4 - snack or 2 meal portions.

### Nutrition Information

- Calories: 184.4
- Total Fat: 6.7
- Sodium: 177.9
- Fiber: 5.1
- Sugar: 11.4
- Cholesterol: 0
- Protein: 5.7
- Saturated Fat: 1.1
- Total Carbohydrate: 29.2

## 253. Peach Surprise

*Serving: 1 serving(s) | Prep: 0S | Ready in:*

### Ingredients

- 1/3-1/2 cup vanilla yogurt
- 1/2 peach (we used canned peach halves in light syrup)

## Direction

- Spread yogurt into circle on plate, using the back of a spoon.
- Place peach half, flat side down, in the center of the yogurt.
- Repeat for each serving desired.

## Nutrition Information

- Calories: 79
- Cholesterol: 10.6
- Protein: 3.5
- Total Fat: 2.8
- Saturated Fat: 1.7
- Sodium: 37.5
- Sugar: 10.1
- Fiber: 1.1
- Total Carbohydrate: 11

## 254. Peanut Butter Banana Dogs!

*Serving: 1 serving(s) | Prep: 5mins | Ready in:*

## Ingredients

- 1 hot dog bun
- peanut butter, -to your liking (Creamy or Chunky)
- 1 banana
- raisins (optional)

## Direction

- Spread the peanut butter on the inside of the hot dog bun as much as you'd like spreading it evenly over each side.
- When that's done simply peal a banana place it inside of the hotdog bun!
- For more flavor you can sprinkle a few raisins on top (Optional).
- Now you're done ready to eat!

## Nutrition Information

- Calories: 225
- Sodium: 207.2
- Fiber: 4
- Sugar: 17.1
- Total Carbohydrate: 48.2
- Cholesterol: 0
- Protein: 5.4
- Total Fat: 2.2
- Saturated Fat: 0.6

## 255. Peanut Butter Jam "sandwich" Muffins

*Serving: 12 muffins | Prep: 10mins | Ready in:*

## Ingredients

- 1 egg
- 1 cup smooth peanut butter
- 1/4 cup oil
- 1/2 cup firmly packed brown sugar
- 1 cup milk
- 1 cup flour
- 1 tablespoon baking powder
- 1/2 teaspoon baking soda
- 1/2 teaspoon salt
- 2 tablespoons jam

## Direction

- Preheat the oven to 400°F.
- Beat the egg, 1 cup of peanut butter and the oil in a large bowl with wire whisk until well blended.
- Add sugar and mix well.
- Gradually add the milk, mixing well after each addition.

- Mix dry ingredients together (flour, baking powder, baking soda and salt). Add to the peanut butter mixture, stir until moistened.
- Spoon just enough batter into each of the 12 paper lined muffin cups to cover the bottom of the cup. Spoon a dollop of jam over the batter (approx. 1/2 tsp.). Cover evenly with the remaining batter.
- Bake for 15-20 minutes until lightly browned. Cool in pan 5 minutes then remove to wire rack. Cool completely.
- Enjoy with a cold glass of milk.

## Nutrition Information

- Calories: 268
- Sodium: 359.4
- Fiber: 1.6
- Total Carbohydrate: 24.6
- Cholesterol: 20.5
- Total Fat: 16.6
- Saturated Fat: 3.4
- Sugar: 12.5
- Protein: 7.7

### 256. Peanut Butter Banana "ice Cream"

*Serving: 1 serving(s) | Prep: 5mins | Ready in:*

## Ingredients

- 1 banana, frozen
- 2 tablespoons peanut butter (natural honey roasted is great!)
- 1/2 cup milk (more or less to desired thickness)

## Direction

- Cut up banana with a fork or knife. Add peanut butter and milk. It is helpful to let the banana thaw a little (a minute) once you pour on the milk. This will make it easier to work everything together with your fork.

## Nutrition Information

- Calories: 371.3
- Sodium: 207.8
- Total Fat: 21
- Saturated Fat: 6.2
- Sugar: 17.4
- Total Carbohydrate: 38.9
- Cholesterol: 17.1
- Protein: 13.3
- Fiber: 5

### 257. Peanut Butter Crunch

*Serving: 1 small cookie sheet | Prep: 10mins | Ready in:*

## Ingredients

- 1 cup sugar
- 1 cup white Karo
- 1 cup peanut butter
- 1 (1 large) boxpost toasties corn flakes

## Direction

- Mix together in a large pot the sugar and karo syrup almost to a boiling point.
- Add 1 cup of peanut butter and mix well.
- Turn off the heat and add the corn flakes.
- Pour onto a buttered cookie sheet and used a buttered rolling pin to roll out.
- Let cool and cut into squares.

## Nutrition Information

- Calories: 3256.1
- Total Fat: 130.7
- Sodium: 1395.6
- Fiber: 15.5
- Cholesterol: 0
- Protein: 64.7
- Saturated Fat: 26.6
- Sugar: 314.9

- Total Carbohydrate: 512.3

## 258. Peanut Butter Granola Balls

*Serving: 24 balls, 24 serving(s) | Prep: 15mins | Ready in:*

### Ingredients

- 1/3 cup honey
- 1/4 cup natural-style peanut butter
- 2 tablespoons unsalted butter
- 1 cup crisp rice cereal
- 1 cup old fashioned oats (not quick cooking)
- 1/4 cup dried fruit (such as cherries, raisins, or cranberries)

### Direction

- In a small saucepan over medium, heat honey, peanut butter, and butter. Stir until loosened and smooth, 1-2 minutes. Remove from heat; stir in cereal, oats, and dried fruit.
- Drop mixture by the tablespoon into mini paper cupcake or candy liners. Place on a rimmed baking sheet, and refrigerate until set, about 15 minutes. To store, refrigerate in an airtight container up to 1 week.

### Nutrition Information

- Calories: 61.2
- Total Fat: 2.5
- Sodium: 10.2
- Fiber: 0.7
- Total Carbohydrate: 9.1
- Cholesterol: 2.5
- Saturated Fat: 0.9
- Sugar: 4.2
- Protein: 1.4

## 259. Peanut Butter And Jelly Bites

*Serving: 6 balls, 2 serving(s) | Prep: 10mins | Ready in:*

### Ingredients

- Peanut Butter Balls
- 1 (1 g) packet Splenda caramel flavor accents for coffee
- 1 (1 g) packet Splenda french vanilla flavor accents for coffee
- 1 tablespoon sugar-free hot cocoa mix
- 1 tablespoon graham cracker crumbs
- 2 tablespoons peanut butter
- 1 1/2 teaspoons fat free cream cheese
- Garnish
- 2 tablespoons graham cracker crumbs
- 2 teaspoons sugar-free jam (or no sugar added)

### Direction

- Mix all peanut butter ball ingredients together in a small bowl. Roll into six balls. Roll balls in graham cracker crumbs.
- Press a small indentation in center with fingertip. Fill with jam. Serve immediately.

### Nutrition Information

- Calories: 127.4
- Fiber: 1.2
- Sugar: 3.9
- Total Carbohydrate: 9.2
- Cholesterol: 0
- Total Fat: 8.9
- Saturated Fat: 1.8
- Sodium: 121.1
- Protein: 4.6

## 260. Peanut Butter And Raisin Stuffed Apples

*Serving: 1 serving(s) | Prep: 5mins | Ready in:*

### Ingredients

- 1 small granny smith apple, cored
- 3 tablespoons peanut butter, approximate
- 2 tablespoons raisins, to taste

### Direction

- Fill the cored apple with peanut butter (mix a few raisins in if desired).
- Cover the peanut butter at each end with raisins.
- Cut into slices or serve whole, or wrap in plastic wrap and send in a lunchbox.

### Nutrition Information

- Calories: 396.6
- Cholesterol: 0
- Saturated Fat: 5
- Fiber: 6.2
- Total Carbohydrate: 39.7
- Protein: 12.9
- Total Fat: 24.5
- Sodium: 223.6
- Sugar: 27.2

## 261. Peppermint Rice Krispies Candy

*Serving: 16-20 pieces | Prep: 15mins | Ready in:*

### Ingredients

- 1/3 cup butter
- 1/2 lb marshmallows
- 1/2 teaspoon vanilla
- 1 -2 drop peppermint extract
- red food coloring, as desired
- 5 -6 cups Rice Krispies
- crushed peppermint candy cane

### Direction

- Make the basic Rice Krispie Candy recipe: Melt butter, marshmallows, and vanilla over a double boiler. Add a drop or two of peppermint extract and red food coloring to tint a nice pink color. At this stage, the pink color should not be too delicate because it will not show up at all when the cereal is mixed in.
- Put Rice Krispies in a large buttered bowl. Pour marshmallow mixture over and stir to mix. Add crushed peppermint candy canes and mix in.
- You may press this mixture into a buttered 9- x 9- x 2-inch pan and cut into bars. Or with well-buttered hands, you may shape portions of the mixture into candy cane shapes. Or you may pat thin and cut with cookie cutters as described above.

### Nutrition Information

- Calories: 113.3
- Protein: 0.8
- Sodium: 121.7
- Fiber: 0.1
- Sugar: 9
- Total Carbohydrate: 19
- Cholesterol: 10.2
- Total Fat: 4
- Saturated Fat: 2.5

## 262. Pepperoni Pizza Sticks

*Serving: 20 breadsticks, 8-10 serving(s) | Prep: 20mins | Ready in:*

### Ingredients

- 1 (8 ounce) packageHormel pepperoni slices
- 2 (10 ounce) packages refrigerated parmesan breadsticks, with garlic

- 1 1/4 cups finely shredded mozzarella cheese
- 2 cups of your favorite pizza sauce, divided, 1/2 cup reserved

## Direction

- Remove breadsticks from package and place in single layer on ungreased baking sheets.
- Spread about 1/2 tablespoon of reserved pizza sauce lightly on each breadstick.
- Top each with 5 slices of pepperoni and 1 tablespoon shredded Mozzarella cheese.
- Bake at 375F for 10-12 minutes or until cooked through.
- Serve pizza sticks warm with remaining pizza sauce warmed also.
- Note: The original recipe does not include spreading pizza sauce on the breadsticks, but I enjoy them even more like this!
- If you do also, spread very lightly, as putting too much sauce on your breadsticks could cause them to become a bit soggy.

## Nutrition Information

- Calories: 224.8
- Sugar: 1.3
- Total Carbohydrate: 5.8
- Cholesterol: 45.1
- Protein: 11.6
- Total Fat: 16.9
- Saturated Fat: 6.8
- Sodium: 689.1
- Fiber: 1.3

## 263. Perfect Health Pancakes (7 Points Per Serving On Weight Watchers

*Serving: 4 serving(s) | Prep: 20mins | Ready in:*

## Ingredients

- 3/4 cup oats (old fashioned or quick oats will work. I use old fashioned though)
- 3/4 cup wheat flour
- 1 tablespoon vital wheat gluten
- 1/4 cup winter squash (Pureed. Can be found in the freezer aisle next to the frozen spinach)
- 2 tablespoons sugar (or honey)
- 2 teaspoons baking powder
- 1/2 teaspoon salt
- 2 large eggs
- 1 1/2 cups skim milk (any milk should be fine though)
- 3 tablespoons vegetable oil (or some other fat such as melted butter)
- 1/4 teaspoon cinnamon

## Direction

- Measure and combine dry ingredients into one bowl. Mix to combine ingredients well.
- Measure and combine wet ingredients in another bowl. Use a whisk to combine thoroughly.
- Pour the wet ingredients into the dry ingredients and mix gently. You want to combine all ingredients well without over mixing. Overmixing will make a tough pancake.
- Set bowl aside for at least 10 minutes. The oats need some time to get soft and incorporate well into the batter.
- In the meantime, turn on a griddle to 325 degrees or a large skillet to about medium heat.
- Apply a thin layer of oil to the griddle or skillet. (I pour a blob of oil on there and then wipe gently with a paper towel so there is just a thin film left).
- Stir the batter gently a couple of times to redistribute the oats in the batter and pour pancake batter onto preheated griddle with a scant 1/4 cup measure.
- When small bubbles appear on the surface of the pancake, it's time to flip (about 2 or 3 minutes per side).
- Serve with maple syrup or any other yummy pancake topping. To avoid sugar, try peanut

butter or cream cheese.  My 20 month old son likes his this way.
- *This recipe is very versatile.  Add fruit, flax seeds, chocolate chips, or whatever to the batter before cooking for a little change.

## Nutrition Information

- Calories: 383.2
- Saturated Fat: 2.7
- Fiber: 6
- Sugar: 6.7
- Total Fat: 15.4
- Sodium: 563.7
- Total Carbohydrate: 48.6
- Cholesterol: 107.6
- Protein: 14.9

### 264. Pickle And Ring Bologna Sandwich Spread

*Serving: 8 sandwiches, 6-8 serving(s) | Prep: 15mins | Ready in:*

## Ingredients

- 1 lb pickled ring bologna
- 1 (24 ounce) jar baby dill pickles
- 5 tablespoons light mayonnaise

## Direction

- Using a grinder, grind up and your bologna and all your pickles in a bowl.
- Next add about 5 tablespoons of light mayo, or more to your taste, and mix well.
- Finally enjoy on your favorite bread, or stuff in pita pockets for quick and easy snacks.

## Nutrition Information

- Calories: 876.8
- Total Fat: 69.8
- Saturated Fat: 25.5
- Sodium: 3062.3
- Fiber: 1.3
- Cholesterol: 164.4
- Sugar: 13.8
- Total Carbohydrate: 18.7
- Protein: 41.3

### 265. Pineapple Carrot Juice

*Serving: 1 serving(s) | Prep: 3mins | Ready in:*

## Ingredients

- 4 large carrots (washed, topped and tailed)
- 1/2 fresh pineapple (top and skin removed)

## Direction

- Juice the fruit, stir and serve!

## Nutrition Information

- Calories: 344.3
- Saturated Fat: 0.1
- Sodium: 203.2
- Fiber: 14.4
- Total Carbohydrate: 87
- Total Fat: 1.2
- Sugar: 58.2
- Cholesterol: 0
- Protein: 5.1

### 266. Pizza Cookie I

*Serving: 48 cookies | Prep: 15mins | Ready in:*

## Ingredients

- Crust
- 3/4 cup all-purpose flour
- 1/2 teaspoon baking powder
- 1/2 teaspoon baking soda

- 1 pinch salt
- 1/2 cup vegetable shortening
- 3/4 cup packed light brown sugar
- 1 large egg
- 1 teaspoon vanilla extract
- 1 cup rolled oats
- 1/2 cup flaked coconut
- Topping
- 1 cup semi-sweet chocolate chips (6 ounces)
- 1 cup walnuts, chopped
- 1/2 cup M's plain chocolate candy

## Direction

- Preheat the oven to 350 degrees F.
- Lightly grease a 14 to 15-inch pizza pan.
- Combine the flour, baking powder, baking soda, and salt.
- In a large bowl, cream the vegetable shortening and brown sugar.
- Beat in the egg and vanilla.
- Gradually blend in the dry ingredients.
- Fold in the oats and coconut.
- Press the dough evenly into the prepared pan.
- Sprinkle the chocolate chips and walnuts evenly over the top.
- Bake for 12 to 15 minutes, until lightly colored.
- Sprinkle the M's over the hot cookies.
- Cool in the pan on a wire rack for a few minutes before cutting into wedges.

## Nutrition Information

- Calories: 94.2
- Sodium: 26.8
- Sugar: 7
- Cholesterol: 4.7
- Protein: 1.2
- Saturated Fat: 1.9
- Fiber: 0.7
- Total Carbohydrate: 10.4
- Total Fat: 5.7

## 267. Pizza Jaffle

*Serving: 2 jaffles | Prep: 5mins | Ready in:*

## Ingredients

- 30 g ham, diced
- 1/2 cup tasty cheese, grated
- 1/3 cup capsicum, diced
- 1/4 cup fresh tomato, diced
- 1/2 cup mushroom, sliced
- 1/4 cup onion, finely diced
- 1/4 teaspoon dried basil
- 1/2 teaspoon garlic, crushed
- 2 teaspoons tomato paste
- 4 slices bread
- margarine or butter, to coat

## Direction

- Plug in the sandwich maker to heat up.
- In a medium size mixing bowl combine all ingredients except tomato paste and bread.
- Spread butter onto one side of the bread and tomato paste onto the other. Place 2 of these bread slices into the jaffle maker, butter side down. Top with pizza filling.
- Place remaining slices of bread on top, paste side facing into the pizza filling.
- Cook until browned to your liking.

## Nutrition Information

- Calories: 315
- Sugar: 5.3
- Total Carbohydrate: 31.7
- Cholesterol: 42.5
- Total Fat: 13.6
- Saturated Fat: 7.7
- Sodium: 818.8
- Fiber: 2.6
- Protein: 16.8

## 268. Pizza By The Slice

*Serving: 8 serving(s) | Prep: 10mins | Ready in:*

### Ingredients

- 1 medium tomatoes
- 2 ounces sliced hard salami (about 6 slices)
- 2 ounces mozzarella cheese, shredded (1/2 C)
- 1 (8 ounce) package refrigerated crescent dinner rolls
- 1/2 teaspoon dried oregano

### Direction

- Preheat oven to 375°F.
- Remove stem end of tomato and cut tomato into several large chunks, then coarsely chop.
- Stack salami slices, two at a time and cut into small wedges.
- Unroll crescent dough on cutting board and separate into 8 triangles.
- Arrange the triangles on a flat baking stone or pizza pan so they do not touch.
- Sprinkle triangles with equal amounts of tomato (or sauce), salami, cheese and oregano.
- Bake 15-18 minutes or until edges are golden brown.

### Nutrition Information

- Calories: 117.8
- Sugar: 1.7
- Protein: 4.8
- Total Carbohydrate: 15.6
- Cholesterol: 21.5
- Total Fat: 3.9
- Saturated Fat: 1.6
- Sodium: 233.6
- Fiber: 1.3

## 269. Platanutres (Plantain Chips)

*Serving: 4-6 serving(s) | Prep: 20mins | Ready in:*

### Ingredients

- 4 green plantains
- vegetable oil
- salt

### Direction

- Trim off both ends from each of the plantains with a sharp knife, then make a few slits through the skin the length of each plantain. Push your thumb between the skin and the flesh and pry skin away from flesh. It will come off in pieces, like bark from a tree. Trim off any woody fiber stuck to plantains. Slice plantains crosswise into thin rounds.
- Pour oil into a large heavy skillet to a depth of 1/2", then heat to 350° on a candy thermometer over medium-high heat. Add plantain slices a few at a time to the oil to prevent them from sticking to one another, and fry them in batches until lightly golden and crisp, about 3 minutes.
- Transfer plantain chips with a slotted spoon to paper towels to drain. Season to taste with salt while still hot.

### Nutrition Information

- Calories: 218.4
- Saturated Fat: 0.3
- Total Carbohydrate: 57.1
- Protein: 2.3
- Cholesterol: 0
- Total Fat: 0.7
- Sodium: 7.2
- Fiber: 4.1
- Sugar: 26.9

## 270. Portabella Burger

*Serving: 8 serving(s) | Prep: 15mins | Ready in:*

### Ingredients

- 1 medium onion, minced
- 2 shallots, minced
- 1/8 teaspoon salt
- 1 cup dried portabella mushroom (I just use all fresh)
- 2 cups stemmed fresh portabella mushrooms
- 12 ounces extra firm tofu
- 1/3 cup toasted wheat germ
- 1/3 cup breadcrumbs
- 3/4 cup quick-cooking oats
- 2 tablespoons low sodium soy sauce or 2 tablespoons soy sauce
- 2 tablespoons Worcestershire sauce
- 1 teaspoon liquid smoke
- 1/2 teaspoon garlic granules

### Direction

- Preheat oven to 375 degrees.
- Lightly coat a heavy skillet with cooking spray and sauté onion, shallots and salt in olive oil for about five minutes.
- Stem softened dry mushrooms and mince with fresh mushrooms in a food processor.
- Add to onions and cook another 10 minutes, stirring occasionally to prevent sticking.
- Mix mushrooms with mashed tofu and add remaining ingredients.
- Mix well.
- Measure eight 1/2-cup portions.
- Wet hands with water to prevent sticking and form into patties.
- Place them side by side on a cookie sheet coated with cooking oil spray.
- Bake for 25 minutes, turning after 15 minutes.
- Before serving the burgers, heat them in a heavy skillet coated with cooking spray and grill a few minutes on each side.

### Nutrition Information

- Calories: 115.8
- Cholesterol: 0
- Fiber: 2.7
- Sugar: 2.5
- Total Carbohydrate: 16.3
- Protein: 7.4
- Total Fat: 3.1
- Saturated Fat: 0.6
- Sodium: 254.5

## 271. Potato, Bacon And Sauerkraut Patties

*Serving: 6-8 patties, depending on size, 6 serving(s) | Prep: 6mins | Ready in:*

### Ingredients

- 1 teaspoon oil
- 3 slices bacon, chopped
- 1 onion, finely minced
- 2 cups mashed potatoes
- 1/2 tablespoon sour cream (your mashed potatoes may already be adequately creamy) (optional)
- 410 g edgell sauerkraut, well drained
- 1 egg, lightly beaten
- 1 teaspoon brown sugar, to taste
- 1 teaspoon caraway seed
- fresh ground pepper, to taste
- salt, to taste (depends on how much salt has already been added to the potato and sauerkraut)
- 2 tablespoons oil, for cooking

### Direction

- Heat 1 teaspoon of oil in a large (preferably non-stick) pan, add the bacon and cook for about a minute, then add the onions and cook for another minute, or until the onion is just beginning to soften. Put the pan aside for use later in cooking the patties.
- In a medium-to-large bowl, combine the mashed potato, (optional) sour cream, the

- well-drained Edgell Sauerkraut, the egg, the cooked onion and bacon, the brown sugar, the caraway seeds and freshly ground black pepper, and (if necessary) salt, and mix well to combine all the ingredients.
- Shape the mixture into 1/2 cup patties. Heat 2 tablespoons of oil in the pan used for cooking the bacon and onions, add the patties and cook for 2-3 minutes on each side or until golden brown.
- Serve as part of a "big breakfast" or with barbecued sausages.
- TIP: Chopped fresh herbs such as parsley or thyme can be added in step 2.

## Nutrition Information

- Calories: 193.7
- Fiber: 3.1
- Sugar: 3.9
- Total Carbohydrate: 18.1
- Cholesterol: 44.4
- Protein: 4.6
- Total Fat: 11.8
- Saturated Fat: 2.9
- Sodium: 770

## 272. Praline Pecan Crunch

*Serving: 10 cups | Prep: 0S | Ready in:*

## Ingredients

- 8 cups Quaker Oatmeal Squares Cereal
- 2 cups pecan pieces
- 1/2 cup light corn syrup
- 1/2 cup brown sugar, firmly packed
- 1/4 cup margarine (1/2 stick) or 1/4 cup butter (1/2 stick)
- 1 teaspoon vanilla
- 1/2 teaspoon baking soda

## Direction

- Heat oven to 250 F.
- Combine cereal and pecans in 13x9-inch baking pan; set aside.
- In large microwaveable bowl, combine corn syrup, brown sugar and margarine. Microwave at HIGH 1 minute 30 seconds; stir. Microwave an additional 30 seconds to 1 minute 30 seconds or until boiling.
- Stir in vanilla and baking soda and pour over cereal mixture; stir to coat evenly.
- Bake 1 hour, stirring every 15 minutes.
- Spread on baking sheet to cool; break into pieces.

## Nutrition Information

- Calories: 451.8
- Sodium: 330.1
- Sugar: 23.4
- Total Carbohydrate: 62.1
- Cholesterol: 0
- Total Fat: 22.2
- Saturated Fat: 2.7
- Fiber: 5.3
- Protein: 7

## 273. Pretzel Butterflies

*Serving: 1 serving(s) | Prep: 3mins | Ready in:*

## Ingredients

- 1 caramel squares
- 2 curly pretzels
- 2 straight pretzels

## Direction

- Press two curly pretzels into the sides of a caramel square for wings.
- Position two straight pretzels at the top to serve as antennas.

## Nutrition Information

- Calories: 38.6
- Protein: 0.5
- Total Fat: 0.8
- Fiber: 0
- Sugar: 6.6
- Cholesterol: 0.7
- Saturated Fat: 0.2
- Sodium: 24.8
- Total Carbohydrate: 7.8

## 274. Princess Spam's Polynesian Pizza

*Serving: 6 serving(s) | Prep: 15mins | Ready in:*

### Ingredients

- 1 (12 ounce) package Spam
- 16 ounces mozzarella cheese
- 1 (4 ounce) can pineapple tidbits
- 1 cup pizza sauce
- 1 pre-made pizza crust

### Direction

- Princess Spam's Polynesian Pizza.
- Spread sauce over crust. Evenly sprinkle pineapple tidbits over sauce. In a large bowl pour all cheese and then grate all of spam into cheese (with a cheese grater). Very gently fold cheese and spam together then arrange over pizza. Bake for 12 minutes. KIDS love this.

### Nutrition Information

- Calories: 432.9
- Saturated Fat: 15.7
- Fiber: 1.1
- Total Carbohydrate: 9.5
- Cholesterol: 100.3
- Total Fat: 32.7
- Protein: 25.2
- Sodium: 1319.4
- Sugar: 3.4

## 275. Puppy Chow Snack Mix

*Serving: 10-12 serving(s) | Prep: 20mins | Ready in:*

### Ingredients

- 1 (12 ounce) bag chocolate chips
- 1/2 cup butter
- 1 cup peanut butter
- 1 (12 ounce) box Crispix cereal or 1 (12 ounce) boxsimilar cereal
- 1 lb confectioners' sugar

### Direction

- Melt chocolate chips, butter peanut butter over medium heat. Stir to blend.
- Pour over Crispix in large bowl.
- Pour confectioners' sugar in paper grocery bag.
- Add Crispix and shake vigorously until it breaks apart. Serve in new doggie dish.

### Nutrition Information

- Calories: 701.1
- Sugar: 69.4
- Total Carbohydrate: 101.2
- Protein: 10.3
- Sodium: 459.6
- Saturated Fat: 14.7
- Fiber: 3.9
- Cholesterol: 24.4
- Total Fat: 32.8

## 276. Puree Verte Potato, Fennel, And Fava Mash

*Serving: 8 serving(s) | Prep: 20mins | Ready in:*

### Ingredients

- 3 lbs unshucked fava beans
- boiling water
- ice
- tap water
- 3 lbs yukon gold potatoes
- 1 large fennel bulb
- 1 cup half-and-half
- 1/2 cup butter
- kosher salt
- fresh ground black pepper, to taste

### Direction

- Shuck the fava beans (remove them from the shells - most of the prep time for this recipe is during this step).
- In a large pot, bring water to a boil.
- In a bowl, combine ice and tap water to make ice water; set aside.
- Add the shelled favas to the boiling water and let cook for about 3 minutes, then remove from saucepan and immediately plunge into the ice water to halt the cooking.
- Let the beans cool, then peel the outer skin from each of them; discard skins, set favas aside.
- Peel and cut potatoes into 1/2-inch pieces; cut the fennel bulb into 1/2-inch pieces (you can save the fronds for another recipe, or use them as garnish).
- Place potato and fennel pieces into a deep pot and cover with cold water; bring water to a boil and simmer for 20 minutes or until tender.
- Add the shucked/blanched/peeled favas and cook for another 5 minutes.
- Drain well, then pass everything through a food mill - do not use an electric mixer to combine the mixture - a food mill will give the best texture for this dish.
- Over medium low temperature, heat together the half and half and butter until the butter is melted.
- Add liquid mixture to the milled puree a little at a time until desired consistency is reached (you might not end up using all the liquid).
- Stir well to incorporate, season to taste with salt and freshly ground pepper, and serve.

### Nutrition Information

- Calories: 486.4
- Saturated Fat: 9.6
- Sodium: 126.2
- Sugar: 4.6
- Total Carbohydrate: 71.4
- Total Fat: 15.9
- Cholesterol: 41.7
- Protein: 17.5
- Fiber: 13.3

## 277. Purple Dazzle Shakes

*Serving: 2-3 serving(s) | Prep: 10mins | Ready in:*

### Ingredients

- 1 (6 ounce) canpurple frozen grape juice concentrate, thawed
- 1/2 cup milk
- 1 tablespoon lemon juice
- 3 scoops vanilla ice cream
- Topping ingredients (if desired)
- additional vanilla ice cream
- purple jelly beans
- purple sprinkles (from Halloween) or purple sugar (from Halloween)

### Direction

- Place grape juice concentrate, milk and lemon juice in a blender and blend for 1 minute. Add ice cream and blend until smooth.

- Pour into serving glasses. If desired top with a small scoop of ice cream and jelly beans and/or sprinkles.
- Serve immediately.

## Nutrition Information

- Calories: 273.7
- Total Fat: 8.6
- Sugar: 40.7
- Cholesterol: 32.3
- Saturated Fat: 5.1
- Sodium: 75.7
- Fiber: 0.8
- Total Carbohydrate: 45.6
- Protein: 5.6

### 278. Purple Monstrosity Fruit Smoothie

*Serving: 4 serving(s) | Prep: 5mins | Ready in:*

## Ingredients

- 2 frozen bananas, skins removed and cut in chunks
- 1/2 cup frozen blueberries
- 1 cup orange juice
- 1 tablespoon honey (optional)
- 1 teaspoon vanilla extract

## Direction

- Place bananas, blueberries and juice in a blender and puree.
- Add honey and/or vanilla to taste.
- Add more or less orange juice depending on the thickness you want for your smoothie.

## Nutrition Information

- Calories: 106.7
- Total Fat: 0.4
- Sodium: 1.6
- Sugar: 18.2
- Cholesterol: 0
- Protein: 1.2
- Saturated Fat: 0.1
- Fiber: 2.3
- Total Carbohydrate: 26.4

### 279. Quick Chewy/Crunchy Coconut Yogurt

*Serving: 1 snack, 1 serving(s) | Prep: 5mins | Ready in:*

## Ingredients

- 1/4 cup yoplait custard style blackberry yogurt (or any other brand or flavor)
- 1/4 cup sweetened flaked coconut

## Direction

- *For a chewy snack, leave coconut untoasted and mix thoroughly with yogurt.
- *For a crunchy and more coconuty snack, spread coconut evenly on an ungreased baking sheet.
- Toast in a 300 degree oven until lightly brown, about 4-5 minutes.
- Mix with yogurt.

## Nutrition Information

- Calories: 116.5
- Sodium: 60.9
- Fiber: 1.1
- Sugar: 10
- Cholesterol: 0
- Protein: 0.7
- Total Fat: 8.2
- Total Carbohydrate: 11.1
- Saturated Fat: 7.3

## 280. Quick Microwave S'mores

*Serving: 1 serving(s) | Prep: 5mins | Ready in:*

### Ingredients

- 1 graham cracker
- 1 large marshmallows
- 1 teaspoon hot fudge

### Direction

- Break graham cracker in half crosswise.
- Place one half on small paper plate or microwavable plate; top with marshmallow.
- Spread remaining 1/2 of cracker with fudge sauce.
- Place cracker with marshmallow in microwave.
- Microwave at HIGH 12 to 14 seconds or until marshmallow puffs up.
- Immediately place remaining cracker, fudge side down, over marshmallow.
- Press crackers gently to even out marshmallow layer.
- Cool completely.

### Nutrition Information

- Calories: 74.2
- Sugar: 8.3
- Total Carbohydrate: 15.1
- Protein: 0.9
- Fiber: 0.4
- Saturated Fat: 0.4
- Sodium: 70
- Cholesterol: 0.1
- Total Fat: 1.3

## 281. Quick Raw Apple Sundae

*Serving: 2 sundaes, 2 serving(s) | Prep: 7mins | Ready in:*

### Ingredients

- 2 apples
- 2 tablespoons almond butter
- 1/4 cup maple syrup
- 1 1/2 teaspoons almond extract
- 2 tablespoons sliced almonds
- 2 tablespoons desiccated coconut, grated

### Direction

- Coarsely chop almonds and set aside for topping.
- In a small mixing bowl, blend the almond butter, maple syrup, and almond extract until smooth. It should be similar in consistency to a caramel sauce. (Drool).
- Core the apples into quarters and dice them. Divide between two serving bowls.
- Drizzle the sauce over the two bowls of apples and top with almonds and coconut. Serve immediately.

### Nutrition Information

- Calories: 341.9
- Sugar: 41.7
- Total Carbohydrate: 53.1
- Protein: 4.1
- Total Fat: 14.1
- Saturated Fat: 2.5
- Sodium: 89
- Fiber: 4.8
- Cholesterol: 0

## 282. Quinoa Granola Bars

*Serving: 40 bars | Prep: 4hours | Ready in:*

### Ingredients

- Granola
- 1/2 cup soaked quinoa (1/4 cup dry)
- 2 cups rolled oats
- 1/4 cup wheat germ

- 1/4 cup slivered almonds (optional)
- 1/4 cup sunflower seeds
- 1/4 cup sesame seeds
- 1/4 cup coconut
- 1/4 cup cooking oil
- 1/4 cup honey
- Granola Bars
- 2 cups cooked quinoa (3/4 cup dry)
- 1/2 cup mixed dried fruit (I used apricot, pear, apple, and cranberry)
- 1/2 cup raisins
- 1/2 teaspoon salt
- 1 teaspoon lemon juice
- 1/2 teaspoon vanilla
- 1/2-1 banana
- granola cereal
- 1/2 cup chopped dates or 1/2 cup other dried fruit
- 1/2 cup raisins

## Direction

- Soak dry quinoa in 1/2 cup of water for two hours.
- To make the granola, mix all dry granola ingredients, including the soaked quinoa, in a bowl.
- Preheat oven to 250 degrees.
- Heat oil and honey in a small saucepan until thin; stir into dry ingredients until mixed.
- Pour the granola mixture into a jelly roll pan and toast for 1 hour at 250 degrees, stirring occasionally.
- Store in a plastic bag until ready to use.
- Cook mixed dried fruit with 2 cups water at a simmer half the water has evaporated (about 45 minutes).
- Add 3/4 cup dry quinoa and enough water to cover plus a quarter inch and cook over medium heat 20 minutes, adding more water as needed.
- Preheat oven to 400 degrees.
- Set aside 1 cup cooked quinoa; pour the rest of the quinoa with cooking liquid and fruit pieces into a blender.
- Blend until large fruit pieces are chopped up.
- Add 1/2 cup raisins, the salt, lemon juice, vanilla, and banana.
- Blend.
- (Mixture will be thick; stop the blender and push with spoon if you have to, adding water if needed) Spoon blender mixture into a bowl, stirring in granola, 1/2 cup dried fruit, and 1/2 cup raisins.
- Press into a greased and floured glass baking dish and bake at 400 degrees for 15 minutes.
- Cool.
- Cut into desired number of bars.

## Nutrition Information

- Calories: 113.4
- Protein: 2.8
- Total Fat: 3.6
- Saturated Fat: 0.7
- Sodium: 32.8
- Fiber: 1.9
- Sugar: 5.6
- Total Carbohydrate: 18.8
- Cholesterol: 0

## 283. Raspberry Peach Smoothie (Diabetic)

*Serving: 12 oz, 2 serving(s) | Prep: 5mins | Ready in:*

## Ingredients

- 1/2 cup nonfat milk
- 1/4 cup nonfat plain yogurt (Greek was suggested in the recipe)
- 1/2 cup frozen peaches
- 1/2 cup frozen raspberries
- 1/2 small peeled apple
- 1/2 tablespoon honey
- 1/2 tablespoon artificial sweetener (Splenda)

## Direction

- Place all ingredients in the blender and process on high until smooth.
- NOTE: I had to add more milk than the recipe called for, as mine was too thick.

## Nutrition Information

- Calories: 191.4
- Fiber: 4.5
- Total Carbohydrate: 44.6
- Saturated Fat: 0.1
- Sodium: 60.3
- Protein: 4.8
- Total Fat: 0.4
- Sugar: 40
- Cholesterol: 1.8

### 284. Red, White And Green French Bread Pizza

*Serving: 6 serving(s) | Prep: 5mins | Ready in:*

## Ingredients

- 1/2 cup prepared pesto sauce
- 1 (8 ounce) jarfire roasted red peppers, drained and sliced
- 1 cup shredded part-skim mozzarella cheese
- 1 loaf French bread, split lengthwise

## Direction

- Preheat broiler.
- Spread pesto over each halve of French bread. Top with pepper slices and then with shredded cheese.
- Place on baking sheet and broil for 1-2 minutes or until cheese is melted.
- Cut each pizza into thirds and serve immediately.

## Nutrition Information

- Calories: 310
- Total Fat: 8.4
- Sugar: 0.6
- Protein: 16.1
- Saturated Fat: 4.3
- Sodium: 1211.9
- Fiber: 2.7
- Total Carbohydrate: 41.8
- Cholesterol: 24.2

### 285. Reese's Snack Mix

*Serving: 1/2 cup, 12 serving(s) | Prep: 3mins | Ready in:*

## Ingredients

- 1 cup peanut butter cookie crisp cereal
- 2 cups Reese's Puffs cereal
- 1 cup Reese's pieces
- 10 ounces peanut butter chips

## Direction

- Mix all ingredients together, being careful not to crush or smash the cereal.
- Store in a large ziplock bag, or an airtight container.

## Nutrition Information

- Calories: 241.1
- Fiber: 1.6
- Sugar: 21.3
- Sodium: 141.3
- Saturated Fat: 5.8
- Total Carbohydrate: 27.9
- Cholesterol: 0
- Protein: 6.8
- Total Fat: 11.6

### 286. Refresher Smoothie

*Serving: 1 serving(s) | Prep: 2mins | Ready in:*

## Ingredients

- 2 large pineapple slices
- 2 pears, skinned cored
- 4 strawberries
- 1 dash orange juice or 1 dash apple juice

## Direction

- Blend all ingredients until smooth.

## Nutrition Information

- Calories: 288.6
- Total Fat: 0.7
- Saturated Fat: 0
- Sodium: 5.5
- Sugar: 50.3
- Fiber: 13.6
- Total Carbohydrate: 76.2
- Cholesterol: 0
- Protein: 2.5

## 287. Rice Krispies " Apple Pie"

*Serving: 1 serving(s) | Prep: 3mins | Ready in:*

## Ingredients

- 1/2 cup Rice Krispies
- 2 tablespoons reduced-calorie maple syrup
- 1/4 cup no-sugar-added fat free vanilla ice cream
- 1/2 teaspoon cinnamon

## Direction

- Measure out 1/2 cup rice krispies into a microwavable bowl.
- Add cinnamon and the 2 T. of syrup.
- Microwave for about 20 seconds or until bubbly, remove and stir until mixed evenly.
- Add ice cream and enjoy the flavors of faux apple pie!

## Nutrition Information

- Calories: 57.4
- Fiber: 0.8
- Protein: 1
- Total Fat: 0.1
- Saturated Fat: 0
- Sodium: 78.7
- Cholesterol: 0
- Sugar: 1.4
- Total Carbohydrate: 13

## 288. Roasted Honey And Spice Nuts

*Serving: 4 serving(s) | Prep: 5mins | Ready in:*

## Ingredients

- 1 1/2 ounces butter
- 2 tablespoons clear honey
- 1 -2 teaspoon mild chili powder (according to taste)
- 1/2 teaspoon salt
- 1 pinch fresh ground black pepper
- 10 ounces mixed unsalted nuts, e.g. almonds, cashews, pecans, hazelnuts, walnuts, peanuts

## Direction

- Preheat the oven to 300°F Place the butter in a saucepan and heat gently, until melted.
- Stir in the honey and season with chili powder, salt and freshly ground black pepper.
- Add the nuts and stir together until thoroughly coated. Transfer to a large, shallow non-stick baking tray and roast for 20-25 minutes, or until glazed, stirring two to three times.
- Allow to cool slightly and eat warm, or cool completely and store in an airtight container for up to 1 week.

## Nutrition Information

- Calories: 186.7
- Protein: 3.2
- Sodium: 604.9
- Fiber: 8.6
- Total Carbohydrate: 22.3
- Cholesterol: 22.9
- Total Fat: 12.8
- Saturated Fat: 6.2
- Sugar: 10.4

## 289. S'mores Pretzels Quesadillas

*Serving: 6 serving(s) | Prep: 5mins | Ready in:*

### Ingredients

- 2 flour tortillas (burrito sized)
- 1/2 cup milk chocolate chips
- 1/2 cup pretzel, broken into small pieces
- 6 large marshmallows, cut in half
- cooking spray

### Direction

- Preheat oven to 250 degrees. On a surface that you can easily slide the tortillas off of, spray with the cooking spray one side of the tortilla, and place sprayed side down.
- Divide the chocolate chips and pretzels evenly between the two tortillas, and spread evenly. Top with the marshmallows.
- Slide the tortillas onto the oven rack, and bake about 5 minutes until chocolate has melted. Switch the oven to broil until the marshmallows have browned.
- Remove from oven and fold each tortilla in half. Cut each tortilla into 3 wedges and serve.

### Nutrition Information

- Calories: 200.3
- Sugar: 11.9
- Protein: 4
- Sodium: 337.2
- Saturated Fat: 2.9
- Fiber: 1.4
- Total Carbohydrate: 34.2
- Cholesterol: 3.2
- Total Fat: 5.4

## 290. Salami Cheese Bread

*Serving: 4 serving(s) | Prep: 10mins | Ready in:*

### Ingredients

- 40 g butter
- 100 g salami, chopped
- 4 green onions, chopped
- 1 small French baguette
- 1/2 cup tasty cheese, grated

### Direction

- Combine softened butter, salami and green onions in a bowl, beat until well combined.
- Split the bread in half lengthways, spread salami mixture over the cut surfaces of the bread.
- Press cheese on lightly, cut bread into quarters crossways.
- Cook under a hot grill until cheese is melted.

### Nutrition Information

- Calories: 382.4
- Sodium: 836.9
- Cholesterol: 56.5
- Protein: 13.2
- Total Fat: 21
- Saturated Fat: 11.5
- Fiber: 2.3
- Sugar: 1
- Total Carbohydrate: 35

## 291. Salt Pepper Dirty Potato Chips

*Serving: 8-10 serving(s) | Prep: 15mins | Ready in:*

### Ingredients

- 4-5 large potatoes
- 2 tablespoons kosher salt
- 1 tablespoon ground black pepper
- 1/2 teaspoon white pepper
- 1/4 teaspoon garlic powder
- 1/4 teaspoon onion powder
- safflower oil (for frying)

### Direction

- Wash potatoes making sure skin is free of dirt. If you prefer "clean" chips, peel the potatoes.
- Mix together all spices in a small dish and set aside.
- Slice on a mandolin and drop into cold, salted water. You can try to slice by hand, but it's very difficult to get them thin enough.
- In deep iron skillet pour oil about 1 1/2 " deep and heat to 365°F. As oil is heating pour water off potatoes and gently pat dry.
- Drop slices 1 at a time into hot oil until a single layer is cooking (about 15-20 slices depending on your pan). Let cook until golden brown. Remove into paper bag to soak up excess oil.
- When potatoes are all done, sprinkle spiced salt mix to taste over chips and shake bag to evenly coat. Add a little at a time, you can always add more, but it's darn difficult to pick off those grains of salt if there are too many.

### Nutrition Information

- Calories: 145.1
- Saturated Fat: 0.1
- Sodium: 1755.6
- Fiber: 4.3
- Sugar: 1.5
- Total Carbohydrate: 33
- Protein: 3.9
- Total Fat: 0.2
- Cholesterol: 0

## 292. Sarah's Party Roast Beef Rounds

*Serving: 10 rounds, 10 serving(s) | Prep: 5mins | Ready in:*

### Ingredients

- 1 lb roast beef
- 1 French baguette
- 1 English cucumber
- 1 cup mayonnaise
- 3 tablespoons prepared horseradish
- 2 tablespoons fresh dill
- 4 tablespoons parmesan cheese
- 3 tablespoons garlic powder

### Direction

- Mix together: a good amount of mayo, horseradish to taste depending on how hot you want the spread, tons of dill, a good amount of park cheese and four shakes of garlic powder. Place spread in refrigerator for as long as possible. You can even leave it overnight. The longer the better.
- When ready to put together.
- Cut baguette into little toasts and place on baking sheet and in a 350° oven until golden brown on both sides. Then let cool before assembly.
- Cut roast beef to fit on baguette toasts.
- Cut cucumber thin as possible.
- Assembly: toast, spread, cucumber, and roast beef.

### Nutrition Information

- Calories: 217.6
- Saturated Fat: 3

- Sodium: 272
- Sugar: 2.6
- Total Carbohydrate: 13
- Total Fat: 12.4
- Fiber: 0.7
- Cholesterol: 43.2
- Protein: 14.6

## 293. Saratoga Chips

*Serving: 4 serving(s) | Prep: 35mins | Ready in:*

### Ingredients

- 4 large oval idaho potatoes
- salt
- black pepper
- peanut oil (for frying) or vegetable oil (for frying)
- ice water
- 1/2 cup smoky barbecue sauce (optional)
- brown paper (bags)
- paper, toweling

### Direction

- Pare potatoes and slice thinly and evenly (a mandolin works well for this).
- Submerge potatoes in ice water and allow to sit for about 30 minutes, separating slices so the starch on each is rinsed.
- Heat oil in a large kettle or fryer to 375°F.
- Drain potatoes from the water and pat dry using paper toweling, making sure they are completely dry.
- Fry potatoes in small batches, until golden.
- Drain potatoes and place on clean brown paper, and season to your liking.
- Keep potatoes in oven on low temperature to keep warm while finishing other potatoes, if necessary.
- Serve chips with smoky barbecue sauce.

### Nutrition Information

- Calories: 284.1
- Fiber: 8.1
- Sugar: 2.9
- Total Carbohydrate: 64.5
- Protein: 7.5
- Total Fat: 0.3
- Saturated Fat: 0.1
- Sodium: 22.1
- Cholesterol: 0

## 294. Sassy Citrus Dip

*Serving: 4 serving(s) | Prep: 2mins | Ready in:*

### Ingredients

- 1 cup no-sugar-added nonfat lemon yogurt (8 oz. container)
- 1 tablespoon lemon juice
- 3 packets sugar substitute
- cantaloupe, cut to bite size

### Direction

- Mix all ingredients.
- Serve as dip with cantaloupe chunks.

### Nutrition Information

- Calories: 3.7
- Sodium: 0
- Total Carbohydrate: 1
- Cholesterol: 0
- Protein: 0
- Total Fat: 0
- Saturated Fat: 0
- Fiber: 0
- Sugar: 0.7

## 295. Sausage Rolls Cheese Pufs

*Serving: 30 pieces | Prep: 50mins | Ready in:*

### Ingredients

- 250 g margarine
- 200 g sour cream
- 500 g self rising flour
- 15 small sausages
- 1 egg
- 200 g feta cheese
- pepper

### Direction

- For the dough.
- Mix the margarine, the flour and the sour cream. Knead the dough for 4 minutes.
- Roll the dough into a big circle and cut into small ones, by using a mug. Continue until all the dough is finished.
- Fill half of the little circles with sausages and the others with cheese.
- For the ham rolls, place one sausage at the middle of the circle and pinch the edges.
- For the cheese filling. Mix the egg with the feta cheese and a little pepper. This should be done at the last minute before filling or else it gets "soggy". Put into the circles one spoon of the filling and pinch the edges.
- Bake in preheated oven at 350°F for 40 minutes until done.

### Nutrition Information

- Calories: 252.5
- Sodium: 601.4
- Fiber: 0.6
- Sugar: 0.3
- Total Carbohydrate: 16.1
- Cholesterol: 36
- Total Fat: 17.3
- Saturated Fat: 5.5
- Protein: 7.7

## 296. Savoury Afternoon Tea / Picnic Tarts / Quiches

*Serving: 12 quiches | Prep: 30mins | Ready in:*

### Ingredients

- butter, for greasing
- 12 ounces ready-to-roll shortcrust pastry
- flour, for dusting
- 2 egg yolks
- 2 whole eggs
- 2/3 cup single cream
- flaked sea salt  freshly ground black pepper
- For the goat cheese and tomato filling
- 3 1/2 ounces mild goat cheese
- 1 tablespoon basil leaves, shredded
- 2 tomatoes, thinly sliced
- for the ham
- 3 1/2 ounces cooked ham, cut into small pieces
- 3 1/2 ounces mature cheddar cheese, grated
- 2 teaspoons coarse grain mustard

### Direction

- Preheat the oven to 350F and lightly butter a 12-hole deep muffin tin.
- Roll out the pastry on a lightly floured surface. Using a 4-5in pastry cutter, cut out 12 circles. Loosely press them into the muffin tin, retaining a frilly or wobbly edge to them, rather than pressing in firmly around the edges. Chill in the refrigerator.
- In a mixing bowl, beat together the egg yolks, whole eggs and cream and season with salt and pepper. This is your basic mixture, ready to add your chosen flavours.
- If you are doing the goat cheese and tomato filling, crumble the goat cheese into the chilled pastry cases and scatter over the basil. Pour over the egg mixture and then top each tart with thin slices of tomato.
- If you are doing the ham, cheddar and mustard filling, stir the ham, cheese and

- mustard into the egg mixture and divide it between the chilled pastry cases.
- Place the tarts in the oven for 30-35 minutes until the pastry is lightly golden and the eggs have set. Cool for about 10 minutes before removing from the tin. Serve warm or cold as a savoury afternoon treat.

## Nutrition Information

- Calories: 269.2
- Total Fat: 19.5
- Sodium: 254.8
- Sugar: 0.9
- Cholesterol: 98.5
- Protein: 9.7
- Saturated Fat: 8.3
- Fiber: 1.2
- Total Carbohydrate: 13.8

## 297. Season's Severed Finger Banana Muffins (Low Fat)

*Serving: 12 muffins | Prep: 10mins | Ready in:*

## Ingredients

- 2 cups whole wheat flour
- 1/2 cup sugar or 1/2 cup brown sugar
- 1 teaspoon baking powder
- 1 teaspoon baking soda
- 1 dash salt
- 1 egg
- 3 bananas
- 1 cup applesauce (chunky)
- 1/8 cup oil
- 1 teaspoon orange juice concentrate
- 1 cup nuts, chopped (optional)
- sugar (optional)
- cinnamon (optional)
- strawberry jam (optional)

## Direction

- Use either candy applesauce which is already red or add enough red food coloring to achieve a "red" color.
- Stir together all the dry ingredients and then mix in the wet ingredients - making sure not to over mix.
- Spoon into a lightly greased muffin tin. You can also at this stage sprinkle with cinnamon and sugar or lightly spoon strawberry jam on top.
- Bake at 350 degrees for 20-25 minutes.

## Nutrition Information

- Calories: 169.6
- Fiber: 3.5
- Sugar: 12.2
- Total Carbohydrate: 34.1
- Protein: 3.6
- Total Fat: 3.2
- Saturated Fat: 0.6
- Sodium: 161.2
- Cholesterol: 17.6

## 298. Shami Kebab(mutton Or Chicken)

*Serving: 3-4 per person, 1 serving(s) | Prep: 1hours | Ready in:*

## Ingredients

- 125 g yellow split peas
- 3 medium onions
- 4 cloves garlic
- 2 inches fresh ginger
- 150 ml cooking oil
- 2 teaspoons ground coriander
- 2 teaspoons ground black pepper
- 1 teaspoon ground cloves
- 1 teaspoon ground cinnamon
- 1 teaspoon cardamom powder
- 2 teaspoons red chili powder
- 900 g ground lamb or 900 g minced chicken

- 2 teaspoons salt
- 150 ml natural yoghurt
- 2 -3 eggs
- 2 tablespoons chopped coriander
- oil, for shallow frying

## Direction

- Soak split peas in water for 2 hours, or pour boiling water over and soak for 20 minutes.
- Peel onions and chop roughly.
- Peel and chop ginger and garlic.
- Heat oil in a large, heavy pan and soften onion.
- Add ginger, garlic and all powdered spices and fry for 1 minute.
- Add meat and split peas and stir constantly until all is mixed well and changes colour. Cook till peas soften slightly and the mixture is dry with no water remaining, cool, now add yoghurt.
- Transfer mixture to a processor, and whiz to smooth paste.
- Check seasoning.
- Remove to a bowl, add eggs and mix, preferably by hand.
- Peel and chop the 3rd onion and mix with chopped coriander leaves.
- Form spoonfuls of mixture into walnut-sized balls, press your thumb into each as you form it to indent it.
- Insert a little of the chopped onion mixture and reform ball around it.
- Now flatten on palm of your hands and shallow fry, turning carefully to brown on both sides.
- Drain on kitchen paper and serve, hot with chapati and salad.

## Nutrition Information

- Calories: 4518.1
- Total Carbohydrate: 128.5
- Cholesterol: 1087.8
- Saturated Fat: 113.7
- Sodium: 5443.1
- Fiber: 43.8
- Sugar: 28.3
- Total Fat: 357.5
- Protein: 200.2

## 299. Simple Tuna Salad

*Serving: 4-6 serving(s) | Prep: 2mins | Ready in:*

### Ingredients

- 400 g pasta (2 boxes kraft dinner white cheddar penne 200 gm.each)
- 1 (750 g) canflaked tuna
- 1/4 cup chopped onion

### Direction

- Make Kraft dinner according to package directions. Omit salt
- Add tuna and onions and mix.
- Eat warm or chill.

### Nutrition Information

- Calories: 645.2
- Total Fat: 10.7
- Fiber: 3.3
- Cholesterol: 71.2
- Protein: 56.9
- Saturated Fat: 2.6
- Sodium: 78.4
- Sugar: 2.2
- Total Carbohydrate: 75.7

## 300. Single Serve Cookies

*Serving: 1 serving(s) | Prep: 5mins | Ready in:*

### Ingredients

- 1 teaspoon margarine

- 2 teaspoons egg whites
- 1/2 teaspoon oil
- 1 teaspoon brown sugar
- 1/2 teaspoon white sugar
- 4 teaspoons flour
- 1 pinch baking soda
- 1 teaspoon chocolate chips or 1 teaspoon raisins

### Direction

- Preheat toaster oven to 350. Melt the margarine in a small bowl for about 20 seconds in the microwave. Add in the egg whites, oil and sugars. Mix well. Add in the flour and baking soda, mix to form batter. Add in chocolate chips or raisins. Spoon into two mounds on sprayed toaster oven baking sheet. Bake for ten minutes.

### Nutrition Information

- Calories: 138.8
- Sugar: 8.5
- Cholesterol: 0
- Protein: 2.3
- Total Fat: 7.2
- Saturated Fat: 1.6
- Sodium: 127
- Fiber: 0.5
- Total Carbohydrate: 16.8

## 301. Smoky Grilled Cheese Fries

*Serving: 2 serving(s) | Prep: 10mins | Ready in:*

### Ingredients

- 16 ounces frozen french fries (can use seasoned fries too... mmm!)
- 2 cups cheddar cheese, shredded
- 2 cups monterey jack pepper cheese, shredded
- 1/2 cup cooked bacon, crumbled
- 1/4 cup chives, chopped small
- 1/4 tsp- 1 tsp kosher salt or 1/4 sea salt
- 1/2 cup sour cream
- 1/4-1/2 cup jalapeno pepper, sliced
- ranch dressing (for dipping) (optional)

### Direction

- Spray a cookie sheet or baking dish with cooking spray, then place French fries into dish. Top with kosher salt, half or the bacon, then pepper jack cheese (can use Monterey jack or any other melting cheese for less heat). Then add on the rest of the bacon, the cheddar cheese, the jalapenos, and lastly the chives.
- Bake in oven for about 15-20 minutes on 375 degrees until cheese is melted through and fries are hot. Top with a thick layer of sour cream and serve with ranch dressing on the side for dipping.

### Nutrition Information

- Calories: 1338.3
- Cholesterol: 244.5
- Sodium: 2090.7
- Fiber: 4.8
- Sugar: 2.2
- Total Carbohydrate: 61.8
- Protein: 63
- Total Fat: 94.4
- Saturated Fat: 55.2

## 302. Smucker's Peanut Butter Caramel Dip

*Serving: 1 cup, 4 serving(s) | Prep: 5mins | Ready in:*

### Ingredients

- 1/2 cup smucker's natural creamy peanut butter
- 1/2 cup smucker's sugar-free caramel topping
- 1 teaspoon cinnamon

- 2 tablespoons milk
- 2 apples, cut into wedges

## Direction

- Mix together peanut butter and caramel topping in a medium bowl until blended.
- Stir in cinnamon and milk. Add additional milk, if needed to make a smooth consistency.
- Dip apple wedges into dip or spread on apple wedges.

## Nutrition Information

- Calories: 231.9
- Total Fat: 16.7
- Sodium: 152.6
- Fiber: 3.9
- Total Carbohydrate: 16.6
- Saturated Fat: 3.5
- Sugar: 10.2
- Cholesterol: 1.1
- Protein: 8.5

## 303. Snack Attack Mix, Low Cal

*Serving: 10-11 cups, 20-24 serving(s) | Prep: 10mins | Ready in:*

## Ingredients

- 6 tablespoons light butter (I used Move Over Butter, can also use Smart Balance Light)
- 2 tablespoons Worcestershire sauce
- 1 1/2 teaspoons seasoning salt (use light salt if watching sodium intake)
- 3/4 teaspoon garlic powder
- 1/2 teaspoon onion powder
- 9 cups Crispix cereal (rice or corn chex)
- 1 cup Wheat Chex
- 1 cup ff pretzel (optional)

## Direction

- Melt butter spread in a saucepan.
- Add seasonings; stir with whisk until blended and heated through.
- In large bowl, add Crispix wheat chex together. Also add pretzels if using those.
- Very slowly dribble melted butter mix over the chex mix, stirring as you dribble. You can dribble a small amount on and the shake if you prefer. Repeat until buttery mix is gone.
- Pour mix into an oven safe pan with sides, stir well.
- Bake at 250 degrees, stirring every 15 minutes, for one hour.
- Cool, and store in air-tight container.

## Nutrition Information

- Calories: 79.5
- Total Fat: 2.6
- Fiber: 0.3
- Sugar: 1.9
- Cholesterol: 4.6
- Protein: 1.2
- Saturated Fat: 1.5
- Sodium: 152.8
- Total Carbohydrate: 13.3

## 304. Snowmen On A Stick (Tackled By Tasty !)

*Serving: 8 snowmen on a stick | Prep: 20mins | Ready in:*

## Ingredients

- 24 thick slices bananas
- 8 grapes (red or green)
- 8 carrots, pieces
- 8 apples, slices
- mini chocolate chips or currants
- 16 pretzel sticks

## Direction

- For each snowman, you will need three thick slices of banana, a grape, a sliver of carrot, and a triangular piece of apple. (Tip: Poke a hole in the apple piece with a bamboo skewer first to make assembly easier.).
- Have your kids slide the fruit onto the skewer, then use the carrot slivers for noses, mini chocolate chips or currants for eyes and buttons, and pretzel sticks for arms.

## Nutrition Information

- Calories: 460.9
- Total Fat: 1.9
- Total Carbohydrate: 116.2
- Cholesterol: 0
- Protein: 6.1
- Saturated Fat: 0.5
- Sodium: 209.9
- Fiber: 14.6
- Sugar: 61.5

### 305. Southwest Snack Mix

*Serving: 10 serving(s) | Prep: 15mins | Ready in:*

## Ingredients

- 4 cups popped popcorn
- 3 cups miniature pretzel twists
- 2 cups bagel chips, garlic flavored
- 1 cup corn chips
- 3 tablespoons butter or 3 tablespoons margarine, melted
- 1 teaspoon paprika
- 3/4 teaspoon chili powder
- 1/2 teaspoon cumin
- 1/4 teaspoon onion powder
- 1/4 teaspoon garlic powder
- 1 dash cayenne pepper

## Direction

- Break up garlic flavored bagel chips into bite-size pieces.
- In a large bowl, combine popcorn, pretzels, bagel chips and corn chips.
- In a small bowl, combine remaining ingredients. Pour evenly over mixture; toss gently to coat.
- Store in tightly covered container.
- Makes 10 (1 cup) servings.

## Nutrition Information

- Calories: 45
- Saturated Fat: 2.2
- Sugar: 0.1
- Total Carbohydrate: 2.9
- Cholesterol: 9.2
- Protein: 0.5
- Total Fat: 3.7
- Sodium: 27.1
- Fiber: 0.6

### 306. Sparkling Jello

*Serving: 1-4 serving(s) | Prep: 3mins | Ready in:*

## Ingredients

- 1 (1 1/3 ounce) box jell-o sugar-free raspberry gelatin
- 1 cup diet Sprite
- 1 cup boiling water

## Direction

- Stir boiling water into Jell-O until completely dissolved.
- Add 1 cup Sprite.
- Refrigerate at least 2 hours.
- Other fantastic combinations:
- Diet Coke and cherry jello.
- Orange soda and strawberry jello.
- Fresca and lime jello.
- You can be pretty creative with this --.

## Nutrition Information

- Calories: 73
- Sugar: 0
- Sodium: 336.7
- Fiber: 0
- Cholesterol: 0
- Protein: 6
- Total Fat: 0
- Saturated Fat: 0
- Total Carbohydrate: 29.6

## 307. Spiced Nuts (Splenda)

*Serving: 1 pound nuts | Prep: 15mins | Ready in:*

### Ingredients

- 1/2 cup sugar-free syrup (caramel or vanilla)
- 2 tablespoons sesame oil (or olive oil)
- 1 lb nuts, of choice
- 2 teaspoons Splenda sugar substitute
- 1/2 teaspoon ground allspice
- 1/2 teaspoon ground cinnamon

### Direction

- Heat oil and sugar free syrup in a large skillet; stir while it heats.
- Add nuts; cook over low heat stirring constantly until most of the liquid is absorbed.
- Mix Splenda and spices together; sprinkle over nuts stir coating evenly.
- Spread mixture into a release foil lined cookie sheet pan.
- Bake at 300°F oven for 25 to 40 minutes time depends on type of nuts used--just be careful not to burn them.
- Cool completely before indulging; store in covered container.

## Nutrition Information

- Calories: 2948.7
- Total Carbohydrate: 116.9
- Saturated Fat: 35.3
- Sodium: 3045.1
- Fiber: 41.8
- Sugar: 21.1
- Cholesterol: 0
- Total Fat: 261.4
- Protein: 78.8

## 308. Spicy Apple Chips

*Serving: 125 chips | Prep: 25mins | Ready in:*

### Ingredients

- 5 -10 cored apples, with skin removed (optional)
- 1 cup sugar
- 1 teaspoon allspice
- 1 teaspoon cinnamon
- 1 teaspoon ground cloves
- 1/2 teaspoon hot pepper sauce (e.g. Tabasco)
- 1 cup apple cider
- 1 cup boiling water

### Direction

- Combine all but the apples in a medium stainless steel pot and stir until sugar is dissolved.
- Slice the apples as thin as you dare and soak them in spiced syrup for at least 1 hour.
- Remove apples from syrup with a slotted spoon (allow a few seconds for excess moisture to drip off) and arrange slices in a dehydrator (follow manufacturer's instructions).
- Dehydrate until preferred crispness, between 6-12 hours.
- Store in airtight containers.
- Prep time yield is based on work with 5 apples-- chip quantity also depends on thickness of slices.

### Nutrition Information

- Calories: 6.3
- Total Carbohydrate: 1.6
- Cholesterol: 0
- Saturated Fat: 0
- Sodium: 0.6
- Fiber: 0
- Protein: 0
- Total Fat: 0
- Sugar: 1.6

---

### 309. Spicy Garlic And Lemon Shrimp Bruschetta

*Serving: 2 serving(s) | Prep: 10mins | Ready in:*

### Ingredients

- 4 slices baguette, sliced on an angle
- 1 teaspoon olive oil
- 2 garlic cloves, sliced thinly
- 1 red chili pepper, deseeded and sliced
- 8 ounces jumbo shrimp, raw, butterflied
- 1 lemon, juice
- 2 tablespoons cilantro, chopped
- 2 ounces arugula

### Direction

- Toast the bread and keep warm.
- Heat the oil in a wok or frying pan and cook the garlic and chili until sizzling.
- Turn the heat up, add the shrimp and cook until pink.
- Remove from the heat, then add the lemon juice and cilantro.
- Season and serve piled on the toast and scattered with arugula.

### Nutrition Information

- Calories: 522.5
- Sodium: 959.7
- Cholesterol: 172.4
- Protein: 36.3
- Total Fat: 8.5
- Saturated Fat: 1.6
- Fiber: 7.3
- Sugar: 2.1
- Total Carbohydrate: 77.3

---

### 310. Spinach Nuggets

*Serving: 12 muffins, 12 serving(s) | Prep: 10mins | Ready in:*

### Ingredients

- 16 ounces frozen spinach, cooked drained and chopped if needed
- 3/4 cup seasoned bread crumbs
- 1/4 cup flax seed meal (if you don't have these things add 1/4 cup more bread crumbs) or 1/4 cup wheat germ (if you don't have these things add 1/4 cup more bread crumbs)
- 1 1/2 cups shredded cheddar cheese (you could also try cheddar flavored with sundried tomatoes and basil)
- 3 eggs

### Direction

- Heat oven to 375.
- Lightly coat baking sheet with oil or use a non-stick mini muffin pan.
- Combine all ingredients well.
- Shape into nuggets or spoon into muffin pan and bake for 20-25 minutes. (Turn nuggets over after 15 minutes).
- Serve with Ranch Dressing for dipping.

### Nutrition Information

- Calories: 129.4
- Total Fat: 7.6
- Saturated Fat: 3.7
- Total Carbohydrate: 7.9

- Cholesterol: 67.8
- Sodium: 268.7
- Fiber: 2.3
- Sugar: 1
- Protein: 8.2

## 311. Sticky Fingers

*Serving: 3 serving(s) | Prep: 10mins | Ready in:*

### Ingredients

- 1 tablespoon peanut butter
- 3 slices banana bread, 1/2 inch thick
- 1/2 large banana, sliced
- 3 tablespoons toasted sweetened coconut
- 1 tablespoon honey
- Garnish
- fresh fruit

### Direction

- Spread peanut butter evenly over banana bread; top with banana and coconut. Drizzle with honey. Serve at room temperature or heat in microwave at high for 10 seconds, and serve warm.
- Garnish if desired.

### Nutrition Information

- Calories: 290.3
- Total Fat: 10.6
- Sugar: 11
- Protein: 4.3
- Cholesterol: 25.8
- Saturated Fat: 3.2
- Sodium: 218
- Fiber: 1.8
- Total Carbohydrate: 47

## 312. Sticky Sausages

*Serving: 20 serving(s) | Prep: 1mins | Ready in:*

### Ingredients

- 20 pork cocktail franks
- 4 tablespoons clear honey

### Direction

- Pre-heat oven to 200 degrees
- Place sausages in a shallow roasting tin lined with baking parchment.
- Brush with honey.
- Cook for 25-30 minutes, until they are thoroughly cooked and a sticky dark brown colour.
- Serve while they are still warm.

### Nutrition Information

- Calories: 140.1
- Sodium: 416
- Sugar: 4
- Total Carbohydrate: 4.3
- Total Fat: 11.5
- Saturated Fat: 4.8
- Protein: 5.3
- Fiber: 0
- Cholesterol: 26.7

## 313. Stir Crazy Kettle Corn

*Serving: 1 large bowl of kettle corn, 4-6 serving(s) | Prep: 1mins | Ready in:*

### Ingredients

- 1/2 cup popcorn
- 1/2 cup sugar
- 1/2 cup vegetable oil
- salt

### Direction

- Make sure your Stir Crazy Popcorn Popper is turned off.
- Using your Stir Crazy Popcorn Popper, combine ingredients on the non-stick surface of the machine.
- Cover the Stir Crazy Popcorn Popper with the bowl provided by Stir Crazy.
- Turn on Stir Crazy Popcorn Popper.
- Watch the popcorn pop! It's fun!
- When only 3 seconds remain in between pops, flip Stir Crazy Popcorn Popper over to yield a big bowl of kettle corn.
- Salt to your liking!

## Nutrition Information

- Calories: 337.6
- Total Carbohydrate: 25
- Cholesterol: 0
- Protein: 0
- Total Fat: 27.2
- Sodium: 0.2
- Fiber: 0
- Saturated Fat: 3.5
- Sugar: 24.9

## 314. Strawberry Corn Muffins

*Serving: 12 serving(s) | Prep: 15mins | Ready in:*

### Ingredients

- 1 cup cornmeal
- 1 cup flour
- 1/2 cup sugar
- 1 tablespoon baking powder
- 1/2 teaspoon salt
- 2 eggs
- 1 1/4 cups low-fat buttermilk
- 2 tablespoons unsalted butter, melted
- 1 cup strawberry, sliced

### Direction

- Preheat oven to 350°F.
- Line muffin cups with paper liners or spray with nonstick spray.
- Combine cornmeal, flour, sugar, baking powder and salt in a bowl.
- In a separate mixing bowl, mix together eggs and buttermilk.
- Add dry mixture to egg mixture.
- Fold in butter and strawberries.
- Divide batter among muffin cups.
- Bake for 15-20 minutes or until browned.
- Cool in pan for 10 minutes before transferring to a wire rack to finish cooling completely.

## Nutrition Information

- Calories: 150.8
- Total Fat: 3.5
- Saturated Fat: 1.7
- Fiber: 1.3
- Cholesterol: 41.4
- Protein: 3.9
- Sodium: 230.3
- Sugar: 10.3
- Total Carbohydrate: 26.6

## 315. Sugar And Spice Pecans

*Serving: 4 cups, 16 serving(s) | Prep: 5mins | Ready in:*

### Ingredients

- 1 lb pecan halves
- 3/4 teaspoon salt
- 1 teaspoon cinnamon
- 1 cup sugar
- 1 egg white
- 1 tablespoon water

### Direction

- Beat the egg white and water until frothy but not stiff.
- Stir in the sugar, salt, and cinnamon.

- Add the pecans and stir well until the pecans are completely coated.
- Spread the nuts on a large baking sheet and bake at 200 degree Fahrenheit for 45 minutes, stirring every 15 minutes.
- Remove them from the oven when dry and toasted.
- When cool, store in an airtight container.

## Nutrition Information

- Calories: 245.7
- Fiber: 2.8
- Protein: 2.8
- Total Fat: 20.4
- Saturated Fat: 1.8
- Sodium: 112.5
- Sugar: 13.6
- Total Carbohydrate: 16.6
- Cholesterol: 0

## 316. Sugar Free Snow Cone

*Serving: 1 serving(s) | Prep: 5mins | Ready in:*

## Ingredients

- 1 (6 3/4 ounce) package Kool-Aid Jammers 10 (Sugar-Free)
- ice, crushed

## Direction

- Crush the ice by machine or by hand with mallet.
- Put crushed ice into a cup.
- Pour the Kool-Aid Jammer over the top of ice.
- Serve.

## Nutrition Information

- Calories: 0
- Saturated Fat: 0
- Total Fat: 0
- Sodium: 0
- Fiber: 0
- Sugar: 0
- Total Carbohydrate: 0
- Cholesterol: 0
- Protein: 0

## 317. Sunflower Coconut Balls

*Serving: 24 balls | Prep: 5mins | Ready in:*

## Ingredients

- 1/4 cup cocoa
- 1/2 cup honey
- 1/2 cup peanut butter
- 3/4 cup non-fat powdered milk
- 1 teaspoon vanilla essence
- 1/2 cup sunflower seeds
- 1/4 cup unprocessed natural bran
- coconut, for rolling

## Direction

- Mix cocoa, honey, peanut butter, powdered milk and vanilla in a bowl until combined. Add sunflower seeds and bran.
- Form into balls and roll in coconut.
- Allow to set and store in an airtight container.

## Nutrition Information

- Calories: 87.9
- Total Carbohydrate: 10.4
- Protein: 3.7
- Total Fat: 4.4
- Sodium: 46.8
- Fiber: 1.1
- Saturated Fat: 0.8
- Sugar: 8.5
- Cholesterol: 0.8

## 318. Sunny Toast

*Serving: 1 serving(s) | Prep: 2mins | Ready in:*

### Ingredients

- 1 egg
- 1 piece bread (white or wheat, any kind)
- 1 teaspoon butter

### Direction

- Heat skillet, butter it.
- Make a "sunny side up" egg.
- While cooking the egg, toast the piece of bread.
- When both ready, put the egg on the toast.
- If you want, you can sprinkle salt and pepper on top.
- Enjoy!

### Nutrition Information

- Calories: 173.6
- Total Fat: 9.6
- Saturated Fat: 4.1
- Sodium: 267.2
- Sugar: 1.5
- Protein: 8.2
- Fiber: 0.6
- Total Carbohydrate: 13
- Cholesterol: 221.6

## 319. Super Amazing Bagel Chips

*Serving: 6 dozen, 12 serving(s) | Prep: 5mins | Ready in:*

### Ingredients

- 1/4 cup soy sauce
- 2 tablespoons vegetable oil
- 1 teaspoon garlic, minced
- 1 teaspoon sugar
- 6 bagels, plain

### Direction

- Blend soy sauce, oil, garlic, sugar and 2 tablespoons water, stirring until sugar dissolves.
- Cut 3 bagels crosswise in half into semi-circles; lay on cut edge and cut into 7 or 8 thin slices.
- Brush both sides of slices lightly and evenly with soy sauce mixture, stirring mixture frequently. Place slices, in single layer, on large baking sheet.
- Bake in 250ºF oven 45 minutes.
- Remove chips to wire racks; cool completely. Store chips in well-sealed plastic bags.

### Nutrition Information

- Calories: 169.7
- Cholesterol: 0
- Protein: 6.2
- Sodium: 615.5
- Fiber: 1.3
- Sugar: 0.5
- Total Carbohydrate: 28.8
- Total Fat: 3.1
- Saturated Fat: 0.4

## 320. Super Easy Chocolate Chip Brownies

*Serving: 36 small brownies | Prep: 20mins | Ready in:*

### Ingredients

- 1 (6 ounce) package semisweet chocolate morsels
- 21 graham cracker squares, crushed
- 1 (14 ounce) can sweetened condensed milk (not evaporated milk!)
- confectioners' sugar

### Direction

- Preheat oven to 375 degrees Fahrenheit.
- In a mixing bowl, combine the chocolate morsels, crushed graham crackers, and sweetened condensed milk.
- Grease an 8-inch by 8-inch pan, line with waxed paper, then grease the waxed paper.
- (Sounds odd, but I've never been brave enough to not do this.) Press mixture into prepared pan.
- Bake for 30 minutes.
- Allow to cool slightly, yet turn out of pan while still warm and peel away waxed paper.
- Cut into squares, and roll in confectioners' sugar.

## Nutrition Information

- Calories: 94.3
- Total Fat: 3
- Cholesterol: 3.9
- Protein: 1.6
- Saturated Fat: 1.5
- Sodium: 63.5
- Fiber: 0.5
- Sugar: 11
- Total Carbohydrate: 15.4

## 321. Super Quick Falafel!

*Serving: 4 pitta pockets, 4 serving(s) | Prep: 25mins | Ready in:*

## Ingredients

- 800 g drained canned chick-peas
- 2 teaspoons cumin
- 2 tablespoons fresh coriander, chopped (cilantro)
- 2 garlic cloves, crushed
- 1 fresh green chile, deseeded and finely chopped
- oil (for frying)
- 1 cup Greek yogurt
- salad leaves
- 4 pita breads, to serve

## Direction

- Mash the chickpeas or puree coarsely in a food processor. Mix with the cumin, coriander, garlic and chili. Season and divide into 24 pieces of equal size. Shape each piece into a ball.
- Heat a little oil in a frying pan and cook the balls for approximately 6 minutes each or until crisp and golden. This will probably have to be done in batches unless you have a huge pan!
- Toast the pitta breads and slit the tops. Fill with the falafel and salad leaves, spoon a little yogurt on to the top too.

## Nutrition Information

- Calories: 415.3
- Sodium: 922.8
- Cholesterol: 0
- Protein: 15.9
- Sugar: 1.5
- Total Carbohydrate: 81
- Total Fat: 3.3
- Saturated Fat: 0.4
- Fiber: 10.8

## 322. Super Soft Caramel Popcorn

*Serving: 6 qts | Prep: 5mins | Ready in:*

## Ingredients

- 1 1/4 cups brown sugar
- 1/2 cup light corn syrup
- 1/2 cup margarine or 1/2 cup butter
- 1 dash salt
- 7 ounces sweetened condensed milk (half of a 14 oz can)
- 1/2 teaspoon vanilla

- 6 quarts popped corn

### Direction

- Combine sugar, corn syrup, margarine, and salt in medium saucepan; bring to boil.
- Reduce heat to medium and add stir in milk; cook, stirring frequently, to soft ball stage (240 degrees).
- Remove from heat then stir in vanilla.
- Pour slowly over popcorn, stirring until caramel is evenly distributed throughout.
- Store caramel popcorn in covered container.
- NOTE: You may vary the amount of popcorn used. I like a little less caramel coating and usually make this recipe with 8 quarts of popcorn.

### Nutrition Information

- Calories: 733.6
- Total Fat: 32.6
- Sodium: 284.6
- Fiber: 3.5
- Saturated Fat: 6.9
- Sugar: 70
- Total Carbohydrate: 110
- Cholesterol: 11.2
- Protein: 6.1

## 323. Sweet Savory Meatballs

*Serving: 6-8 serving(s) | Prep: 5mins | Ready in:*

### Ingredients

- 1 (16 ounce) bagfrozen italian style meatballs
- 1 (10 ounce) jar grape jelly
- 1 (12 ounce) jar chili sauce
- 2 tablespoons lemon juice
- salt pepper

### Direction

- Place meatballs in Crockpot (or slow cooker).
- Mix remaining ingredients very well, and add to Crockpot.
- Simmer on low for 2 hours. Stir after 2 hours.

### Nutrition Information

- Calories: 185.9
- Total Fat: 0.2
- Saturated Fat: 0
- Fiber: 3.8
- Total Carbohydrate: 44.7
- Sodium: 772.9
- Sugar: 30.3
- Cholesterol: 0
- Protein: 1.5

## 324. Sweet Cream Cheese Spread.

*Serving: 8 crackers, 4 serving(s) | Prep: 14mins | Ready in:*

### Ingredients

- 3 tablespoons butter or 3 tablespoons margarine
- 4 tablespoons cream cheese
- 2 tablespoons sugar
- 8 Ritz crackers

### Direction

- Put 3 tbs of butter or margarine into microwaveable cup and microwave for 20 seconds or until melted.
- Put 4 tbs of cream cheese in with butter, mix.
- When cheese and butter are about half way mixed, add 1 tbs of sugar.
- When mixed thoroughly, add the other tablespoon of sugar and blend thoroughly.
- Chill mixture in freezer for 10 minutes, or chill in refrigerator for an hour (recommended).
- Stir with butter knife, then spread evenly onto crackers.

## Nutrition Information

- Calories: 182.8
- Protein: 1.6
- Total Fat: 15.2
- Saturated Fat: 8.9
- Sodium: 153.9
- Fiber: 0.1
- Total Carbohydrate: 10.8
- Cholesterol: 38.9
- Sugar: 6.8

### 325. Sweet Malted Chocolate Dessert Sandwiches

*Serving: 4 slices, 4 serving(s) | Prep: 5mins | Ready in:*

## Ingredients

- 4 slices white bread
- 4 tablespoons sweetened condensed milk
- 4 teaspoons chocolate malt powder

## Direction

- Take your slices of bread and spread 1 TBSP of Sweetened condensed milk on EACH slice.
- Sprinkle 1 tsp malt powder evenly on EACH slice.
- Fold the bread into half so that you have 4 rectangles.
- Leave it for about 5 minutes in order to "melt" the powder.
- Pick up and ENJOY!

## Nutrition Information

- Calories: 134.2
- Saturated Fat: 1.3
- Total Carbohydrate: 24.4
- Cholesterol: 6.5
- Sodium: 204.1
- Fiber: 0.7
- Sugar: 12.6
- Protein: 3.5
- Total Fat: 2.5

### 326. Sweet Tortilla Roll Ups

*Serving: 4 serving(s) | Prep: 10mins | Ready in:*

## Ingredients

- 1/2 cup fat-free ricotta cheese
- 1 tablespoon sugar
- 2 teaspoons cinnamon
- 1/4 teaspoon vanilla
- 4 (10 inch) flour tortillas

## Direction

- Set oven to broil.
- In a mixing bowl, blend ricotta cheese, sugar, cinnamon and vanilla.
- Spread about 2 tablespoons of ricotta mixture down center of each tortilla.
- Fold ends of each tortilla in and roll up like a burrito.
- Place on a cookie sheet and broil for approximately 1 minute.
- Serve warm.

## Nutrition Information

- Calories: 234.3
- Total Fat: 5.5
- Saturated Fat: 1.3
- Sugar: 4.5
- Total Carbohydrate: 40
- Cholesterol: 0
- Sodium: 445.5
- Fiber: 2.8
- Protein: 5.8

## 327. Sweet Zucchini Carrot Garden Bread

*Serving: 1 loaf | Prep: 15mins | Ready in:*

### Ingredients

- 2 cups brown sugar
- 3/4 cup vegetable oil
- 2 eggs
- 3 teaspoons vanilla
- 1/2 teaspoon baking powder
- 3 cups flour
- 3 teaspoons cinnamon
- 2 teaspoons nutmeg
- 1/4 cup butter
- 1 cup grated zucchini
- 1 cup grated carrot (adjust to your taste, or omit one or the other to make plain zucchini bread or carrot bread.)

### Direction

- Blend all ingredients together.
- Bake in buttered pan at 350 degrees for approx. 45 minutes.

### Nutrition Information

- Calories: 5167.9
- Protein: 54.9
- Total Fat: 225.6
- Sugar: 435.4
- Cholesterol: 545
- Saturated Fat: 55.4
- Sodium: 919.5
- Fiber: 19.3
- Total Carbohydrate: 739.8

## 328. Taco Bell Quesadillas

*Serving: 4 serving(s) | Prep: 20mins | Ready in:*

### Ingredients

- SAUCE
- 1/4 cup mayonnaise
- 2 teaspoons minced jalapenos, slices
- 2 teaspoons jalapeno juice, from minced jalepenos
- 3/4 teaspoon sugar
- 1/2 teaspoon cumin
- 1/2 teaspoon paprika
- 1/8 teaspoon cayenne pepper
- 1/8 teaspoon garlic powder
- 1 dash salt
- QUESADILLAS
- 4 flour tortillas
- 4 chicken tenderloins
- 1 cup shredded cheddar cheese
- 1 cup shredded monterey jack cheese
- 2 slices process American cheese

### Direction

- Combine sauce ingredients and stir until smooth.
- Grill chicken in vegetable oil and cut into thin slices.
- Preheat skillet over medium heat.
- One at a time, lay tortilla into hot skillet and sprinkle with 1/4 cup of each shredded cheese and 1/2 cheese slice on one side of the tortilla.
- Arrange about 1/4 cup chicken slices over tortilla on the same half covered with cheese.
- On the empty side, spread about one tablespoon of sauce.
- Fold over and press gently with spatula.
- Cook until cheese is melted and slice each into 4 pieces.

### Nutrition Information

- Calories: 365
- Sugar: 2.8
- Total Carbohydrate: 18.2
- Total Fat: 23.8
- Saturated Fat: 14.1
- Sodium: 783.8
- Fiber: 1.1
- Cholesterol: 63.9

- Protein: 19.3

### 329. Taco Cups

*Serving: 10 serving(s) | Prep: 10mins | Ready in:*

## Ingredients

- 1 lb ground beef
- 1 (1 1/4 ounce) package taco seasoning mix
- 1 (10 ounce) can refrigerated buttermilk biscuits
- 1/2 cup shredded cheddar cheese

## Direction

- PREHEAT oven to 400°F
- Brown meat, adding seasoning mix;
- Spray muffin tin with cooking spray.
- PRESS biscuits onto bottoms and up sides of muffin pan cups, making a "bowl".
- Fill with seasoned meat.
- BAKE 15 minutes. Sprinkle with cheese. Bake an additional 2 to 3 minutes or until cheese is melted.

## Nutrition Information

- Calories: 210.4
- Total Fat: 12.5
- Fiber: 0.4
- Cholesterol: 36.8
- Protein: 11.6
- Saturated Fat: 4.8
- Sodium: 378.6
- Sugar: 2.3
- Total Carbohydrate: 12.5

### 330. Taco Tortilla Dogs

*Serving: 8 serving(s) | Prep: 10mins | Ready in:*

## Ingredients

- 8 large hot dogs
- 1 cup refried beans
- 1 cup grated cheddar cheese
- 1/2 cup salsa
- 8 (8 inch) flour tortillas
- shredded lettuce
- 2 large firm tomatoes, chopped

## Direction

- Cook the hot dogs in boiling water for about 5 minutes; drain.
- In a bowl combine beans with cheddar cheese and salsa; microwave on HIGH for 2 minutes or until thoroughly heat, stirring once.
- Spread the mixture on one side of EACH tortilla, then place the hot dog on top of the mixture.
- Sprinkle with shredded lettuce and chopped tomatoes, then roll up.
- Place each tortilla on a small baking sheet.
- Place in a 275 degree oven JUST to warm the tortillas slightly so that they are soft.

## Nutrition Information

- Calories: 422.3
- Sodium: 1150.5
- Cholesterol: 41.2
- Protein: 15.6
- Total Fat: 22.8
- Saturated Fat: 9.5
- Fiber: 4.2
- Sugar: 4.4
- Total Carbohydrate: 38.5

### 331. Teddy Bear Snack Mix

*Serving: 12 cups, 24 serving(s) | Prep: 10mins | Ready in:*

## Ingredients

- 2 cups ramen noodles, crushed
- 5 cups Golden Grahams cereal
- 3 cups bear shaped graham crackers
- 1 cup peanuts or 1 cup sliced almonds
- 1 cup raisins
- 1/2 teaspoon cinnamon
- 1/3 cup butter
- 1/3 cup honey
- 1 teaspoon orange juice

## Direction

- Preheat oven to 375 degrees.
- Discard seasoning package from ramen noodles.
- In a large bowl, mix together noodles, cereal, teddy bear cookies, nuts and raisins.
- In a 4 cup glass measure, combine cinnamon, honey, butter and orange juice.
- Heat in microwave until melted and well mixed.
- Pour this mixture over the cereal mixture.
- Toss to coat well.
- Spread into a large rimmed baking sheet and bake for 10 minutes, stirring once.
- Remove from oven and cool.
- Package in individual baggies, about 1/2 cup per baggie and then place in a larger freezer bag and freeze.

## Nutrition Information

- Calories: 120.7
- Total Fat: 5.9
- Sodium: 94.7
- Total Carbohydrate: 16.6
- Cholesterol: 6.8
- Protein: 2.2
- Saturated Fat: 2.1
- Fiber: 1
- Sugar: 10.6

## 332. Teddy Bear Trail Mix

Serving: 20-25 individual baggies | Prep: 5mins | Ready in:

## Ingredients

- 1 (14 1/2 ounce) packagesweetened honey corn and oat cereal (like Honey Nut Cheerios)
- 1 (10 ounce) package bear shaped graham crackers (Teddy Grahams)
- 1 (10 ounce) bag mini marshmallows
- 1 (12 ounce) bag semi-sweet chocolate chips (or another flavor, if you like)

## Direction

- Combine all ingredients in a large bowl and stir to mix.
- Divide and store in small baggies.

## Nutrition Information

- Calories: 127.2
- Cholesterol: 0
- Protein: 1
- Total Fat: 5.1
- Sodium: 13.3
- Fiber: 1
- Sugar: 17.5
- Total Carbohydrate: 22.5
- Saturated Fat: 3

## 333. Tempura Prawns

Serving: 4-8 serving(s) | Prep: 10mins | Ready in:

## Ingredients

- 1 kg green prawns (remove shells, leave tails on)
- 1 cup chilled soda water (or plain water)
- 1/2 cup all-purpose flour (plain flour)
- 1/2 cup cornstarch
- 1 teaspoon baking soda

- salt and pepper (to taste)
- 1 egg yolk
- oil (for deep frying)

## Direction

- Combine soda water and egg yolk in a large bowl.
- Then add the flours and baking soda.
- Season with salt and pepper.
- Whisk mixture until just combine but still lumpy.
- Dip the prawns in the mixture, coating well.
- Cook in hot oil for about 2-3 minutes.
- Place prawns on paper towel to drain excess oil.
- Serve on their own or with a dipping sauce or serve as a meal with chips (fries) and salad.

## Nutrition Information

- Calories: 307.6
- Total Fat: 3.7
- Saturated Fat: 0.7
- Sodium: 1745.7
- Fiber: 0.6
- Sugar: 0.1
- Cholesterol: 356.5
- Total Carbohydrate: 28.9
- Protein: 36.3

## 334. The "only" Power Cookies

*Serving: 23 serving(s) | Prep: 20mins | Ready in:*

## Ingredients

- 2 ounces pumpkin seeds, raw
- 2 ounces sunflower seeds, raw
- 1 1/2 tablespoons flax seeds
- 4 ounces canola oil
- 2 large eggs
- 4 ounces honey
- 5 ounces unsweetened applesauce
- 3 1/2 ounces warm water
- 1 ounce dried cherries
- 1 ounce dried cranberries
- 1 1/2 ounces raisins
- 20 ounces whole wheat flour
- 2 1/2 ounces wheat germ
- 5 1/2 ounces rolled oats
- 1 ounce mini chocolate chip
- 2 1/2 teaspoons baking powder
- 1 tablespoon baking soda
- 3/4 teaspoon iodized salt

## Direction

- Preheat oven to 375 degrees.
- Toast seeds in preheated oven for about 5 minutes, until oils release.
- Mix wet ingredients together.
- Mix all dry ingredients together. Except chocolate chips.
- Mix wet and dry to form a batter.
- Scoop on sheet pan with parchment paper. 12/sheet.
- Place 8-10 mini chocolate chips on each cookie.
- Bake 6 minutes, then rotate tray and bake for 3 more minutes.
- Pull from oven and cool.
- Wrap and serve as a nutritious snack.

## Nutrition Information

- Calories: 232.8
- Protein: 6.9
- Saturated Fat: 1.3
- Sugar: 6.8
- Total Carbohydrate: 32.4
- Cholesterol: 16.2
- Total Fat: 9.8
- Sodium: 287.4
- Fiber: 4.6

## 335. The Full Monty F E B Full English Breakfast

*Serving: 1 Full English Breakfast, 1 serving(s) | Prep: 5mins | Ready in:*

### Ingredients

- 2 links good quality sausages
- 2 -3 slices bacon
- 2 flat mushrooms
- 1 -2 ripe tomatoes
- 1 large egg
- 1 slice bread
- Optional Extras
- 1 slice black pudding (optional)
- baked beans (optional)
- cooked potato, thinly sliced (optional)

### Direction

- Heat the flat grill plate over a low heat, on top of 2 rings/flames if it fits, and brush sparingly with light olive oil or vegetable oil.
- For the sausages.
- Always buy sausages with a high meat content. Cook these first. Add the sausages to the hot grill plate/the coolest part if there is one and allow to cook slowly for about 15-20 minutes, turning occasionally, until golden. After the first 10 minutes, increase the heat to medium before beginning to cook the other ingredients. If you are struggling for space, completely cook the sausages and keep hot on a plate in the oven.
- For the bacon.
- Choose between back or streaky, smoked or unsmoked bacon; generally, dry-cure has the best flavour. Snip a few small cuts into the fatty edge of the bacon. Place the bacon straight on to the grill plate and fry for 2-4 minutes each side or until your preferred crispiness is reached. Like the sausages, the cooked bacon can be kept hot on a plate in the oven.
- For the mushrooms.
- Brush away any dirt using a pastry brush and trim the stalk level with the mushroom top. Season with salt and pepper and drizzle over a little olive oil. Place stalk-side up on the grill plate and cook for 1-2 minutes before turning and cooking for a further 3-4 minutes. Avoid moving the mushrooms too much while cooking, as this releases the natural juices, making them soggy. (Alternatively, you can slice your mushrooms, as shown in my photo.).
- For the tomatoes.
- Cut the tomatoes across the centre/or in half lengthways if using plum tomatoes, and with a small, sharp knife remove the green 'eye'. Season with salt and pepper and drizzle with a little olive oil. Place cut-side down on the grill plate and cook without moving for 2 minutes. Gently turn over and season again. Cook for a further 2-3 minutes until tender but still holding their shape.
- For the fried bread.
- For 'proper' fried bread it's best to cook it in a separate pan. Ideally, use bread that is a couple of days old. Heat a frying pan to a medium heat and cover the base with oil. Add the bread and cook for 2-3 minutes each side until crispy and golden. If the pan becomes too dry, add a little more oil. For a richer flavour, add a knob of butter after you turn the slice.
- For the fried eggs.
- Break the egg straight into the pan with the fried bread and leave for 30 seconds. Add a good knob of butter and lightly splash/baste the egg with the butter when melted. Cook to your preferred stage, season and gently remove with a fish slice.
- Once all the ingredients are cooked, serve on warm plates and enjoy straight away with a good squeeze of tomato ketchup, Worcestershire sauce or brown sauce, and don't forget the toast and marmalade with a pot of good English Breakfast tea.
- Optional Extras.
- Black Pudding.
- Cut the black pudding into 3-4 slices and remove the skin. Place on the grill plate and

cook for 1½-2 minutes each side until slightly crispy.
- Baked Beans.
- Heat up the baked beans in a saucepan and serve on top of the fried bread, or on the side.
- Fried Potatoes:
- Fry the sliced cooked potatoes in a little butter until crispy and golden brown. Season with a little salt and black pepper.

## Nutrition Information

- Calories: 547.9
- Sugar: 5.3
- Total Carbohydrate: 19.3
- Protein: 24.1
- Total Fat: 41.4
- Saturated Fat: 13.5
- Sodium: 982
- Fiber: 2.4
- Cholesterol: 282.6

## 336. The Traditional Cyprus Sandwich With Halloumi, Onions And Tomato

*Serving: 1 Cyprus Sandwich, 1 serving(s) | Prep: 5mins | Ready in:*

### Ingredients

- 1 large finger rolls or 1 pita bread or 1 hoagie roll
- 4 slices halloumi cheese
- 1 tablespoon olive oil
- 1/4 onion, peeled and sliced
- 1/2 large fresh tomato, sliced
- 1/4 fresh lemon
- fresh oregano leaves (Rigoni leaves)
- lettuce leaf, to serve
- black olives, to serve

### Direction

- Put 2 teaspoons of the olive oil into a frying pan and cook the onions over a medium heat until soft and slightly coloured, set aside.
- Put the remaining 1 teaspoon of oil into the frying pan and fry the halloumi slices over a medium to high heat on both sides, until golden brown and crispy around the edges.
- Cut the roll in half, and place the halloumi slices on one half and then squeeze the lemon juice over the cooked cheese slices. Sprinkle a few oregano leaves over the cheese before adding the sliced tomatoes and cooked onions.
- Place the other half of the roll on top of the cheese and the filling. Gently press the two halves together.
- Put the filled roll into a pre-heated griddle, Panini, George Foreman or sandwich grill for about 2 minutes, or until the bread roll is crisp and golden brown.
- Serve immediately with fresh lettuce leaves and a handful of black olives -- and don't forget the ice cold Keo or Efes beer!

## Nutrition Information

- Calories: 313.7
- Protein: 6.8
- Total Fat: 16.2
- Saturated Fat: 2.2
- Sodium: 316
- Sugar: 4.6
- Total Carbohydrate: 36.1
- Cholesterol: 0
- Fiber: 2.9

## 337. Three Little Pigs Snack Mix

*Serving: 3 cups, 4 serving(s) | Prep: 5mins | Ready in:*

### Ingredients

- 1 cup potato sticks
- 1 cup pretzel stick

- 1 cup semisweet chocolate chunk (or regular Hershey bars, broken into marked rectangular pieces)

### Direction

- Mix together and serve.

### Nutrition Information

- Calories: 341.2
- Total Fat: 18
- Saturated Fat: 9.7
- Sugar: 30.2
- Protein: 3.1
- Sodium: 24.2
- Fiber: 4.1
- Total Carbohydrate: 42.3
- Cholesterol: 1.7

## 338. Tim Horton's Style Lemon Cranberry Muffins

*Serving: 12 muffins | Prep: 20mins | Ready in:*

### Ingredients

- 3 cups oats
- 3/4 cup all-purpose flour
- 4 teaspoons baking powder
- 1/2 teaspoon salt
- 1 cup cranberries, rough chopped
- 1 cup low-fat plain yogurt
- 1/2 cup oil
- 1/2 cup brown sugar
- Egg Beaters egg substitute (enough for two eggs worth)
- 2 teaspoons finely grated lemon peel
- 1 teaspoon cinnamon
- 1/2 teaspoon vanilla

### Direction

- Preheat oven to 350 degrees F.
- Mix oats, flour, baking powder, salt and chopped cranberries in one bowl; set aside.
- In second bowl mix yogurt, oil, brown sugar, Egg Beaters, lemon peel, cinnamon and vanilla together. Fold all ingredients together in one bowl. Place batter into muffin tins (non-stick or lined with paper liners).
- Bake at 350 degrees F for 35 minutes.
- Allow to cool on wire rack out of the tins.

### Nutrition Information

- Calories: 321.4
- Sodium: 234.5
- Total Carbohydrate: 46.2
- Cholesterol: 0.8
- Protein: 8.3
- Total Fat: 12.1
- Saturated Fat: 1.8
- Fiber: 4.8
- Sugar: 13.1

## 339. Toddler Teething Cookies

*Serving: 24 approximate cookies | Prep: 5mins | Ready in:*

### Ingredients

- 2 tablespoons shortening
- 2 tablespoons brown sugar
- 2 tablespoons molasses
- 1 teaspoon vanilla
- 1 egg yolk
- 1 cup flour, less 2 tbs
- 1/4 teaspoon salt
- 1 1/2 teaspoons baking powder

### Direction

- Cream together shortening and sugar until light and fluffy. Add molasses, vanilla, egg yolk and mix well. Stir in dry ingredients and mix until well incorporated.

- Roll out 1/4" thick and cut into 1"x1/2" strips.
- Bake in preheated 350 degree F oven for 15-20 minutes.
- Store in airtight container for 1 week or in freezer up to 3 months.

## Nutrition Information

- Calories: 40.3
- Protein: 0.6
- Sugar: 2.1
- Total Carbohydrate: 6.5
- Fiber: 0.1
- Cholesterol: 6.9
- Total Fat: 1.3
- Saturated Fat: 0.3
- Sodium: 48.3

## 340. Toddler Zoobana Bread

*Serving: 2 loaves, 12 serving(s) | Prep: 20mins | Ready in:*

### Ingredients

- 2 cups zucchini, grated
- 2 bananas, mashed
- 1/2 cup kale, steamed and pureed (or more)
- 1/2 cup applesauce
- 3 teaspoons lemon juice or 3 teaspoons vanilla extract
- 1/2 cup olive oil
- 1/2 cup blackstrap molasses
- 2 cups whole wheat flour
- 1 cup all-purpose white flour
- 1 cup oats
- 2 tablespoons cornstarch
- 1 teaspoon baking soda
- 1/4 teaspoon baking powder
- 3 teaspoons cinnamon
- 1/4 teaspoon nutmeg
- 1 teaspoon salt

### Direction

- Preheat oven to 325.
- Grease 2 loaf pans (8x4 or 9x5)
- Combine zucchini, bananas, applesauce, kale, juice/vanilla.
- Measure and add oil, then use same measuring cup for adding molasses to make it flow easier.
- Sift in the remaining dry ingredients.
- Stir until just combined.
- Pour into 2 loaf pans.
- Bake for 50-60 minutes or until a toothpick comes out clean.

## Nutrition Information

- Calories: 314.5
- Saturated Fat: 1.6
- Sodium: 318.7
- Sugar: 10.9
- Total Carbohydrate: 50.9
- Cholesterol: 0
- Protein: 6.5
- Total Fat: 10.7
- Fiber: 5.1

## 341. Tomato Pots

*Serving: 4 serving(s) | Prep: 35mins | Ready in:*

### Ingredients

- 4 large firm tomatoes
- salt and pepper
- 3/4 cup shredded cheese (, Sharp cheddar or parmesan)
- 4 eggs
- 1/4 cup heavy cream
- 3 tablespoons butter

### Direction

- Cut tops off the tomatoes with a sharp knife, remove core and seeds.

- Sprinkle the insides with salt, turn upside down on paper towels to drain for 30 minutes.
- Blot as much moisture as you can from the inside of each tomato and make 4 small slits around the top with a sharp knife.
- Preheat oven to 450 degrees, bake for 5 minutes.
- Remove and put 2 tablespoons cheese into each tomato.
- Break an egg into each tomato and season with salt and pepper.
- Heat the cream to boiling point and spoon it into the eggs, top each with a pat of butter and the remaining cheese.
- Bake for a further 5-10 minutes.

## Nutrition Information

- Calories: 304.1
- Protein: 12.4
- Saturated Fat: 13.8
- Sodium: 350.8
- Fiber: 2.2
- Cholesterol: 268.3
- Total Fat: 24.7
- Sugar: 5.2
- Total Carbohydrate: 9.7

## 342. Tortilla Roll Ups

*Serving: 4-5 dozen pieces, 4-5 serving(s) | Prep: 15mins | Ready in:*

## Ingredients

- 1 (8 ounce) package cream cheese (softened)
- 1/3 cup kraft three cheese ranch dressing
- 1 carrot (finely chopped)
- 2/3 cup broccoli (finely chopped)
- 5 (6 inch) flour tortillas

## Direction

- Mix all ingredients, except tortillas.
- Spread 2 tbsps. of mixture on each tortilla.
- Roll each tortilla tightly.
- Wrap in saran wrap; refrigerate 4hrs or overnight.
- Just before serving, unwrap and slice 1/2inch on the diagonal.
- Makes 4-5 dozen pieces.

## Nutrition Information

- Calories: 471.6
- Total Carbohydrate: 31.8
- Cholesterol: 67.8
- Protein: 9.5
- Total Fat: 34.3
- Sodium: 708.5
- Fiber: 2.5
- Saturated Fat: 15
- Sugar: 2.8

## 343. Touchdown Pepperoni Pizza Sandwich

*Serving: 1 slamwich | Prep: 2mins | Ready in:*

## Ingredients

- For one sandwich
- 2 slices Italian bread
- 2 teaspoons mayonnaise
- 2 teaspoons pizza sauce (or spaghetti sauce)
- 6 slices pepperoni
- 2 slices sharp cheddar cheese (or mozzarella)
- 1 tablespoon grated parmesan cheese (or Asiago)

## Direction

- Spread mayonnaise on one slice and pizza or spaghetti sauce on the other slice.
- Lay pepperoni slices on the pizza sauce and the cheese over the top of that.
- Sprinkle Parmesan on the mayonnaise slice.

- Pop both pieces into the toaster oven (or put together and use a Panini maker) until cheese is bubbly and melted.
- Fold sides together, and serve while warm.
- VARIATION: try this with your favorite pizza toppings OR cheeses.
- SERVING SUGGESTION: Cut on point into four pieces and use as "appetizers" or little kid-wiches.

## Nutrition Information

- Calories: 416.3
- Sodium: 861
- Sugar: 0.7
- Cholesterol: 75.9
- Protein: 22.2
- Total Fat: 26.7
- Saturated Fat: 14.8
- Fiber: 1.1
- Total Carbohydrate: 21.1

## 344. Tropical Smoothie (No Added Sugar)

*Serving: 2 12 oz glasses, 2 serving(s) | Prep: 5mins | Ready in:*

## Ingredients

- 1/2 cup banana, mashed and frozen
- 1/2 cup pineapple chunk, frozen
- 2 ounces coconut milk
- 2 ounces evaporated milk
- 4 ounces yogurt

## Direction

- Throw everything in the blender. 1 -- 37 -- 82 -- HIKE!
- Blend for about 2 minutes or until creamy and well mixed.
- Pour into two lovely cups and enjoy. :)

- NOTES: These are even better chilled in the fridge. Time to make does not including chilling or freezing fruit.

## Nutrition Information

- Calories: 200.4
- Fiber: 2.1
- Total Carbohydrate: 26.3
- Protein: 5.4
- Saturated Fat: 7.2
- Sodium: 72.1
- Total Fat: 9.4
- Sugar: 18.1
- Cholesterol: 15.7

## 345. Tuna Treats

*Serving: 12 snacks, 12 serving(s) | Prep: 3mins | Ready in:*

## Ingredients

- 1 (8 ounce) can tuna
- 2 eggs
- 1 slice bread
- 8 tablespoons peas (fresh or frozen)
- 1/4 cup of shredded cheese

## Direction

- Preheat oven to 350 degrees.
- Mix all the ingredients in a bowl.
- Put about 2 spoonfuls of mixture in to each muffin cup. Do not fill the cup up. (These are snacks, not muffins).
- Sprinkle with shredded cheese.
- Place in oven for 15 minutes.
- Take out of muffin paper. Place on serving dish.
- Serve and enjoy. Can use any kind of dip.

## Nutrition Information

- Calories: 58.4
- Sugar: 0.6
- Total Carbohydrate: 2.4
- Total Fat: 2.4
- Saturated Fat: 0.9
- Fiber: 0.4
- Protein: 6.4
- Sodium: 56.2
- Cholesterol: 43.9

## 346. Turkey Pickle Roll Ups

*Serving: 16 serving(s) | Prep: 5mins | Ready in:*

### Ingredients

- 8 slices turkey slices
- 4 tablespoons whipped cream cheese
- 2 dill pickles, whole

### Direction

- Cut pickle into quarters lengthwise.
- Spread one piece of lunchmeat with 1/2 tablespoon cream cheese, add one pickle piece pickle and roll up, cut in half and serve.

### Nutrition Information

- Calories: 10.2
- Fiber: 0.1
- Total Carbohydrate: 0.4
- Protein: 0.2
- Saturated Fat: 0.6
- Sugar: 0.3
- Cholesterol: 2.8
- Total Fat: 0.9
- Sodium: 111.6

## 347. Uncle Bill's Microwave Potato Chips

*Serving: 4-6 serving(s) | Prep: 10mins | Ready in:*

### Ingredients

- 4 large potatoes (russet, yellow gold, white or red potatoes)
- your choice spices (granulated garlic powder, seasoning salt, cayenne pepper, dried dill weed, granulated garlic powder)
- vegetable oil, for microwave bacon tray

### Direction

- If potatoes are old, peel and slice thin, less than 1/16" in thickness (paper thin), slicing across the potato.
- If the potatoes are new or good skins, DO NOT PEEL, just scrub well, then slice them less than 1/16" in thickness (paper thin), slicing across the potato.
- Place potato slices in a bowl, sprinkle with some salt (if desired) cover with cold water and let sit for 10 minutes.
- Remove potato slices in batches onto paper toweling and pat dry.
- If you have a microwave bacon tray, rub the tray with a vegetable oil, then place the sliced potatoes flat on the tray in a single layer.
- Sprinkle with your choice of herbs or spices or just leave them plain.
- Cover with a microwaveable, round heavy plastic cover.
- Microwave on HIGH (full power) for 5 to 5 1/2 minutes or until they curl slightly and are a very light brown in color.
- Cooking time could vary slightly, depending on the wattage of your microwave and the thickness of the slices. The thinner the slices, the quicker they cook and the tastier they are.
- You do not have to turn the sliced potatoes over.
- If you do not have a bacon tray, use a microwave safe casserole dish.

- Rub the inside of the dish with some olive oil for the first batch of potato chips.
- I do not know why, but I find that if you do not rub oil the first time, some chips will tend to stick to the dish.
- After the first batch is done, you do not have to rub the dish again.
- Continue to microwave the remainder of sliced potatoes as noted above.
- If using a bacon tray, after the first batch is cooked, you can reduce the microwaving time to 4 1/2 minutes and even less as you continue to microwave each batch.
- NOTE: You can also use PARCHMENT PAPER to microwave the potato slices. Lightly spray or rub the parchment paper with some vegetable oil or a Pam spray. Place your potato slices on the parchment paper, then sprinkle them with whatever you like and then place another piece of parchment paper on top. This will help microwave the potatoes more evenly and they should turn out nice and crisp. Microwaving time should be between 5 and 6 minutes.
- ADDITIONAL IDEAS, suggested by Deb K:
- Granulated garlic powder with parsley.
- Cracked black pepper, grated parmesan and sea salt sprinkled after removing from microwave.
- Another, after removing chips from microwave, sprinkle with grated cheddar cheese, zap for a few seconds to melt the cheese, then add a dab of sour cream.
- A great dip is Robert Rothschild Farm Dips:
- Emerald Isle Onion Dill and Horseradish Dip.

## Nutrition Information

- Calories: 284.1
- Total Fat: 0.3
- Sodium: 22.1
- Fiber: 8.1
- Cholesterol: 0
- Protein: 7.5
- Saturated Fat: 0.1
- Sugar: 2.9

- Total Carbohydrate: 64.5

### 348. Very Easy Crispy Cinnamon Treats

*Serving: 8 strips, 1-2 serving(s) | Prep: 5mins | Ready in:*

### Ingredients

- 1 pita bread (preferably pocket-less)
- 3 tablespoons butter, melted
- 3 tablespoons white sugar
- 2 teaspoons ground cinnamon

### Direction

- Preheat an oven to 350*.
- Brush the butter evenly over the pita.
- Sprinkle sugar and cinnamon evenly over the pita.
- Cut into strips or wedges (a pizza slicer works really well).
- Place on baking sheet and bake for 5-8 minutes, or until crispy and slightly golden (watch, ovens can vary).
- Cool and serve with vanilla ice cream.
- Enjoy!

### Nutrition Information

- Calories: 628.6
- Total Carbohydrate: 74.9
- Sugar: 38.7
- Saturated Fat: 22
- Sodium: 568.2
- Fiber: 3.8
- Cholesterol: 91.6
- Protein: 6
- Total Fat: 35.4

## 349. Wally's 1/2 Sour Pickles

*Serving: 1 jar, 6 serving(s) | Prep: 15mins | Ready in:*

### Ingredients

- 3/4 cup white cider vinegar
- 1/2 cup pickling salt or 1/2 cup you can use kosher salt, your choice
- 3 -4 garlic cloves
- 2 sprigs fresh dill or 1 1/2 tablespoons dill seeds
- 5 -6 pickling cucumbers

### Direction

- MAKE SURE YOU USE A ONE GALLON JAR OTHERWISE THEY MIGHT BE TOO SALTY!
- Place one garlic clove and a piece of dill in the bottom of a gallon jar.
- Cut cucumbers into quarters and place 1/2 in jar, standing upright.
- Put another garlic clove in the centre of the pickles, then add remaining pickles to fill jar.
- Put another garlic clove in top of pickles.
- Add in one tablespoon of dill weed or dill seed.
- Add in 3/4 cup vinegar and 1/2 cup of the salt.
- Fill with water to cover.
- Keep refrigerated for 7 to 10 days, turning upside down every day.

### Nutrition Information

- Calories: 46.2
- Saturated Fat: 0.1
- Sodium: 9437.9
- Total Carbohydrate: 9.9
- Cholesterol: 0
- Protein: 1.7
- Total Fat: 0.3
- Fiber: 1.3
- Sugar: 4.3

## 350. Watermelon Orange Popsicles

*Serving: 12-16 popsicles | Prep: 5mins | Ready in:*

### Ingredients

- 1 1/2 cups diced watermelon
- 1 cup orange juice
- 1 cup water
- 1/4 cup sugar

### Direction

- Stir sugar into the orange juice until sugar is dissolved.
- Put everything in a blender and blend until well mixed.
- Pour into Popsicle moulds and freeze until firm.

### Nutrition Information

- Calories: 31.1
- Total Fat: 0.1
- Sodium: 0.8
- Cholesterol: 0
- Protein: 0.3
- Saturated Fat: 0
- Fiber: 0.1
- Sugar: 7.1
- Total Carbohydrate: 7.8

## 351. White Chocolate Peanut Butter Apple Dip For 1

*Serving: 1 serving(s) | Prep: 3mins | Ready in:*

### Ingredients

- 1 (4 ounce) containerweight watchers white chocolate cheesecake nonfat yogurt
- 1/2 tablespoon natural-style peanut butter
- 1 medium honeycrisp apple, sliced

- 1 dash cinnamon

## Direction

- Open yogurt container and measure in 1/2 tablespoon of peanut butter. Stir until combined.
- Sprinkle with cinnamon.
- Dip apple liberally and enjoy.
- Eat any remaining dip with spoon!

## Nutrition Information

- Calories: 119.1
- Fiber: 3.9
- Total Carbohydrate: 20.7
- Cholesterol: 0
- Sugar: 15.1
- Protein: 2.4
- Total Fat: 4.3
- Saturated Fat: 0.9
- Sodium: 2.8

## 352. White Chocolate Salties

*Serving: 1 1/2 pounds | Prep: 10mins | Ready in:*

## Ingredients

- 16 ounces white chocolate or 16 ounces white chocolate chips
- 2 tablespoons shortening or 1/4 block paraffin wax
- 3 cups pretzel sticks
- 1 cup salted peanuts

## Direction

- Melt chocolate and shortening or wax over a double boiler or in the microwave.
- Stir until smooth and combined.
- Pour into a large mixing bowl.
- Stir in pretzels and nuts and spread into a buttered 15 x 10 inch pan.
- Chill 20 minutes or until firm and then break into pieces.
- Store in airtight container in a cool place.

## Nutrition Information

- Calories: 2664.4
- Total Fat: 189.1
- Fiber: 12.1
- Total Carbohydrate: 211.6
- Cholesterol: 42.3
- Saturated Fat: 73.4
- Sodium: 1501.3
- Sugar: 184.9
- Protein: 53.5

## 353. Whole Wheat Banana Muffins

*Serving: 12 muffins | Prep: 15mins | Ready in:*

## Ingredients

- 3 small bananas
- 1 cup sugar
- 1/2 cup unsweetened applesauce
- 1 1/4 cups whole wheat flour
- 1/2 teaspoon salt
- 1 1/2 teaspoons baking soda

## Direction

- Preheat oven to 350 degrees.
- Mash bananas and mix with sugar and applesauce until blended.
- Mix flour, salt and soda together. Fold into banana mixture.
- Scoop into lined muffin tins.
- Bake or 25 minutes.

## Nutrition Information

- Calories: 133.7
- Cholesterol: 0

- Protein: 2
- Sodium: 255.3
- Fiber: 2.3
- Sugar: 19.8
- Total Carbohydrate: 32.6
- Total Fat: 0.3
- Saturated Fat: 0.1

## 354. Wiggly Worm Trail Mix

*Serving: 5 cups, 5-10 serving(s) | Prep: 10mins | Ready in:*

### Ingredients

- 1 cup miniature pretzel
- 1 cup miniature Teddy Grahams honey graham snacks
- 1 cup dry roasted peanuts
- 1 cup M'
- 1 cup gummy worms

### Direction

- Mix together and enjoy.
- This can be stored in individual sized containers (I like to use the 8 oz. size Ziploc plastic containers with lids), snack-sized bags, or a large airtight container.

### Nutrition Information

- Calories: 470
- Total Fat: 31.3
- Saturated Fat: 8.6
- Sodium: 394.1
- Fiber: 4.7
- Sugar: 28.4
- Total Carbohydrate: 39.4
- Cholesterol: 5.8
- Protein: 12.5

## 355. World's Best Chocolate Chip Cookies (By Dorie Greenspan)

*Serving: 45 cookies | Prep: 10mins | Ready in:*

### Ingredients

- 2 cups all-purpose flour
- 1 teaspoon salt
- 3/4 teaspoon baking soda
- 1 cup unsalted butter, at room temperature
- 1 cup sugar
- 2/3 cup packed light brown sugar
- 2 teaspoons pure vanilla extract
- 2 large eggs
- 12 ounces bittersweet chocolate, chopped into chips or 2 cups store-bought chocolate chips or 2 cups semisweet chocolate chunks
- 1 cup finely chopped walnuts (optional) or 1 cup pecans (optional)

### Direction

- Center a rack in the oven and preheat the oven to 375 degrees F. Line two baking sheets with parchment or silicone mats.
- Whisk together the flour, salt, and baking soda.
- Working with a stand mixer, preferably fitted with the paddle attachment, or with a hand mixer in a large bowl, beat the butter at medium speed for about 1 minute, until smooth. Add the sugars and beat for another 2 minutes or so, until well-blended. Beat in the vanilla. Add the eggs one at a time, beating for 1 minute after each egg goes inches Reduce the mixer speed to low and add the dry ingredients in 3 portions, mixing only until each addition is incorporated. On low speed, or by hand with a rubber spatula, mix in the chocolate and nuts.
- Spoon the dough by slightly rounded tablespoonfuls onto the baking sheets, leaving about 2 inches between spoonfuls.
- Bake the cookies- one sheet at a time and rotating the sheet at the midway point- for 10-

12 minutes, or until they are brown at the edges and golden in the center; they may still be a little soft in the middle, and that's just fine. Pull the sheet from the oven and allow the cookies to rest for 1 minute, then carefully, using a wide metal spatula, transfer them to racks to cool to room temperature.
- Repeat with the remainder of the dough, cooling the baking sheets between batches.

## Nutrition Information

- Calories: 89.7
- Fiber: 0.1
- Total Fat: 4.4
- Saturated Fat: 2.7
- Sodium: 77.7
- Sugar: 7.6
- Total Carbohydrate: 11.9
- Cholesterol: 20.2
- Protein: 0.9

## 356. Yogurt Banana Muffins

*Serving: 96 mini-muffins, 24 serving(s) | Prep: 10mins | Ready in:*

## Ingredients

- 1 1/4 cups sugar
- 1/2 cup butter or 1/2 cup margarine, softened
- 2 large eggs
- 3 large bananas, mashed (or 4, to taste)
- 1 (6 ounce) container vanilla yogurt (or plain Greek yogurt and 1 t vanilla)
- 2 1/2 cups all-purpose flour
- 1 teaspoon baking soda
- 1 teaspoon salt
- 1 cup semi-sweet chocolate chips (optional)

## Direction

- Preheat oven to 350, placing rack in lowest position.
- Prepare mini-muffin tins with paper liners.
- Cream sugar and butter in large bowl.
- Mix in eggs with mixer until well blended.
- Add bananas and yogurt, and beat until smooth.
- Add baking soda and salt. Mix.
- Fold in flour until it's all moistened.
- Stir in chips.
- Fill liners in pan about 3/4 of the way. I use a cookie scoop and they go quickly and turn out uniform.
- Bake 20 minutes on bottom rack.

## Nutrition Information

- Calories: 147.1
- Total Fat: 4.7
- Sodium: 192.8
- Cholesterol: 26.6
- Protein: 2.3
- Saturated Fat: 2.8
- Fiber: 0.8
- Sugar: 12.9
- Total Carbohydrate: 24.6

## 357. Yogurt Fruit Bars

*Serving: 8 serving(s) | Prep: 10mins | Ready in:*

## Ingredients

- 1 1/2 cups whole wheat flour
- 1 teaspoon baking soda
- 1/2 teaspoon baking powder
- 1 teaspoon cinnamon
- 1/2 teaspoon ground ginger
- 1 (6 ounce) package mixed dried fruit, coarsely chopped
- 1/3 cup chopped walnuts (optional)
- 1 cup plain fat-free yogurt or 1 cup low-fat plain yogurt
- 1 large egg
- 1/4 cup apple juice concentrate
- 2 tablespoons oil

- nonstick cooking spray

## Direction

- Preheat oven to 350°F.
- In a large bowl, mix all dry ingredients. Add dried fruits and walnuts.
- In a medium bowl, combine yogurt, egg, apple juice concentrate, and oil.
- Make a well in the center of the dry ingredients and add the wet ingredients until blended.
- Coat a 9 X 13 inch pan with vegetable spray, spread batter in pan.
- Bake 45-50 minutes or until done. Cool 10 minutes before slicing.
- Slice into 8 servings. Freeze in individual portions if desired.

## Nutrition Information

- Calories: 202
- Total Fat: 4.8
- Saturated Fat: 0.8
- Sodium: 219.1
- Sugar: 5.9
- Protein: 6.1
- Fiber: 4.3
- Total Carbohydrate: 36.7
- Cholesterol: 23.9

## 358. Yogurt A Go Go C/O Tasty Dish

*Serving: 1 serving(s) | Prep: 5mins | Ready in:*

## Ingredients

- 2/3 cup plain yogurt or 2/3 cup fruit yogurt, your choice flavor
- 1 tablespoon raisins or 1 tablespoon dried cranberries
- 1 tablespoon sunflower seeds, roasted
- 1/4 cup strawberry, sliced (or other favorite seasonal fruit such as diced apples, nectarine, berries, pear chunks, etc.)

## Direction

- Start by placing half the yogurt in the cup.
- Layer with the raisins, the remaining yogurt, and then the sunflower seeds.
- For the final layer, top with the fresh fruit of choice.
- Yummy!
- Ooopsie, I almost forgot to tell you! If you choose to use plain yogurt for the flavored yogurt, Mommy says it would be best to drain the plain yogurt first so it doesn't make everything else mushy. Sometimes Mommy will add a pinch of raw sugar, a few drops of real maple syrup or stir in a swirl of softened honey to the plain yogurt. *WARNING*: DO NOT feed honey to children under 2 years of age.

## Nutrition Information

- Calories: 191.9
- Sugar: 15.5
- Total Carbohydrate: 20
- Cholesterol: 21.2
- Total Fat: 10
- Saturated Fat: 3.8
- Fiber: 1.8
- Protein: 8
- Sodium: 77.4

## 359. Your Basic Quesadilla

*Serving: 2 serving(s) | Prep: 10mins | Ready in:*

## Ingredients

- 1 tablespoon butter
- 2 flour tortillas, whatever size you want

- 1 cup shredded cheddar cheese, more for bigger tortillas
- salsa, however much and whatever heat you desire, for topping (optional)
- sour cream, as much as you like, for topping (optional)

## Direction

- In a pan skillet large enough to hold one of the tortillas flat, melt ½ of the butter.
- Fry one side of one of the tortillas, then remove it from the pan.
- Put the rest of the butter in the pan, then put the unfired tortilla in to cook.
- Immediately sprinkle the cheese on top of the tortilla in the pan, then top with the previously fried tortilla, browned side up.
- Press them together with a spatula and fry the quesadilla until the cheese is melted.
- Remove it from the pan and cut in wedges like a pizza.
- Top with sour cream and/or salsa.
- Enjoy!

## Nutrition Information

- Calories: 372.2
- Fiber: 0.9
- Sugar: 0.9
- Total Carbohydrate: 16.1
- Protein: 16.6
- Saturated Fat: 16.1
- Sodium: 592.4
- Cholesterol: 74.6
- Total Fat: 26.8

## 360. Yummy Frozen Chocolate Covered Bananas!

*Serving: 4 bananas, 4 serving(s) | Prep: 15mins | Ready in:*

## Ingredients

- 2 ripe but firm bananas
- 6 ounces dark chocolate, chopped or 6 ounces semi-sweet chocolate chips
- 2 tablespoons vegetable oil
- 1/2 cup granola cereal, chopped or 1/2 cup pecans (optional) or 1/2 cup walnuts (optional) or 1/2 cup candy sprinkles (optional)

## Direction

- Line a baking sheet with non-stick foil or parchment paper.
- Cut the bananas in half and insert a Popsicle stick into each half. Place them on the baking sheet and freeze for 15 minutes.
- Meanwhile, melt the chocolate with the oil in a Pyrex measuring cup in the microwave (check it every 30 seconds) or in a half-full pan of simmering water (about 2 minutes). Stir until smooth.
- Roll each banana half in the chocolate, then quickly sprinkle with your topping (if using).
- Freeze until the chocolate sets, 30 minutes. Serve or freeze in an airtight container for up to a week.

## Nutrition Information

- Calories: 400.2
- Sugar: 10.7
- Sodium: 14.6
- Fiber: 10
- Cholesterol: 0
- Protein: 8.4
- Total Fat: 32.9
- Saturated Fat: 15.3
- Total Carbohydrate: 34.3

## 361. Yummy Peanut Butter Snack Mix

*Serving: 7-8 serving(s) | Prep: 8mins | Ready in:*

## Ingredients

- 4 1/2 cups miniature marshmallows
- 1/2 cup peanut butter
- 1/4 cup butter
- 3 1/2 cups Rice Chex
- 3 1/2 cups Corn Chex
- 1/2 cup M'

## Direction

- In a microwaveable bowl, melt 4 cups marshmallows, peanut butter, and butter on high for 2 minutes or until melted.
- Stir until smooth and then add in the following order: 1/2 cup marshmallows, Rice Chex, M's, and Corn Chex.
- Stir after each item is added and until everything is coated.
- Pour into a jelly roll pan or 9x13 pan and allow to cool before serving.

## Nutrition Information

- Calories: 444.5
- Saturated Fat: 8.1
- Fiber: 1.9
- Protein: 7.7
- Total Fat: 19.3
- Sodium: 426.6
- Sugar: 32.3
- Total Carbohydrate: 63.9
- Cholesterol: 19.5

## 362. Yummy Pepperoni With Cheese

*Serving: 15 slices, 3-5 serving(s) | Prep: 5mins | Ready in:*

## Ingredients

- 15 pepperoni slices (you can buy them frozen if you like, I prefer that)
- 6 ounces cheese (preferred cheddar or if you like, any cheese )

## Direction

- Place pepperoni slices on a paper towel which is on a plate.
- Place cheese on top of the slices (its ok to add as much as you want).
- Put the plate in the microwave for about 23 seconds
- After that let them cool for about 1min then enjoy!

## Nutrition Information

- Calories: 187.7
- Protein: 11.2
- Saturated Fat: 8.7
- Sodium: 547.7
- Fiber: 0
- Sugar: 0
- Total Carbohydrate: 4.7
- Cholesterol: 36.3
- Total Fat: 13.9

## 363. Yummy Pizza Sauce

*Serving: 1 large pizza bottom, 4 serving(s) | Prep: 20mins | Ready in:*

## Ingredients

- 3 tablespoons olive oil (plain)
- 1 tablespoon margarine
- 5 big onions
- 5 garlic cloves
- 1200 g chopped tomatoes (canned)
- 150 g tomato puree
- 2 tablespoons dried basil
- 2 tablespoons dried oregano
- 1 tablespoon salt
- 1 tablespoon sugar
- 2 teaspoons ground black pepper
- 4 bay leaves
- 7 tablespoons parmesan cheese

## Direction

- In a large pot, melt the margarine and oil. Add onions and sauté. After a couple of minutes, add the garlic. Let everything go a bit soft and shiny.
- Add tomato ingredients.
- Add everything except the bay leaves and parmesan and stir well. Bring to a simmer and lay the bay leaves on top. Simmer for an hour or more, until the sauce is thick.
- Remove the bay leaves and add the parmesan cheese.
- (Our favourite dough for the pizza is herbed pizza dough - my recipe or chef Texas moms).

## Nutrition Information

- Calories: 327.4
- Protein: 9.1
- Saturated Fat: 3.7
- Sodium: 1944.2
- Sugar: 21.1
- Total Fat: 16.6
- Fiber: 8.4
- Total Carbohydrate: 41.2
- Cholesterol: 7.7

## 364. Yummy And Healthy Popsicles

*Serving: 4 serving(s) | Prep: 2mins | Ready in:*

## Ingredients

- wooden popsicle sticks
- juice or yogurt

## Direction

- Pour in yogurt or juice into mould (or cup and place stick in).
- Freeze.
- Enjoy!
- For Vegan use just the juice or a soy yogurt.

## Nutrition Information

- Calories: 0
- Saturated Fat: 0
- Total Carbohydrate: 0
- Cholesterol: 0
- Sodium: 0
- Fiber: 0
- Sugar: 0
- Protein: 0
- Total Fat: 0

## 365. Zucchini Oat Carrot Bars With Butter Cream Cheese Frosting

*Serving: 3 dozen | Prep: 10mins | Ready in:*

## Ingredients

- 2 1/4 cups sugar
- 1 cup oil (not olive oil)
- 3 large eggs
- 2 cups flour
- 1 teaspoon cinnamon
- 1 teaspoon salt
- 2 teaspoons baking powder
- 1/4 teaspoon baking soda
- 2 teaspoons vanilla
- 2 cups shredded zucchini, unpeeled
- 1 small carrot, shredded
- 3/4 cup rolled oats
- 1 cup chopped walnuts
- FROSTING
- 1 cup butter, softened
- 1 1/2 teaspoons almond extract
- 3 teaspoons vanilla
- 5 cups confectioners' sugar
- 1 (8 ounce) package cream cheese, softened

## Direction

- Set oven to 350 degrees.
- Grease a 15 x 10-inch jelly roll pan or cookie sheet, and line with parchment paper.
- In a large bowl, beat the eggs oil, vanilla and sugar until smooth (about 2 minutes).
- Sift together flour, cinnamon, salt baking powder, baking soda.
- Add the flour mixture into the oil/egg mixture and blend well to combine (about 2 minutes).
- Fold in zucchini, carrots, oats and nuts; blend well to combine.
- Transfer to prepared pan.
- Bake for about 22-25 minutes.
- To make frosting: Mix/beat all ingredients together until smooth, adding more confectioners' sugar to achieve desired consistency to spread.
- Spread on cooled cake.
- Cut into bars.

## Nutrition Information

- Calories: 3566.7
- Sodium: 1877.8
- Fiber: 8.6
- Sugar: 351.2
- Cholesterol: 457.3
- Total Fat: 193.3
- Saturated Fat: 69.3
- Total Carbohydrate: 441
- Protein: 31.6

# Index

## A

Almond 3,11,17

Apple 3,4,5,6,7,14,16,34,39,51,60,66,80,87,89,114,124,131,140,150,153,163,184

Apricot 3,17

Avocado 5,125

## B

Bacon 3,4,6,20,36,58,145

Bagel 5,6,97,168

Banana 3,4,5,6,7,11,20,21,22,61,65,69,90,98,105,108,109,130,137,138,158,185,187,189

Beans 177

Beef 6,155

Berry 3,23,24

Biscuits 3,6,31,135,136

Blueberry 3,4,25,69

Bran 4,90

Bread 3,4,5,6,7,11,25,50,54,98,100,105,108,152,154,172,179

Brie 4,58

Brioche 3,29

Buns 4,75,77

Burger 3,6,32,145

Butter 3,4,5,6,7,44,47,54,60,64,83,86,91,106,115,135,137,138,139,140,146,160,161,184,189,191

## C

Cake 3,4,5,17,18,20,63,69,70,113

Caramel 3,6,33,34,160,169

Carrot 4,6,7,52,142,172,191

Celery 5,129

Cheddar 3,4,35,36,73,114

Cheese 3,4,5,6,7,34,36,37,38,39,52,58,60,63,73,100,111,120,154,157,160,170,190,191

Cherry 3,44

Chicken 3,4,5,6,18,42,43,75,101,104,114,118,130,158

Chilli 12

Chips 4,5,6,7,62,67,73,92,106,131,144,155,156,163,168,182

Chocolate 3,4,5,6,7,11,29,44,45,46,47,48,49,53,82,96,109,119,168,171,184,185,186,189

Chorizo 5,120

Cinnamon 4,7,19,51,52,81,183

Coconut 4,6,53,54,80,149,167

Couscous 4,56,83

Crab 4,70,114

Crackers 3,4,8,20,34,35,49,55

Cranberry 3,4,7,32,73,178

Cream 3,4,5,6,7,8,23,34,45,52,55,58,59,63,82,110,124,127,130,133,137,138,170,178,187,191

Crisps 3,38

Croissant 4,58

Cucumber 5,124

Currants 17

## D

Dijon mustard 37,58

Dill 3,5,24,94,183

Dumplings 3,21

## E

Egg 3,4,5,11,49,72,110,123,128,178

English muffin 71

# F

Falafel 6,169

Fat
4,5,6,8,9,10,11,12,13,14,15,16,17,18,19,20,21,22,23,24,25,26,27,28,29,30,31,32,33,34,35,36,37,38,39,40,41,42,43,44,45,46,47,48,49,50,51,52,53,54,55,56,57,58,59,60,61,62,63,64,65,66,67,68,69,70,71,72,73,74,75,76,77,78,79,80,81,82,83,84,85,86,87,88,89,90,91,92,93,94,95,96,97,98,99,100,101,102,103,104,105,106,107,108,109,110,111,112,113,114,115,116,117,118,119,120,121,122,123,124,125,126,127,128,129,130,131,132,134,135,136,137,138,139,140,141,142,143,144,145,146,147,148,149,150,151,152,153,154,155,156,157,158,159,160,161,162,163,164,165,166,167,168,169,170,171,172,173,174,175,177,178,179,180,181,182,183,184,185,186,187,188,189,190,191,192

Fennel 6,148

Feta 3,5,6,24,27,112,116,135

Fish 4,74

Flapjacks 4,85

French bread 63,152

Fruit
3,4,5,6,7,10,13,35,79,80,81,82,83,84,107,117,133,136,149,187

Fudge 4,62

# G

Garlic 3,5,6,19,40,105,106,164

Gin 6,132,133

Grapefruit 133

# H

Halloumi 7,177

Ham 3,4,37,88

Honey 3,4,6,37,41,44,54,58,61,77,95,135,136,153,174

Horseradish 183

# I

Icing 113

# J

Jam 6,137,167

Jelly 6,139

Jus 5,17,30,99,119,125,180

# K

Kidney 5,102

# L

Lemon 5,6,7,106,164,178

Lime 5,106

# M

Macaroni 5,111

Mandarin 80

Mango 5,80,112

Meat 4,5,6,75,101,170

Melon 5,114

Milk 3,5,22,109,126

Molasses 5,118

Mozzarella 4,5,62,120,141

Muffins
3,4,5,6,7,11,16,25,40,65,69,90,109,115,130,137,158,166,178,185,187

Mustard 41

# N

Nut
3,4,5,6,8,9,10,11,12,13,14,15,16,17,18,19,20,21,22,23,24,25,26,27,28,29,30,31,32,33,34,35,36,37,38,39,40,41,42,43,44,45,46,47,48,49,50,51,52,53,54,55,56,57,58,59,60,61,62,63,64,65,66,67,68,69,70,71,72,73,74,75,76,77,78,79,80,81,82,83,84,85,86,87,88,89,90,91,92,93,94,95,96,97,98,99,100,101,102,103,104,105,106,107,108,109,110,111,112,113,114,115,116,117,118,119,120,121,122,123,124,125,126,127,1

28,129,130,131,132,134,135,136,137,138,139,140,141,142,143,144,145,146,147,148,149,150,151,152,153,154,155,156,157,158,159,160,161,162,163,164,165,166,167,168,169,170,171,172,173,174,175,177,178,179,180,181,182,183,184,185,186,187,188,189,190,191,192

## O

Oatmeal 3,5,6,16,115,127,130,132,146

Oil 4,32,65,67

Olive 5,67,132

Onion 3,7,37,75,177,183

Orange 6,7,132,133,162,184

## P

Pancakes 3,5,6,36,119,127,141

Paprika 3,40

Parfait 3,4,10,61

Parmesan 3,5,30,35,107,116,132,180

Pasta 5,6,101,135

Peach 5,6,80,99,136,151

Peanuts 5,95

Pecan 4,6,55,58,77,146,166

Peel 8,15,21,22,36,67,78,81,92,99,100,121,124,125,148,159

Pepper 4,5,6,7,68,116,140,155,180,190

Pickle 4,5,6,7,84,94,142,182,184

Pie 3,4,6,14,66,79,94,105,153

Pineapple 4,5,6,80,88,129,142

Pizza 4,5,6,7,59,112,115,117,132,140,142,143,144,147,152,180,190

Plantain 6,144

Popcorn 4,5,6,68,82,86,93,129,166,169

Port 6,145

Potato 3,4,5,6,7,10,12,30,62,67,68,92,145,148,155,177,182

Praline 6,146

Prawn 7,174

Pulse 35

## Q

Quinoa 6,150

## R

Raisins 54,83

Raspberry 6,151

Rhubarb 4,69,70

Rice 3,4,5,6,28,45,49,53,60,62,86,106,140,153,190

## S

Salad 3,6,13,35,159

Salami 6,154

Salsa 4,5,81,99

Salt 6,7,19,42,67,155,166,185

Sausage 6,157,165

Savory 6,170

Sea salt 67

Seasoning 71

Soda 31

Soup 75

Spaghetti 5,122

Spinach 4,5,6,88,116,134,164

Strawberry 3,4,5,6,11,48,61,78,114,166

Sugar 4,5,6,7,8,9,10,11,12,13,14,15,16,17,18,19,20,21,22,23,24,25,26,27,28,29,30,31,32,33,34,35,36,37,38,39,40,41,42,43,44,45,46,47,48,49,50,51,52,53,54,55,56,57,58,59,60,61,62,63,64,65,66,67,68,69,70,71,72,73,74,75,76,77,78,79,80,81,82,83,84,85,86,87,88,89,90,91,92,93,94,95,96,97,98,99,100,101,102,103,104,105,106,107,108,109,110,111,112,113,114,115,116,117,118,119,120,121,122,123,124,125,126,127,128,129,130,131,132,133,134,135,136,137,138,139,140,141,142,143,144,145,146,147,148,149,150,151,152,153,154,155,156,157,158,159,160,161,162,163,164,165,166,167,168,169,170,171,172,173,174,175,177,178,179,180,181,182,183,

184,185,186,187,188,189,190,191,192

# T

Tabasco 20,125,163

Taco 6,7,172,173

Tea 6,133,136,157

Tempura 7,174

Tomato 3,4,7,40,63,177,179

Turkey 3,7,32,182

# V

Vegan 116,191

# W

Watermelon 7,184

Worcestershire sauce 42,59,102,123,145,161,176

Wraps 4,74,75

# Y

Yam 5,96

Yoghurt 4,89

# Z

Zest 133

# Conclusion

Thank you again for downloading this book!

I hope you enjoyed reading about my book!

If you enjoyed this book, please take the time to share your thoughts and post a review on Amazon. It'd be greatly appreciated!

Write me an honest review about the book – I truly value your opinion and thoughts and I will incorporate them into my next book, which is already underway.

Thank you!

If you have any questions, **feel free to contact at:** *author@jumbocookbook.com*

Edith Traylor

jumbocookbook.com

Made in United States
Orlando, FL
30 March 2025